- Basics of body proportions
- Freehand sketching for fashion figure
- Cutting method for fashion figure croquis
- Figure croquis manipulations
- Faces and hands drawing

HOW TO DRAW FASHION FIGURE

Essential figure drawing techniques for women's wear designers

IRINA V. IVANOVA

FASHION DRAWING: STYLISH AND ACCURATE

With dedication to memory of Maya F. Rybalkina.
Teacher, mother and friend.

How to draw fashion figure

Essential figure drawing techniques for women's wear designers

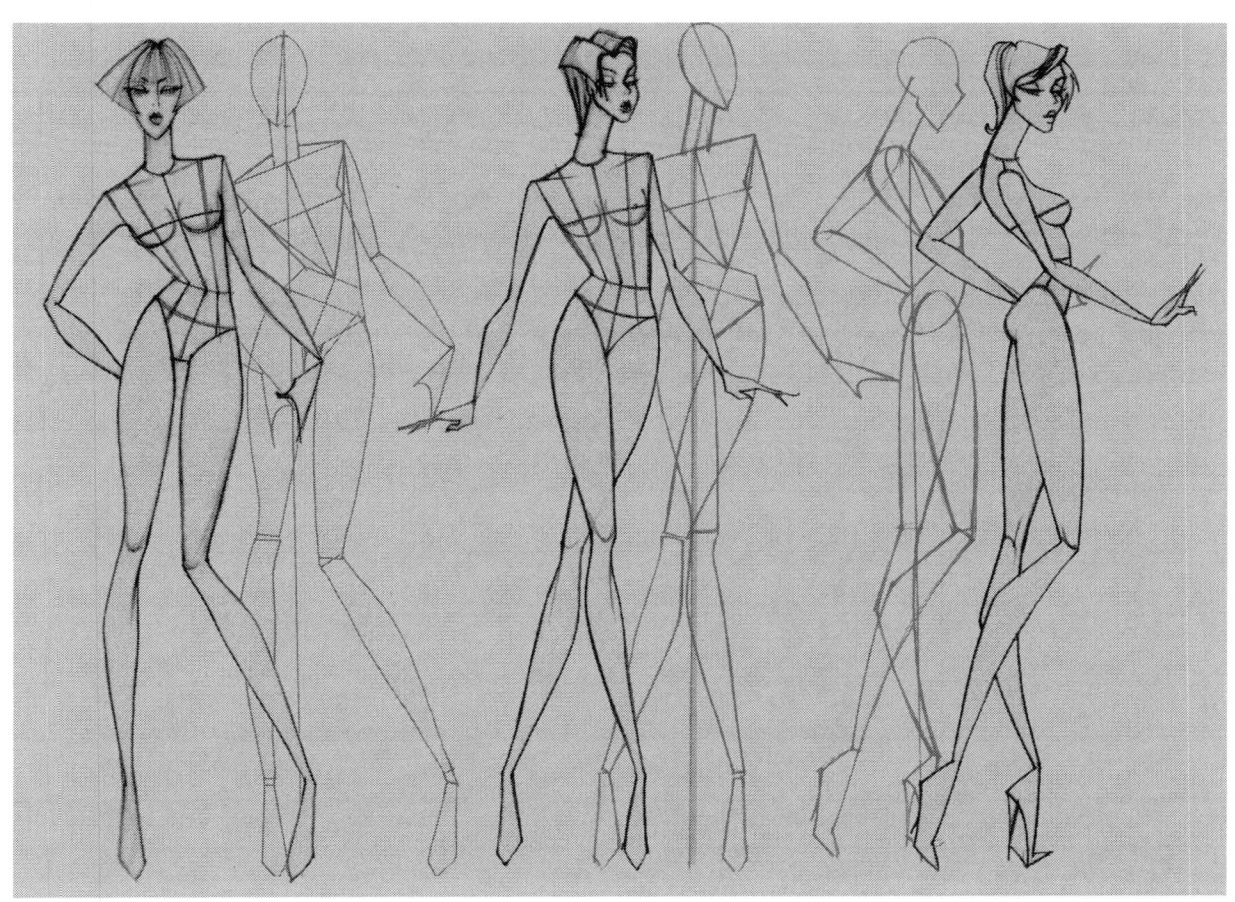

by Irina V. Ivanova

Art Design Project, Inc

How to draw fashion figure.

Essential figure drawing techniques for women's wear designers

by Irina V. Ivanova

Copyright © 2019 by Irina V. Ivanova

Cover by Andre L. Milman

All rights reserved. No part of this book may be reproduced in any form by any electronic or mechanical means including photocopying, recording, or information storage and retrieval without permission in writing from the author.

Any form of reproduction by any other means, whether it be in a book, electronic, or in any other design resource, is strictly prohibited and is a violation of our copyright.

For permission for additional use please contact Permissions, Art Design Project, Inc. www.artdesignproject.com/permissions.html

ISBN-13: 978-0-9843560-4-1
ISBN-10:0-9843560-4-5

Book Website
www.fashioncroquis .com
Email: contact@artdesignproject.com

Give feedback on the book at:
contact@artdesignproject.com

Art Design Project, Incorporated

Printed in U.S.A

CONTENTS:

Chapter 1:
Basics of body proportions
Pages 9-25

- About this book.....10
- Basic body proportions for figure drawing.....10
- Basic requirements for any figure drawing.....11
- Standard 10 heads tall fashion women's figure. Basic lines.....12
- Women's croquis with different head/body proportions.....14
- Women's croquis with different shape/weight distribution.....16
- Women's croquis with different waist size.....17
- Women's croquis with different hip size.....18
- Women's croquis with different shoulders size.....19
- Women's croquis with different posture.....20
- Women's figure by size: apparel industry standards.....22
- Historical overview of women body proportions in art.....24

Chapter 2:
Fashion figure schematics
(wire skeleton study)
Pages 27-35

- Study body in static (no motion) position for front and side views.....28
- Study body in movement.....30
- Different body positions with wire skeleton.....32
- Common balance mistakes in figure drawing....34

Chapter 3:
Sketching strategy
Pages 37-45

- Step by step sketching strategy....38
- Step #1. Choose the head -body proportions.....38
- Step #2. Choose the body style.....39
- Step #3. Focus on the right body movement.....40
- Step #4. Avoid sitting figure for fashion illustration.....44
- Step #5. Do not use excessive movement.....44
- Step #6. Avoid stiff static body poses.....45
- Step #7. Make sure your figure drawing is accurate.....45
- Step #8. Have strategy in place......45
- Step #9. Develop a set of croquis......45
- Step #10. Be patient......45
- Step #11. Never be discouraged by mistakes!......45

Chapter 4:
Freehand sketching for 10 heads tall fashion figure (front view)
Pages 47-61

- Freehand sketching of front view croquis.....48
- Freehand sketching of front view croquis at a glance.....60

Chapter 5 :
Freehand sketching for 10 heads tall fashion figure (side view)
Pages 63-75

- Side view. Static (no motion) position.....64
- Templates with different heel height.....65
- Freehand sketching of side view croquis.....66

Chapter 6:
Cutting method for fashion figure croquis
Pages 77-91

- Cutting method for front view croquis.....78
- Cutting method for front view croquis at a glance.....90

Chapter 7:
Figure croquis manipulations
Pages 93-125

- Manipulation #1. Creating plus size croquis using croquis with streamline body proportions.....94
- Manipulation #2. Creating back view croquis using the front.....100
- Manipulation #3. Creating croquis with right supporting leg using croquis with the left supporting leg.....110
- Manipulation #4. Creating croquis for maternity wear using streamline style croquis.....118
- Manipulation #5. Creating 9½ and 10½ heads tall croquis using 8½ heads croquis.....120
- Manipulation #6. Using the cutting method for creating a croquis with a new movement for arms and legs.....122

Chapter 8:
Faces and hands drawing
Pages 127-147

- Face shape styles.....128
- Step by step front view face drawing.....129
- Step by step side view face drawing.....133
- Step by step 3/4 view face drawing.....136
- Hairstyles.....140
- Gallery of hands.....144

Index:
Pages 148-149

About the author:
Pages 150-151

Contents:

Chapter 1. Pages 9-25
Basics of body proportions

Chapter 2. Pages 27-35
Fashion figure schematics (wire skeleton study)

Chapter 3. Pages 37-45
Sketching strategy

Chapter 4. Pages 47-61
Freehand sketching for 10 heads tall fashion figure (front view)

Chapter 5. Pages 63-75
Freehand sketching for 10 heads tall fashion figure (side view)

Chapter 6. Pages 77-91
Cutting method for fashion figure croquis

Chapter 7. Pages 93-125
Figure croquis manipulations

Chapter 8. Pages 127-147
Faces and hands drawing

Index
Pages 148-149

About the author
Pages 150-151

Chapter 1

Basics of body proportions

About this book

Do you want to draw fashion illustration but do not know where to start? This book can help with an overview of the essential principles of fashion figure drawing.

Do you want to develop your style in fashion drawing? Let's try! Just a reminder: a solid understanding of dos and don'ts in figure drawing is a must for any style of fashion illustration. We focus on fundamental principles and main logical concepts of figure drawing for fashion which are true to any style.

This book will help to
- learn the basic proportion for a human body (see page 11)
- chose body proportion for your croquis (see pages 16-21)
- understand the difference between movement and motion (see pages 30-31)
- learn basic rules for movement with wire skeleton (see pages 30-35)

Basic requirements for any figure drawing

No matter how tall, short, skinny, curved, athletic style you chose for your fashion figure drawing, you should follow the basic rule for body proportions. Fashion drawing can look exaggerated (some times even grotesque) and still be accurate and useful. There are methods in every mode of stylization. A figure cannot be distorted arbitrary with no regard to certain rules and methods.
Let's start from the basics.

Check out basic body proportions (see page 11):

- upper arm, as a rule, has the same length as the lower arm (A=B)
- upper leg, as a rule, has the same length as lower leg (C=D)
- elbows and waistline, as a rule, are on the same level (level E)
- length of a hand, as a rule, is equal to face size from chin level to hairline (F=G)
- length of a foot, as a rule, is equal or little bigger head size from chin level to the top of the head (H=I)
- keep fingertips in the middle or close to the middle of the tights
- never allow tips of fingers to reach the level of the knees in a standing figure

Follow the basic requirements for figure drawing, but the rest of body proportions (how wide will the hipline be, how small will the shoulder line be, how long will the neck be, etc.) is up to you.

We are all different! We have different body shapes and proportion.

Basic body proportions for figure drawing

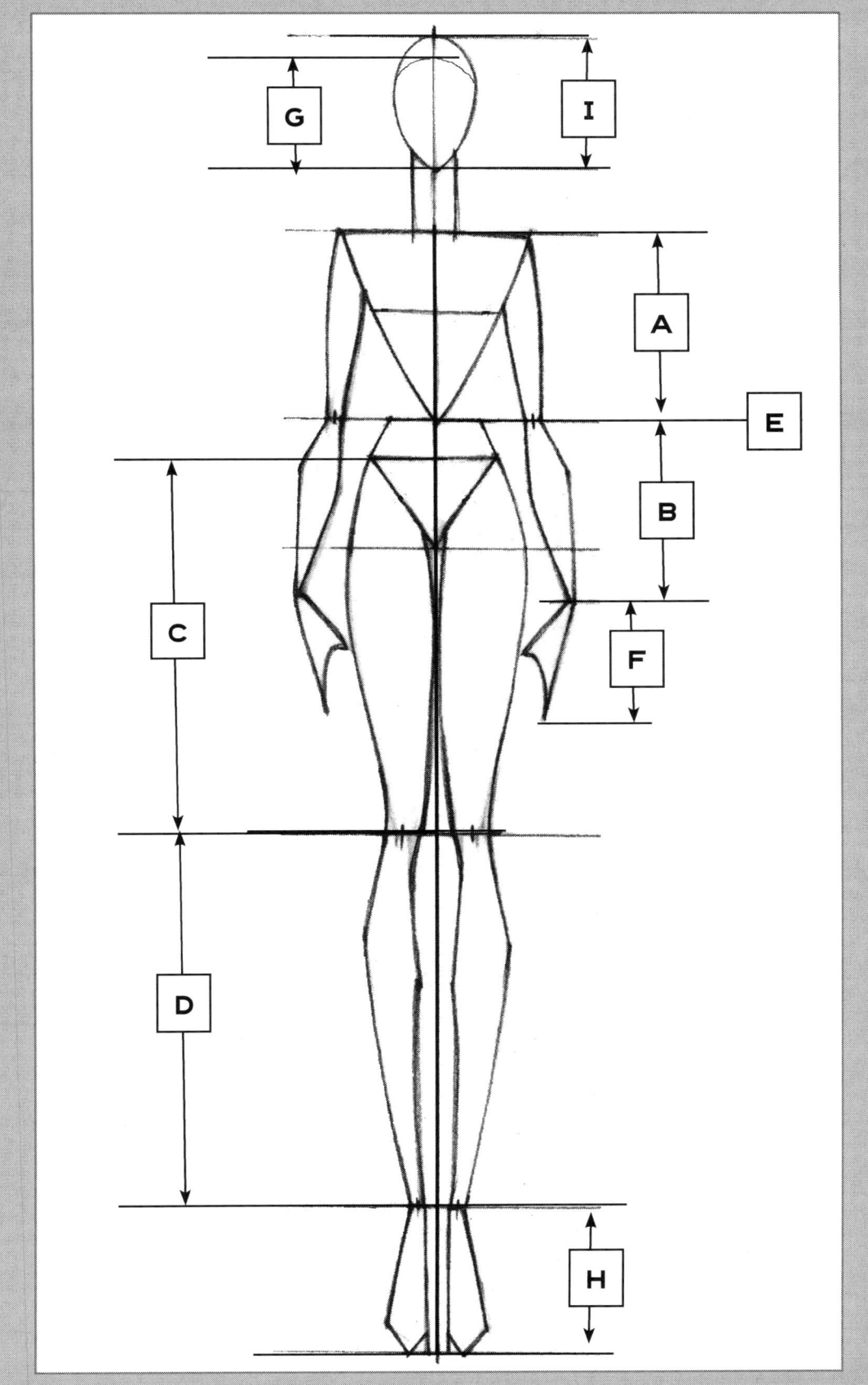

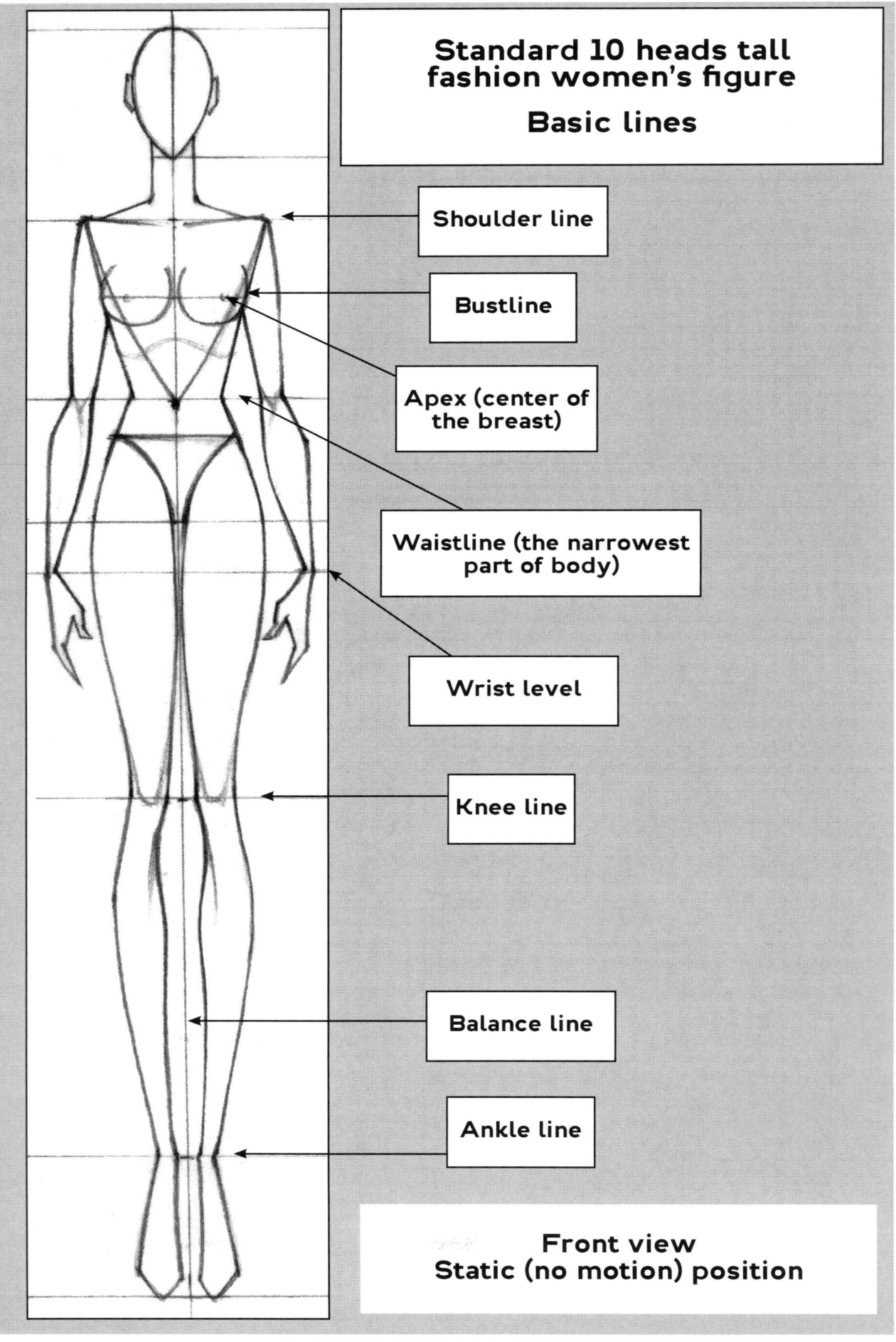

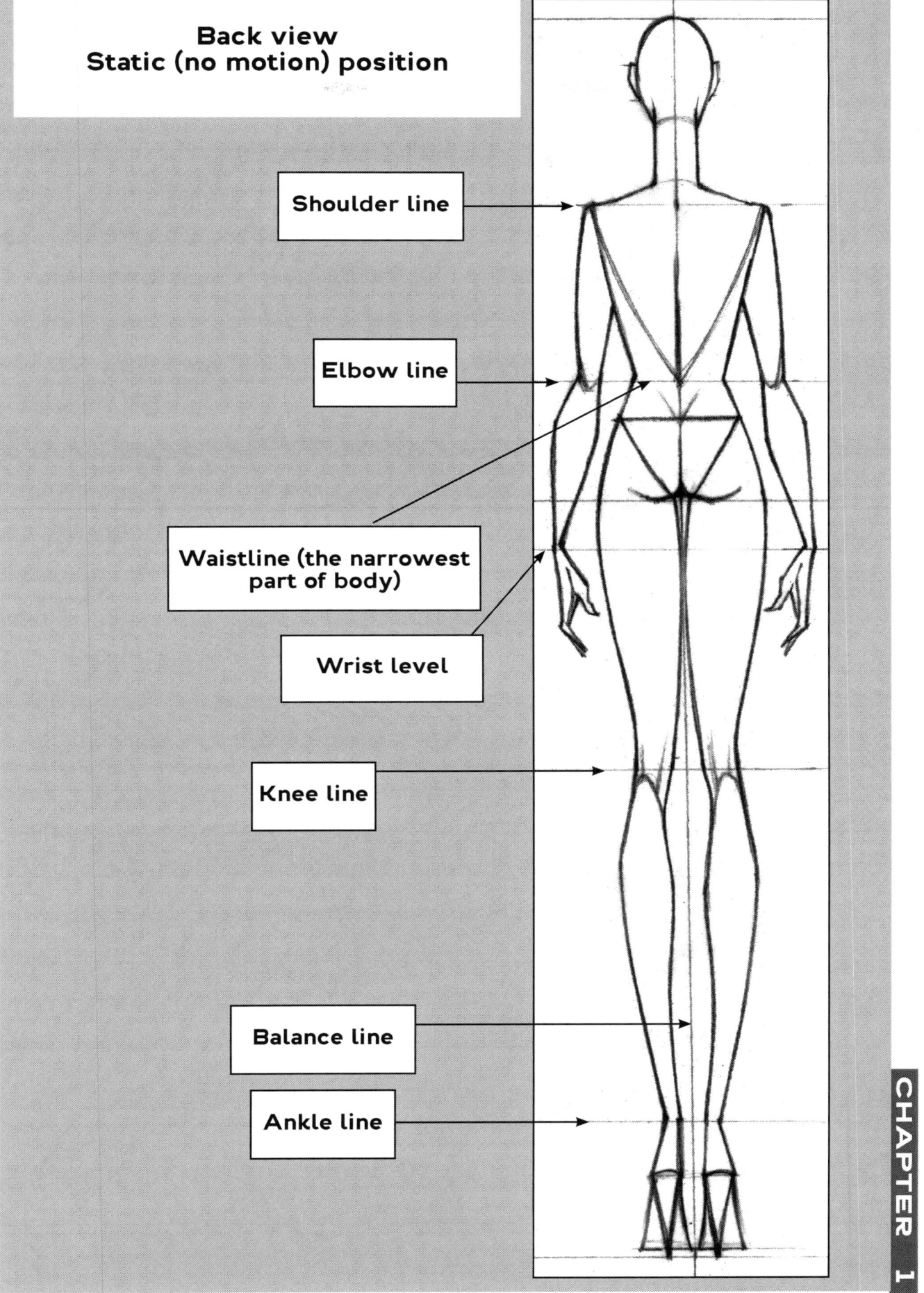

**Back view
Static (no motion) position**

- Shoulder line
- Elbow line
- Waistline (the narrowest part of body)
- Wrist level
- Knee line
- Balance line
- Ankle line

Women's croquis with different head/body proportions

The same length of the body, but different proportions of head to overall size the body

| 8 heads tall croquis | 10 heads tall croquis | 12 heads tall croquis | 14 heads tall croquis |

The **size of the head** in proportion to the body is a starting point for fashion figure drawing. The average human is about 6 ½ -7 ½ heads tall. But when working on a fashion illustration project, you have to follow the different rules.

Fashion illustrators use different proportions and "style" of a body. As a rule, it is a figure with 8 ½, 9, 10 or sometimes even more heads tall with the extra length in the legs and neck.

What is fashion croquis?

- In the art world, term croquis can define a sketch or quick drawing of any kind.
- In the fashion industry, fashion croquis is usually a term for a quick fashion sketch or even (sometimes) fully finished illustration.
- In fashion design, term "croquis" often used as a term for a figure drawing template.

In this book we will use word "croquis" as a term for figure drawing template and will use "template " and "croquis" interchangeably.

There is no absolute fashion figure standard.

The ratio which measures head to body length in fashion figure drawing depends on the style and purpose of fashion illustrator or market for which fashion design is intended for.

Leonardo da Vinci used 8 heads tall figures for most of his drawings, Michelangelo used mostly 9 heads tall body proportion figures.

High fashion (Haute Couture) illustration depicting top-models can be and should be more exaggerated with 10-16 heads tall.

Fashion drawing for product development process for the mass market are required to be realistically or even naturalistically precise to give concrete information for specifications. So, figure drawing with 8-9 heads tall will be more appropriate.

It is practically impossible to cover with one set of proportions all multiplicities of body types by ethnicity, age, and natural anatomy.

You can change body proportion drastically by switching from 8 heads tall to 14 heads tall figure (see page 14), or you can vary body drawing slightly by manipulation with a size of the waistline (see page 17), hip (see page 18) or shoulder (see page 19) area.

Women's croquis with different shape/weight distribution

The same length of the body and the size of the head, but different body shapes

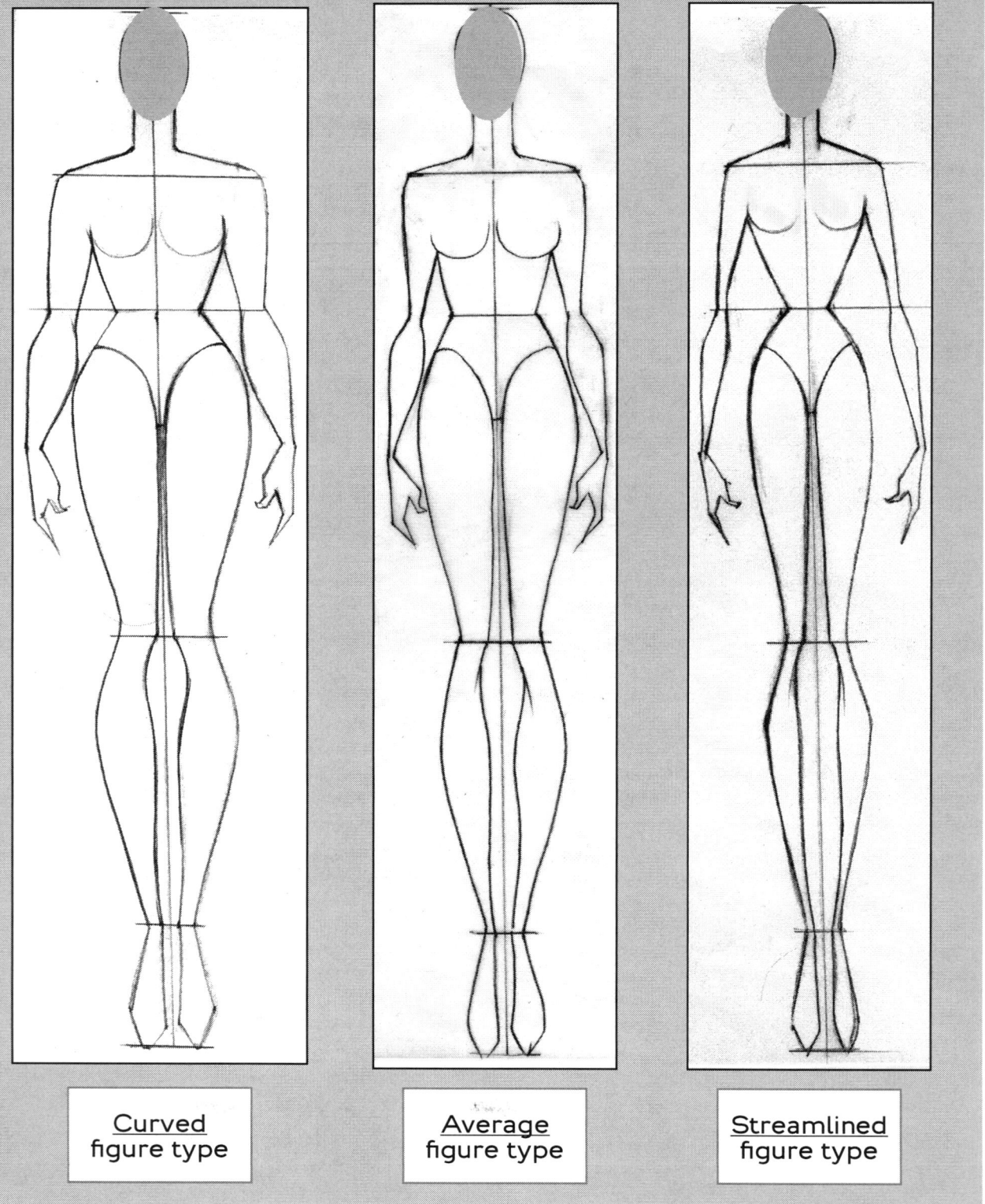

Curved figure type

Average figure type

Streamlined figure type

Women's croquis with a different waist size

The same length of the body and the size of the head, but different waistlines

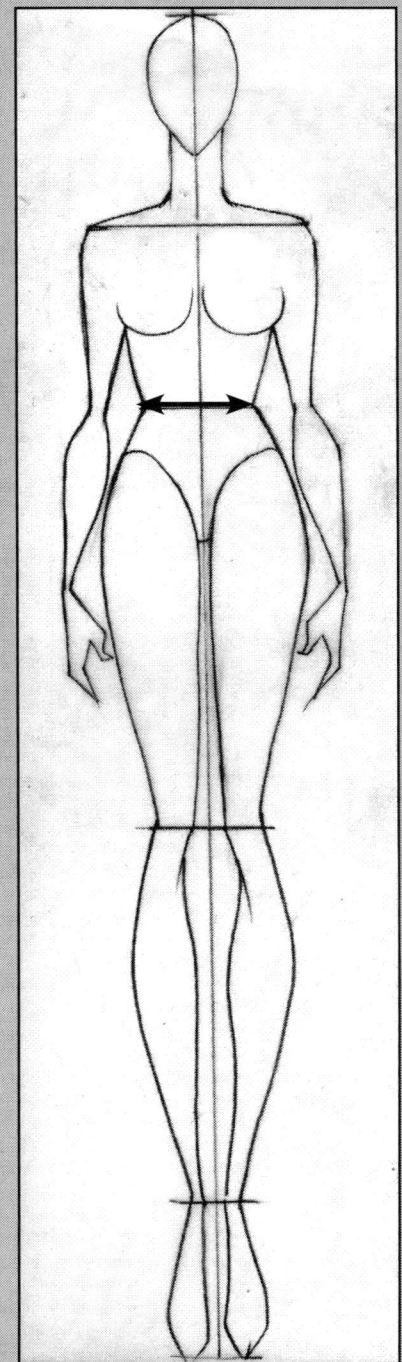

Average figure type
<u>with average waist</u>

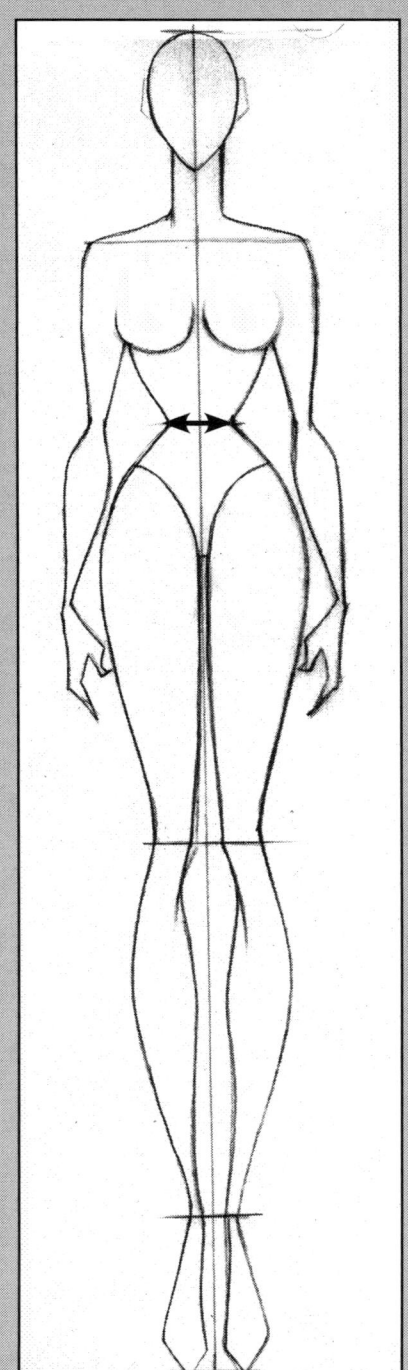

Average figure type
<u>with narrow waist</u>

Women's croquis with different hip size

The same length of the body and the size of the head, but different hip area

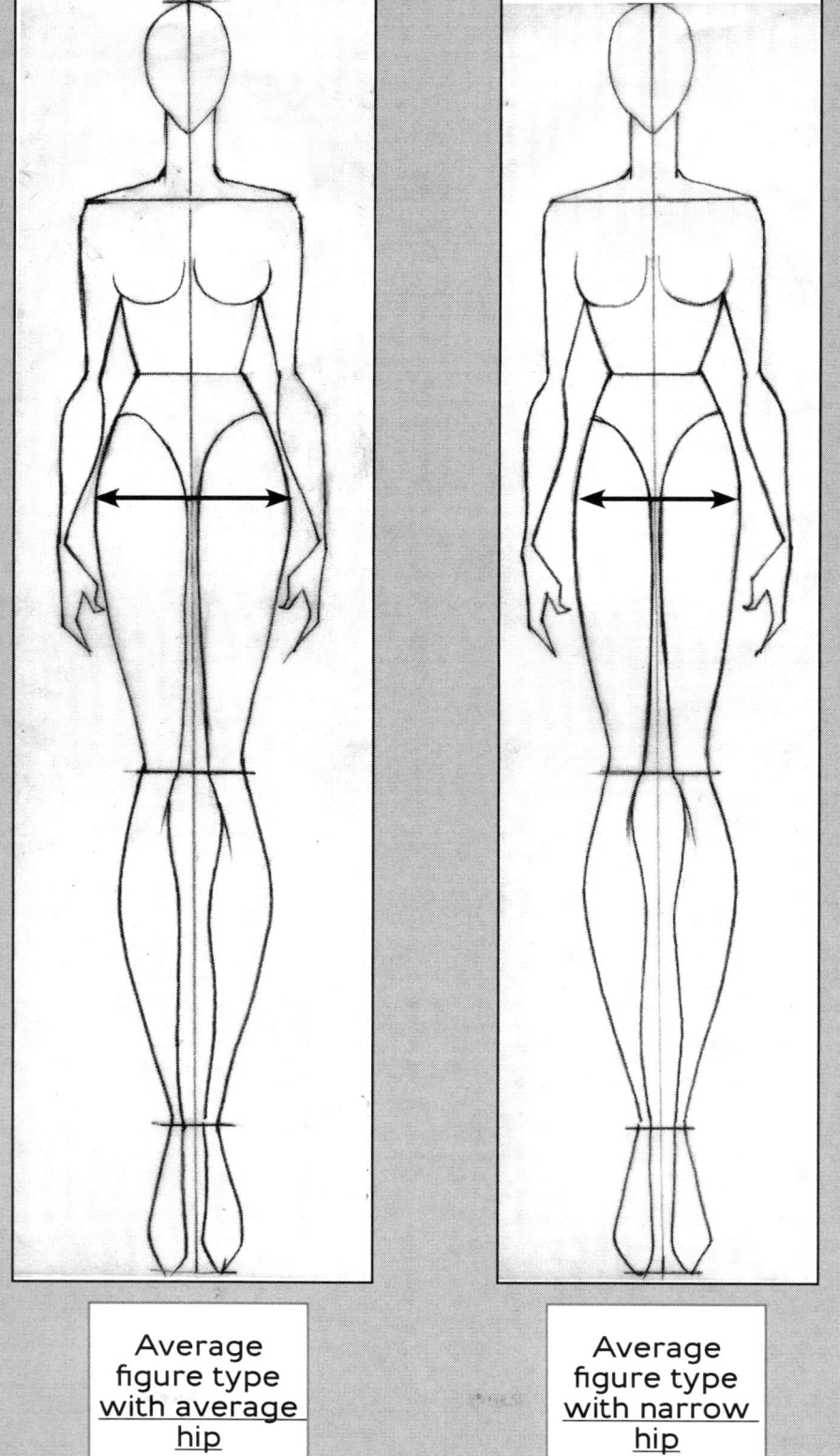

Average figure type with average hip

Average figure type with narrow hip

Women's croquis with different shoulders size

The same length of the body and the size of the head, but different shoulders

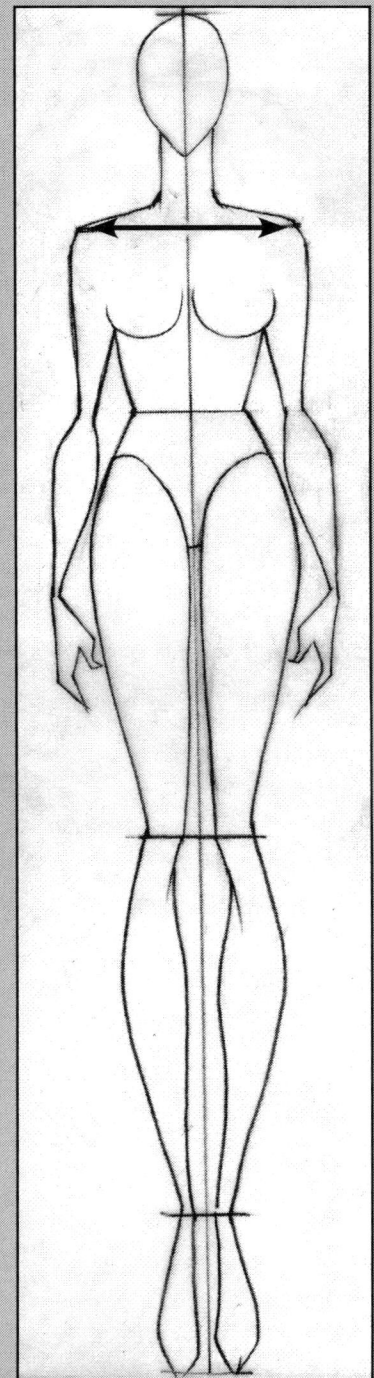

Average figure type with average shoulders

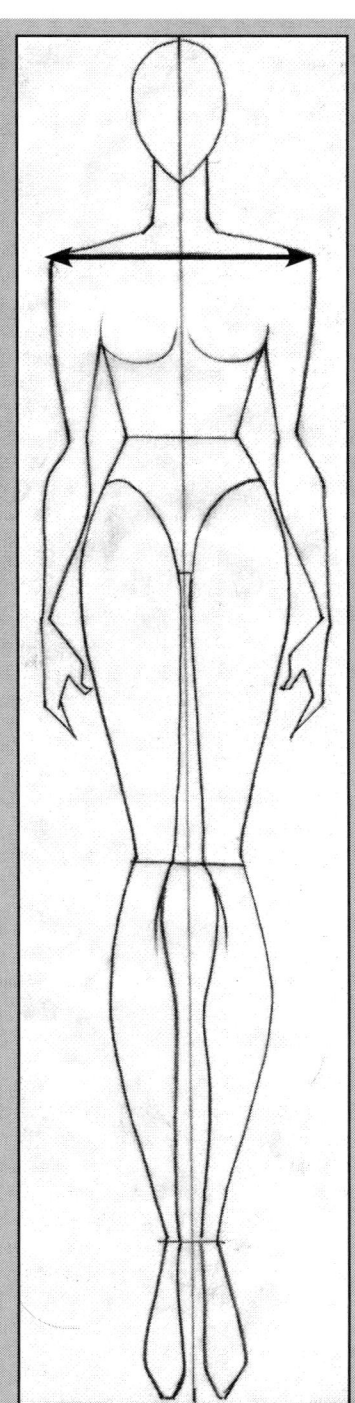

Average figure type with wide shoulders

Women's croquis with different posture

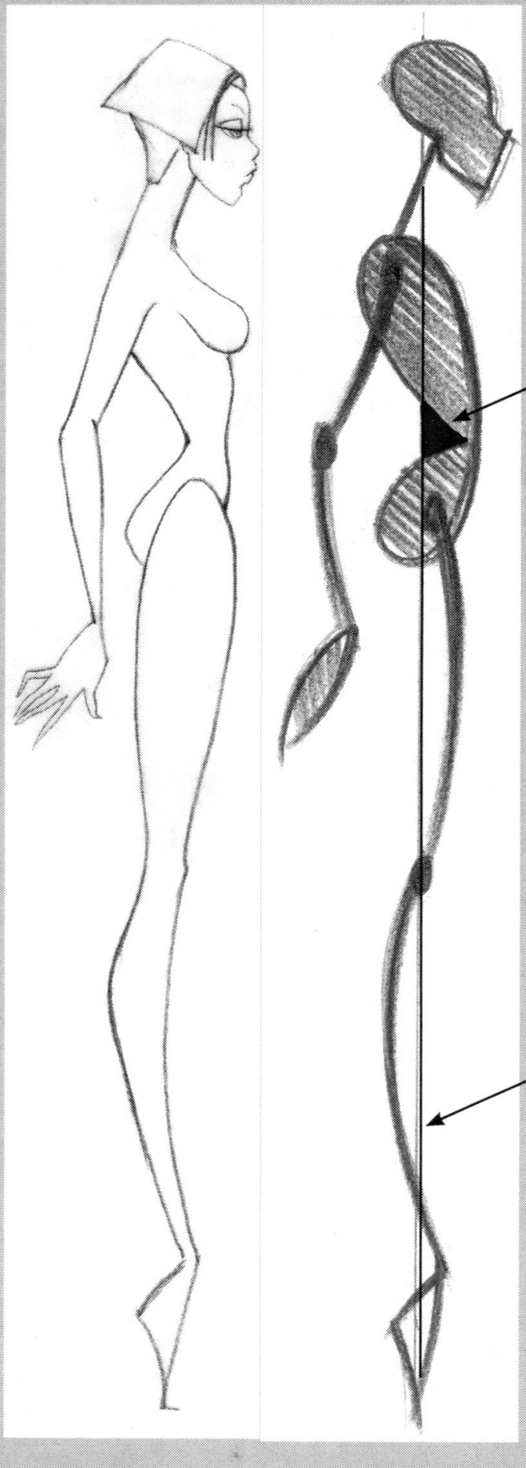

Pay attention to the distance between the body in the waistline area and balance line

Balance line

Additional learning resources for the book available at www.fashioncroquis.com/resources/figuredrawing

Standard posture

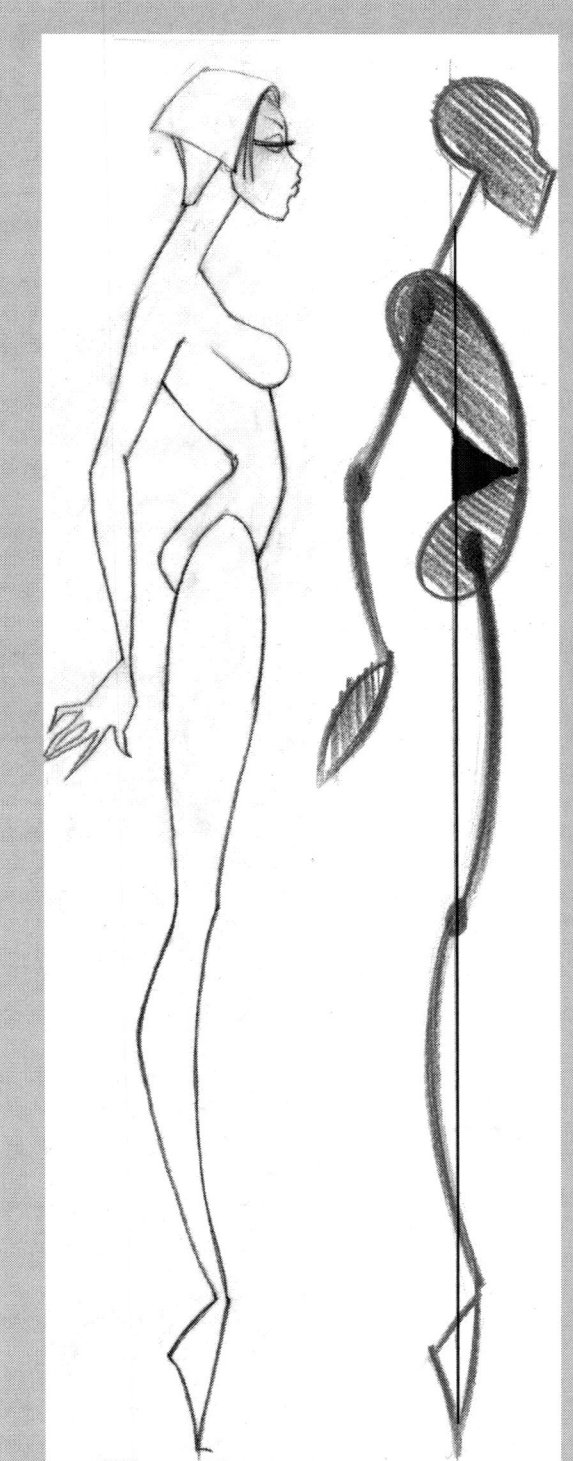

Slumped posture

Avoid placement of waistline area too far from balance line

Too erect posture

Waistline area close to balance line will create a very unnatural side view

Women's figure by size: apparel industry standards

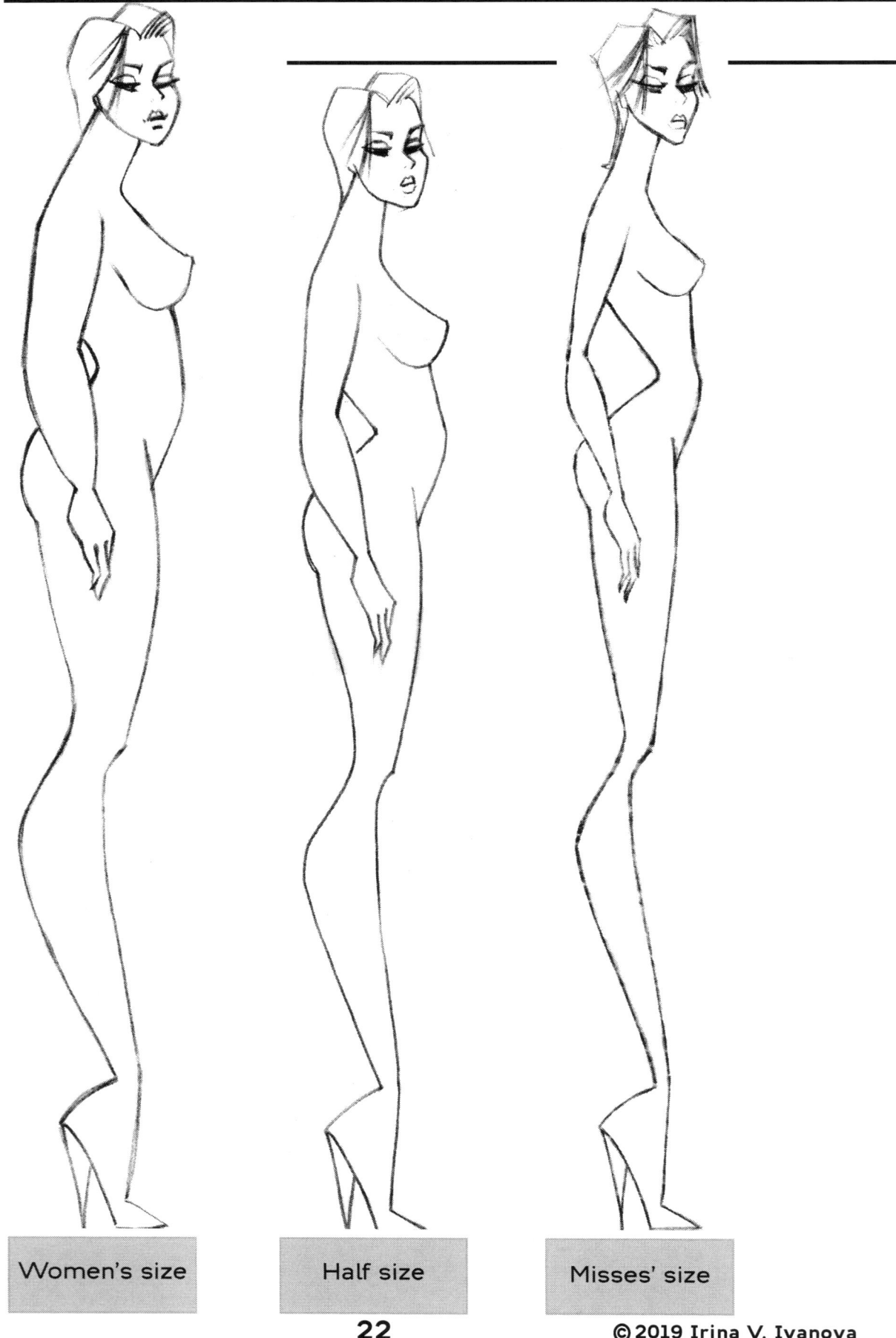

Women's size

Half size

Misses' size

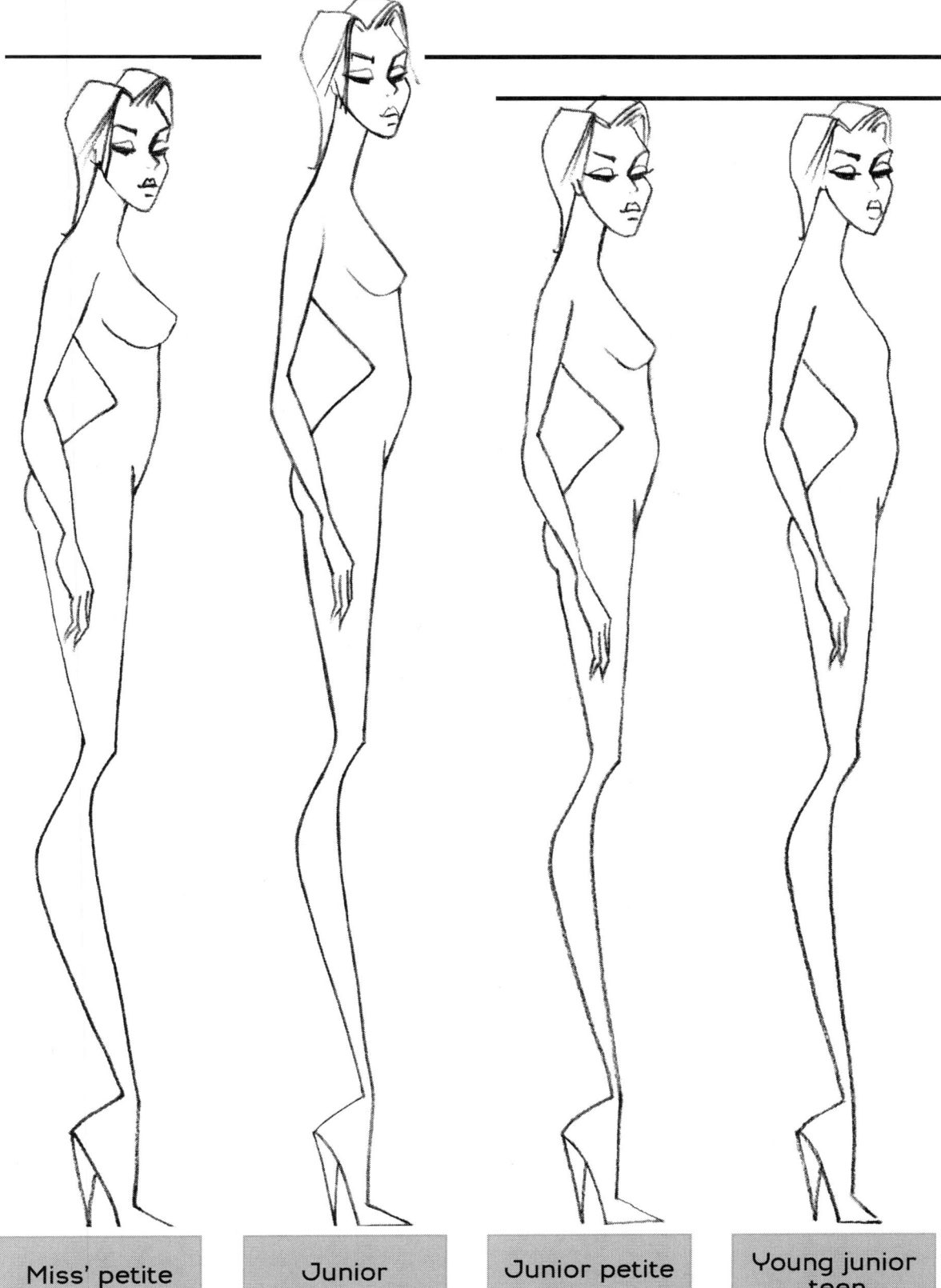

Historical overview of women body proportions in art

| Venus of Willendorf. 25000-21000 B.C. | Egypt. Queen Khamerernebty. 2490-2472 B.C. | Early Greek Statue 650 B.C. |

| Venus De Medici. 3rd century B.C. | Hubert and Jan van Eyck. 1432 | Sandro Botticelli. Birth of Venus. 1482 |

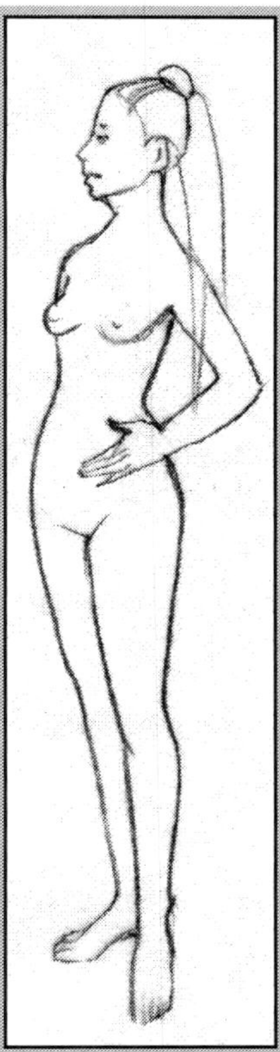

Hieronymus Bosch. about 1500	Albrecht Durer. Eve. 1504	Hans Baldung Grien. about 1540.	Lucas Cranach. Venus. about 1550
Klimt. Nuda Veritas. 1899	Pablo Picasso 1907	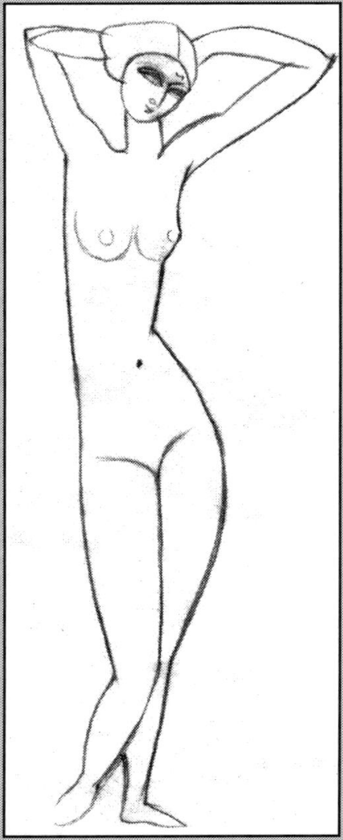	Modigliani. Caryatid. 1911

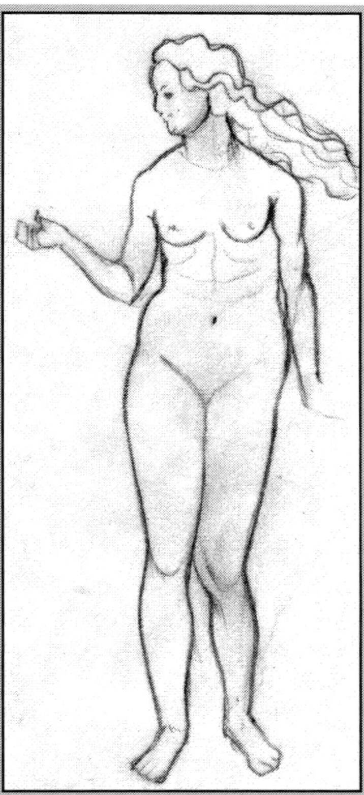

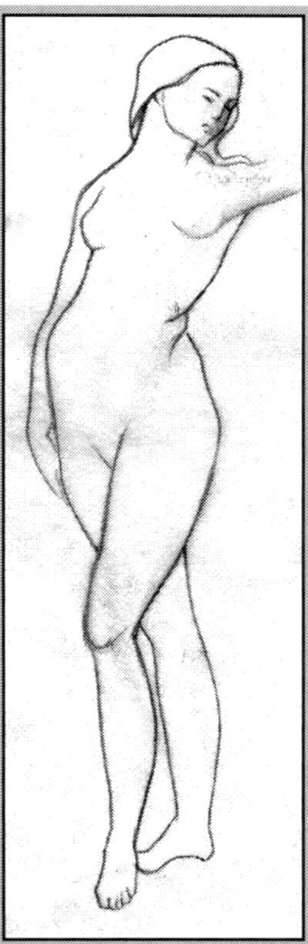

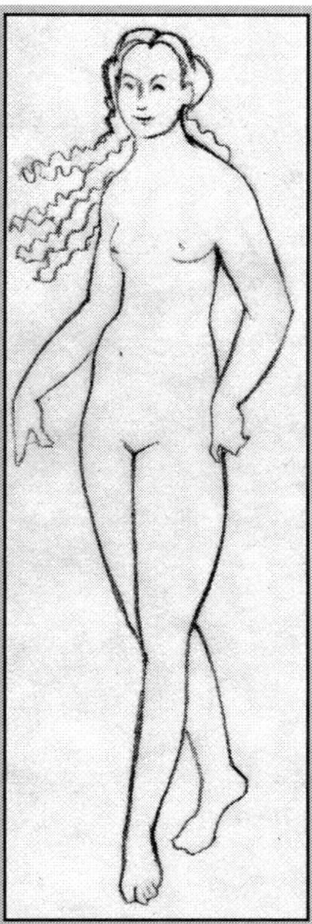

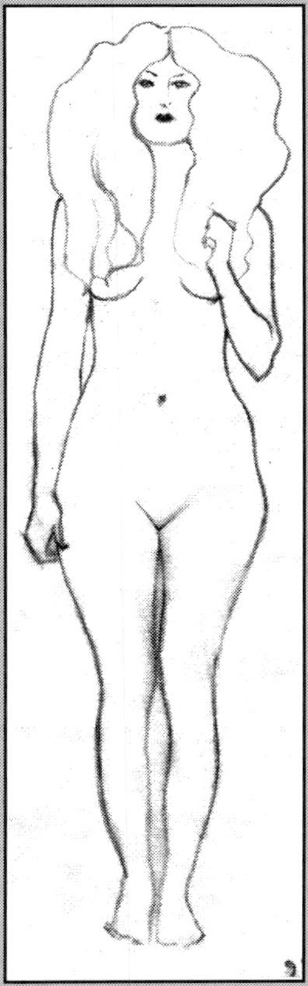

Contents:

Chapter 1. Pages 9-25
Basics of body proportions

Chapter 2. Pages 27-35
Fashion figure schematics (wire skeleton study)

Chapter 3. Pages 37-45
Sketching strategy

Chapter 4. Pages 47-61
Freehand sketching for 10 heads tall fashion figure (front view)

Chapter 5. Pages 63-75
Freehand sketching for 10 heads tall fashion figure (side view)

Chapter 6. Pages 77-91
Cutting method for fashion figure croquis

Chapter 7. Pages 93-125
Figure croquis manipulations

Chapter 8. Pages 127-147
Faces and hands drawing

Index
Pages 148-149

About the author
Pages 150-151

Chapter 2

Fashion figure schematics (wire skeleton study)

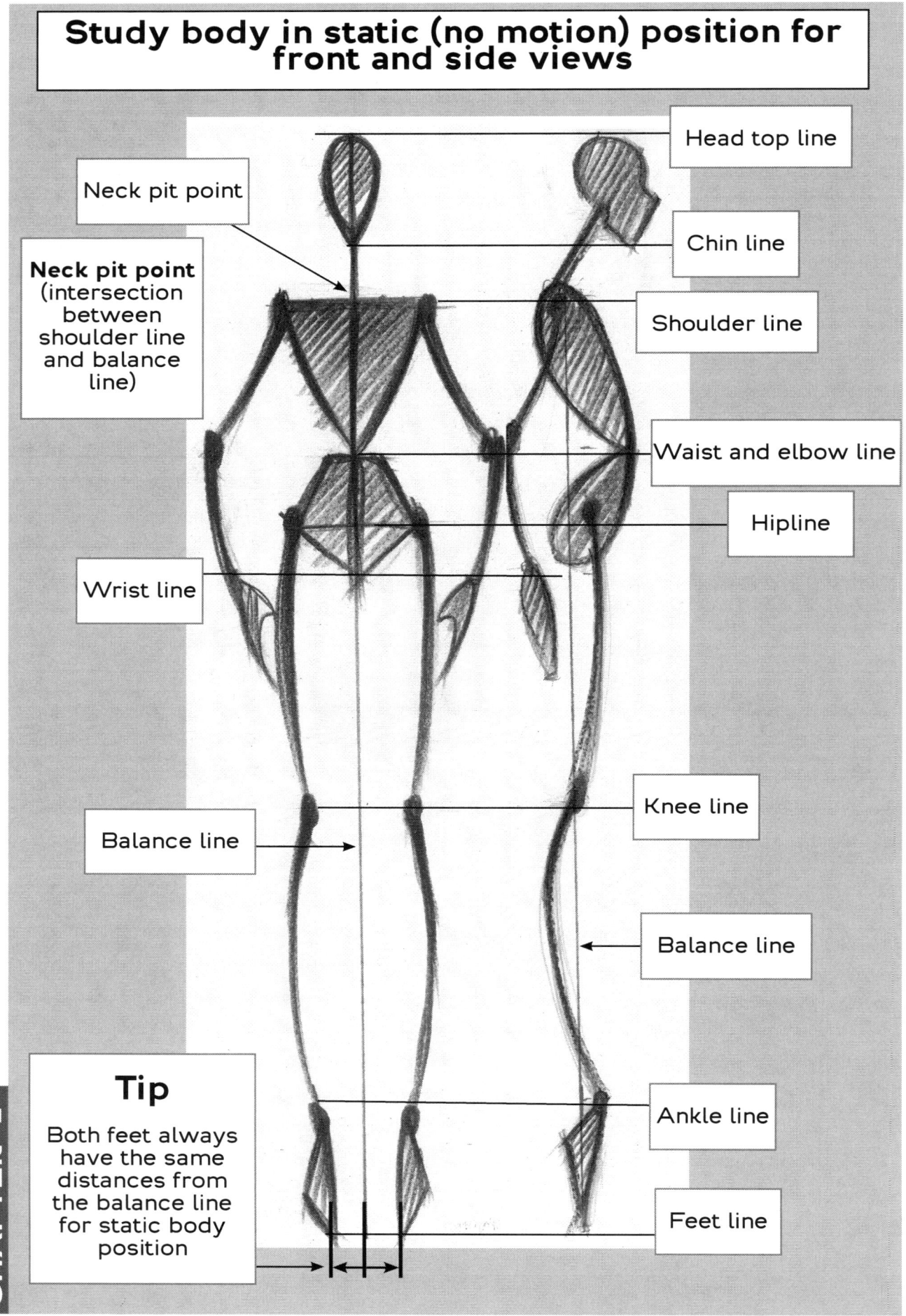

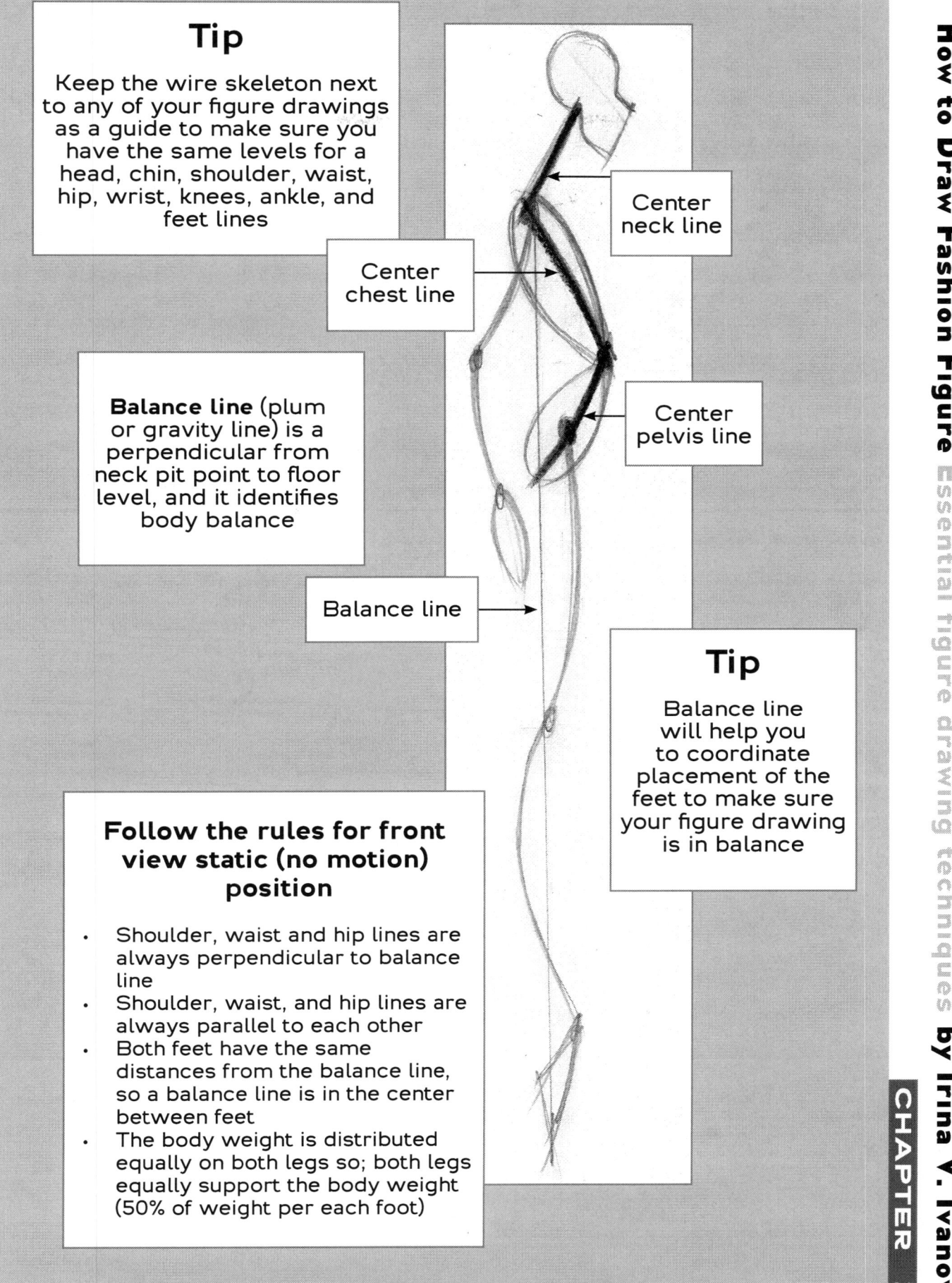

Tip

Keep the wire skeleton next to any of your figure drawings as a guide to make sure you have the same levels for a head, chin, shoulder, waist, hip, wrist, knees, ankle, and feet lines

Center neck line

Center chest line

Center pelvis line

Balance line (plum or gravity line) is a perpendicular from neck pit point to floor level, and it identifies body balance

Balance line

Tip

Balance line will help you to coordinate placement of the feet to make sure your figure drawing is in balance

Follow the rules for front view static (no motion) position

- Shoulder, waist and hip lines are always perpendicular to balance line
- Shoulder, waist, and hip lines are always parallel to each other
- Both feet have the same distances from the balance line, so a balance line is in the center between feet
- The body weight is distributed equally on both legs so; both legs equally support the body weight (50% of weight per each foot)

Study body in movement

You may concentrate all weight of the figure on:

- both feet evenly (static) (see page 28)
- one foot only (movement) (see page 30 figure A)
- both feet unevenly (movement) (see page 30 figure B)

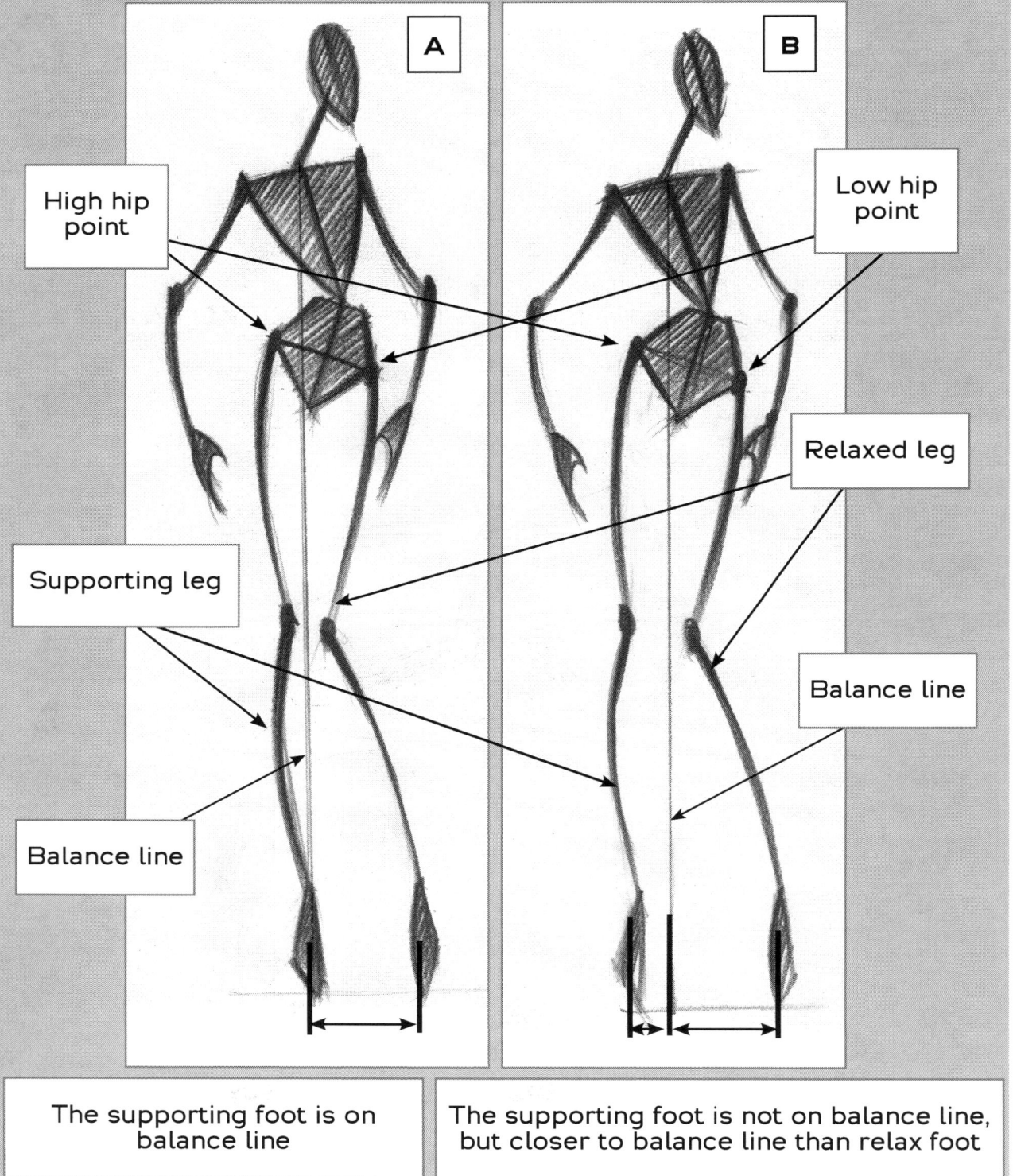

The supporting foot is on balance line

The supporting foot is not on balance line, but closer to balance line than relax foot

Follow the rules for movement

- Shoulder, waist, and hip lines are never perpendicular to balance line in the movement
- Move shoulder and hiplines in the opposite direction to each other
- Always place supporting foot on balance line or closer to balance line than relaxed foot
- Supporting legs always started from the high point of the hipline and keep most or 100% of body weight
- Keep supporting foot precisely on the balance line if you want to carry the weight of the figure on this foot only
- Keep the balance line closer to supporting foot rather than to relaxed foot if you want to spread the weight of the figure on both legs

How would you know which leg is supporting?

- The high hip point indicates the supporting leg (see page 30)
- The supporting foot is always close to balance line or on the balance line
- The supporting leg should always be straight because it carries all or most of the body weight

Tip

Make sure that the balance line will connect the pit point and the supporting foot

Remember, the supporting foot and the balance line are "friends," so keep them together or close to each other

Tip

The relaxed leg is the leg which does not carry the weight of the body at all or carries the less of the body weight

Tip

The balance line always comes closer to the foot supporting the volume of the body weight

Tip

Body balance is a visual equilibrium of a body

Difference between movement (motion) and static (no motion) positions are in the placement of shoulder, waistlines, and supporting legs

© 2019 Irina V. Ivanova

Different body positions with a wire skeleton

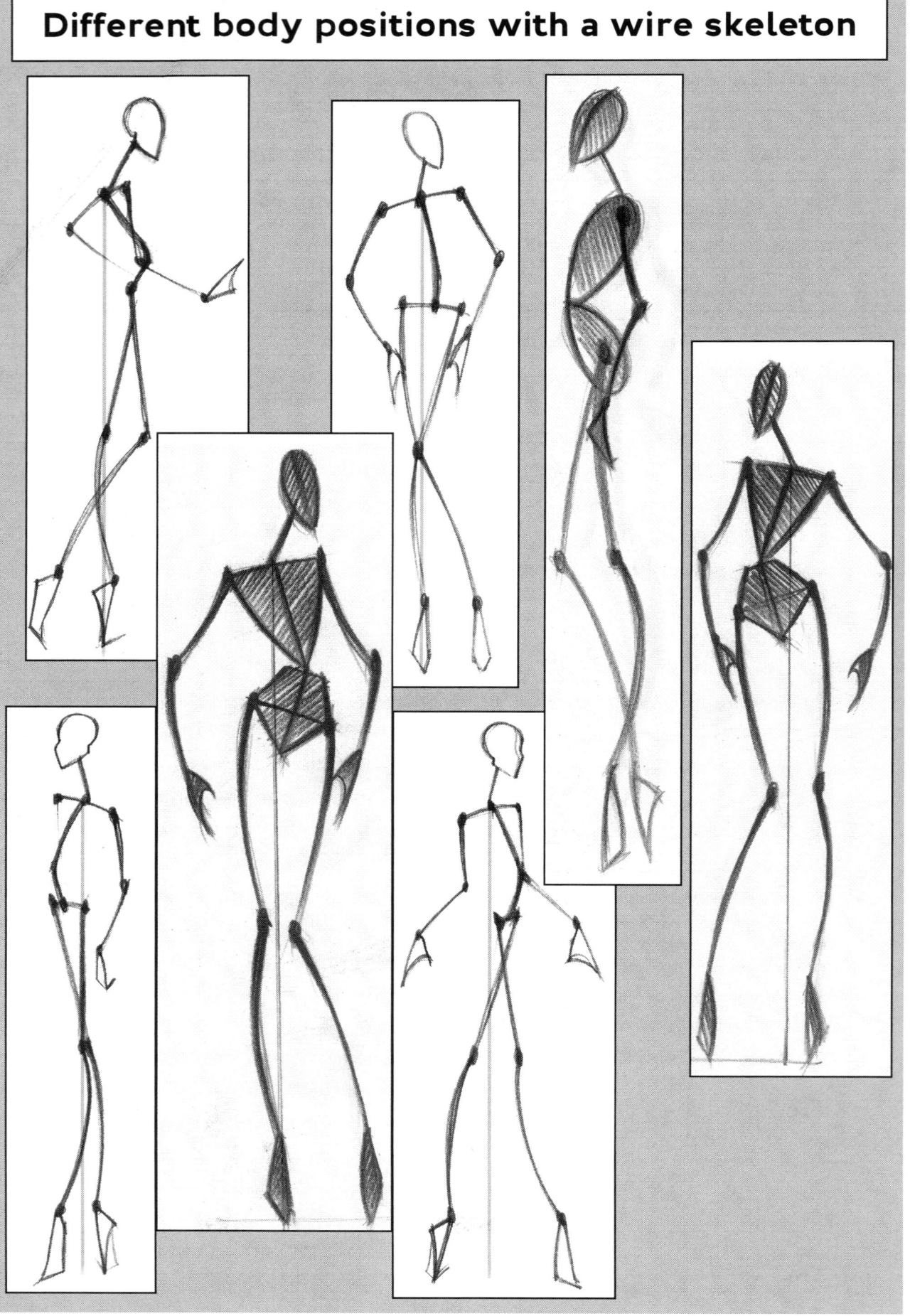

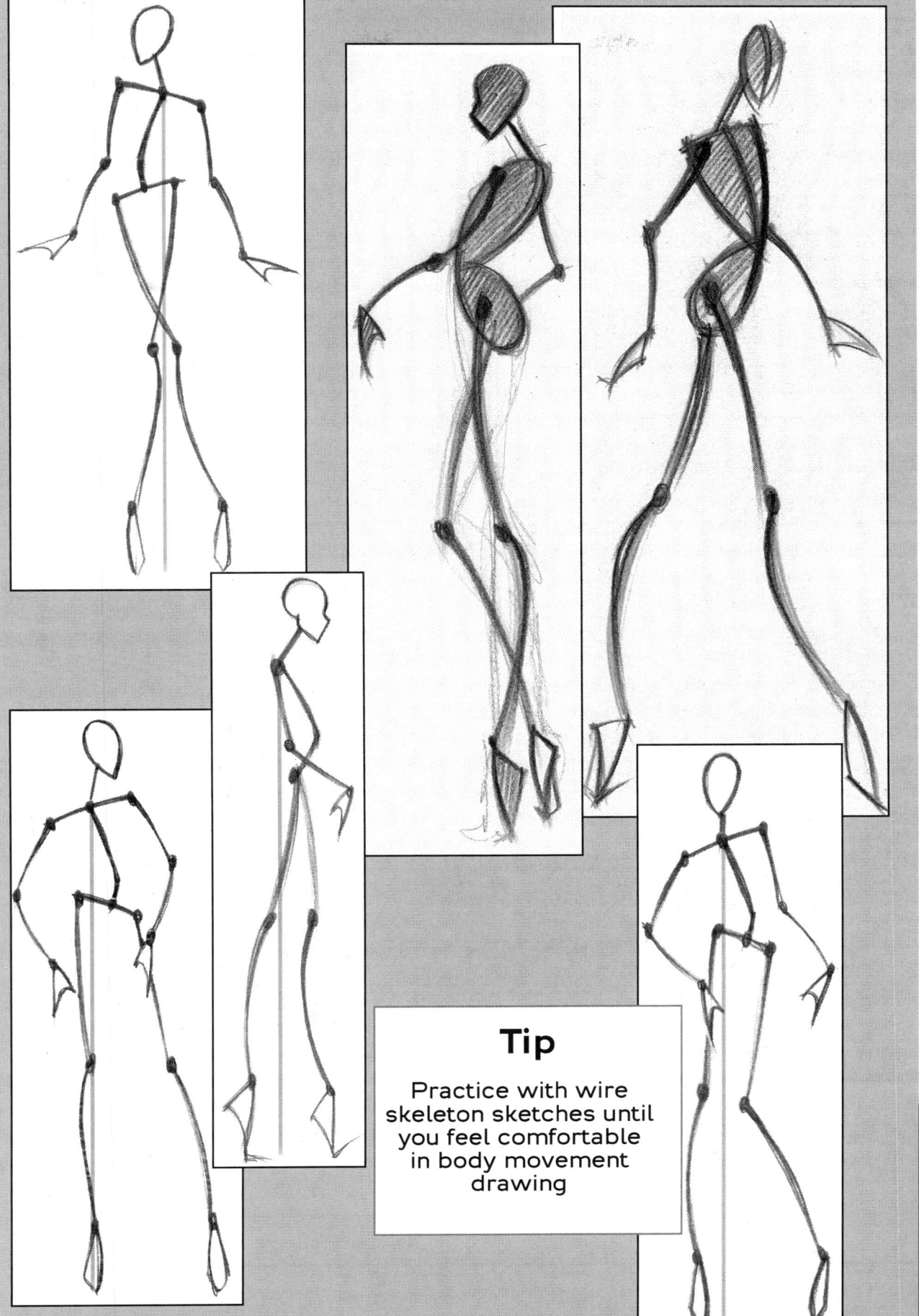

Tip

Practice with wire skeleton sketches until you feel comfortable in body movement drawing

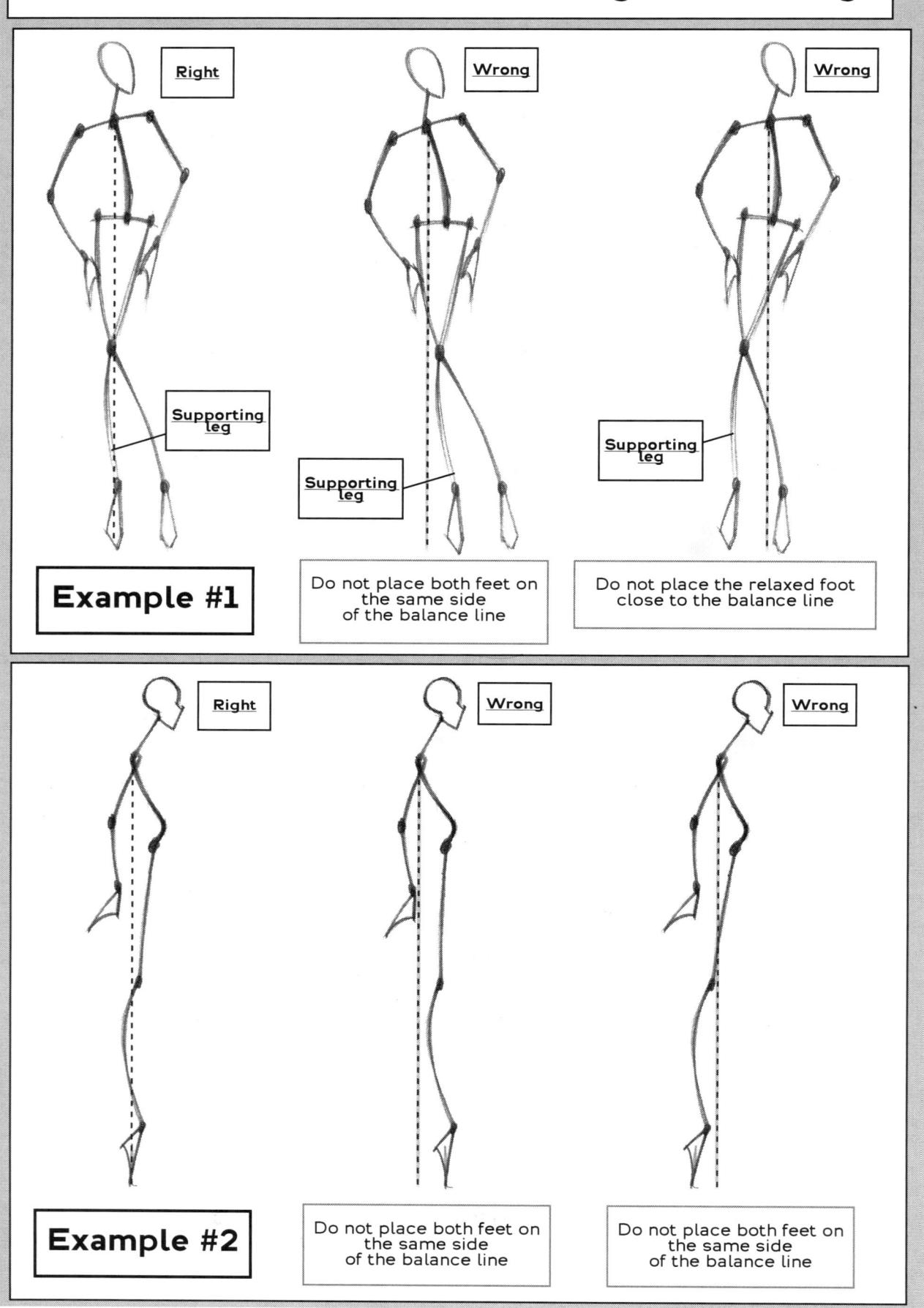

Right
Wrong
Wrong
Supporting leg
Supporting leg
Supporting leg
Example #3
Do not place both feet on the same distance from the balance line for body in movement
Do not place both feet on the same side of the balance line

Right
Wrong
Wrong
Supporting leg
Supporting leg
Example #4
Do not place both feet on the same side of the balance line
Do not place the relaxed foot on the balance line

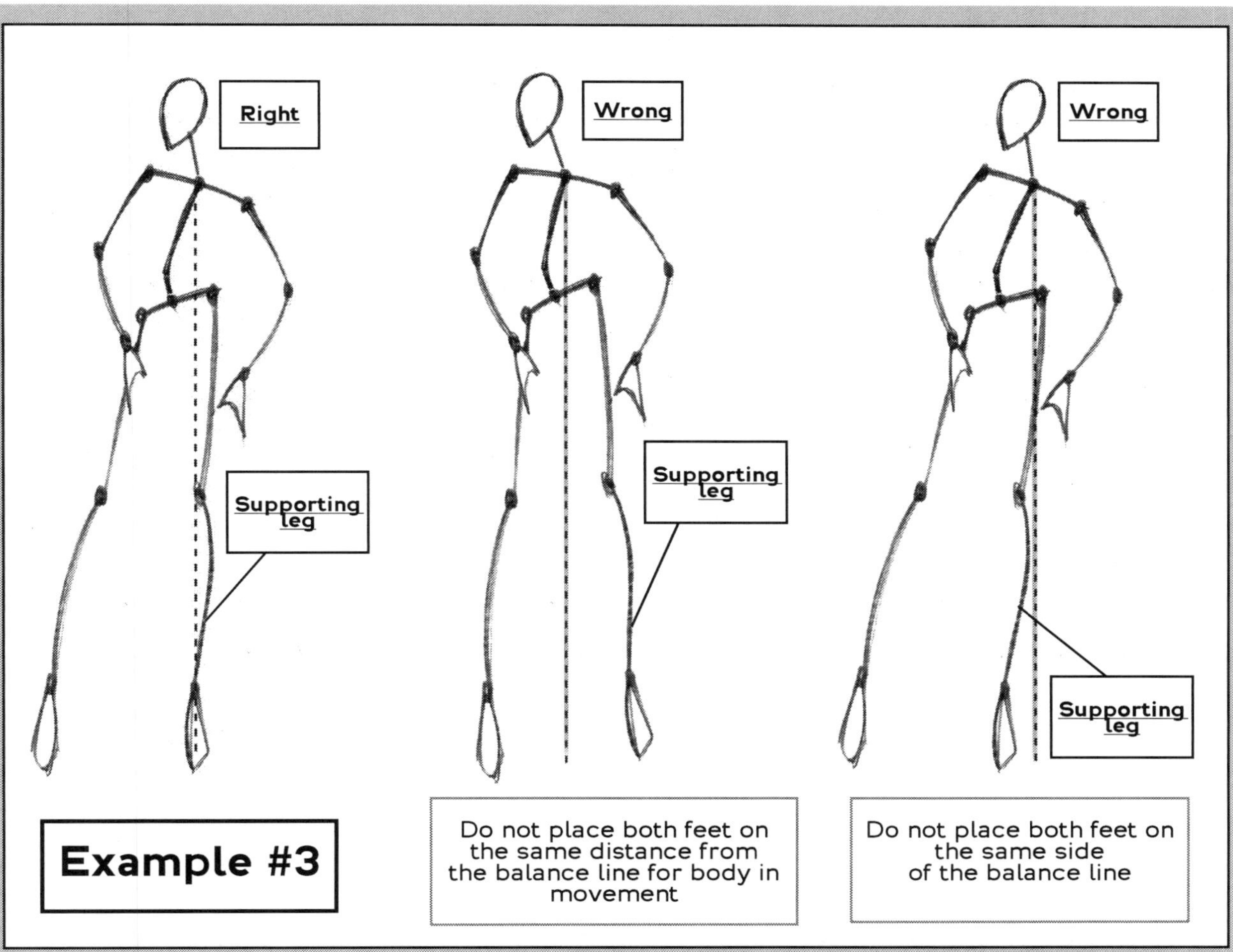

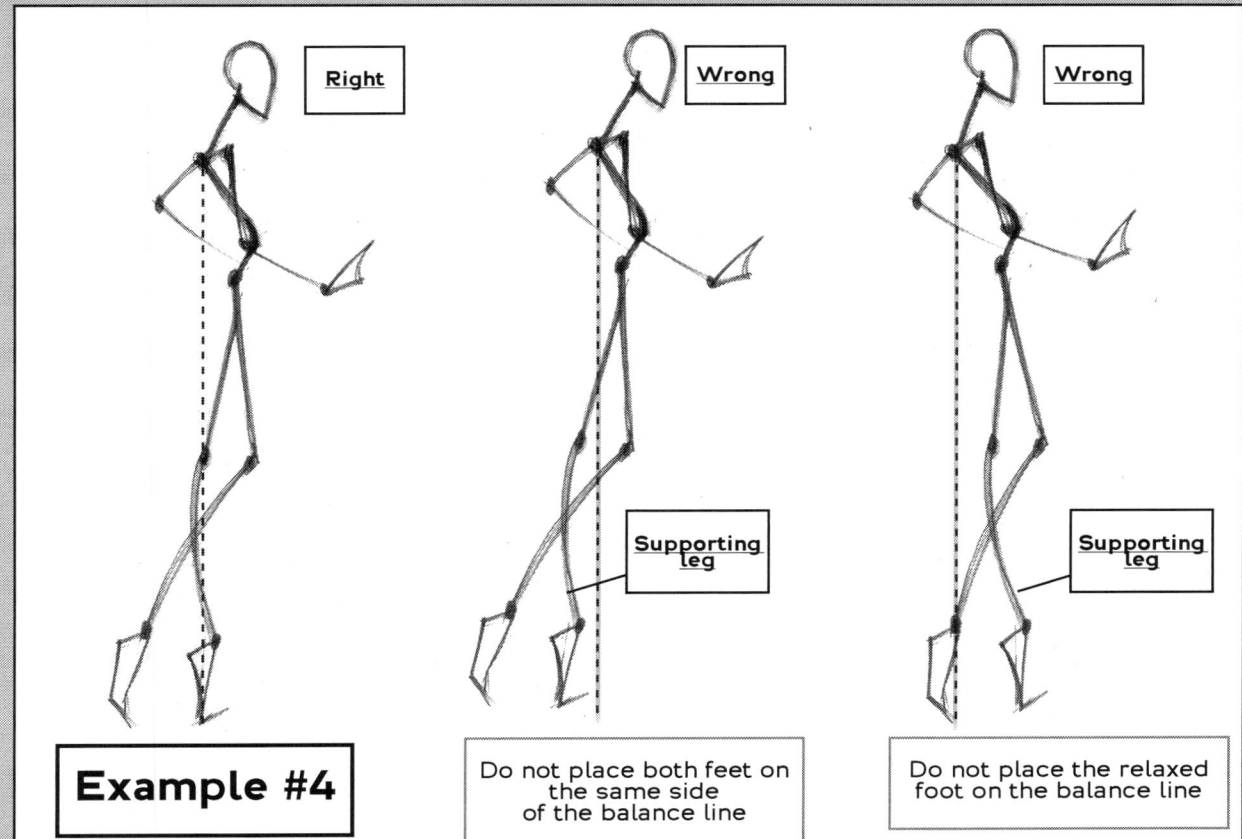

Contents:

Chapter 1. Pages 9-25
Basics of body proportions

Chapter 2. Pages 27-35
Fashion figure schematics (wire skeleton study)

Chapter 3. Pages 37-45
Sketching strategy

Chapter 4. Pages 47-61
Freehand sketching for 10 heads tall fashion figure (front view)

Chapter 5. Pages 63-75
Freehand sketching for 10 heads tall fashion figure (side view)

Chapter 6. Pages 77-91
Cutting method for fashion figure croquis

Chapter 7. Pages 93-125
Figure croquis manipulations

Chapter 8. Pages 127-147
Faces and hands drawing

Index
Pages 148-149

About the author
Pages 150-151

Chapter 3

Sketching strategy

Step by step sketching strategy

Step #1. Choose the head-body proportions

Before you start drawing your croquis, think **how many heads tall** you want your croquis will be.
Ratio of the head to the size of the body is significant for fashion illustration.

Do a few simplified sketches with different size of the head. Look at all of them, choose the best proportions for your project and focus only on these proportions.

Do not draw yet any details. It is not important right now. Just think about overall head-body proportions.

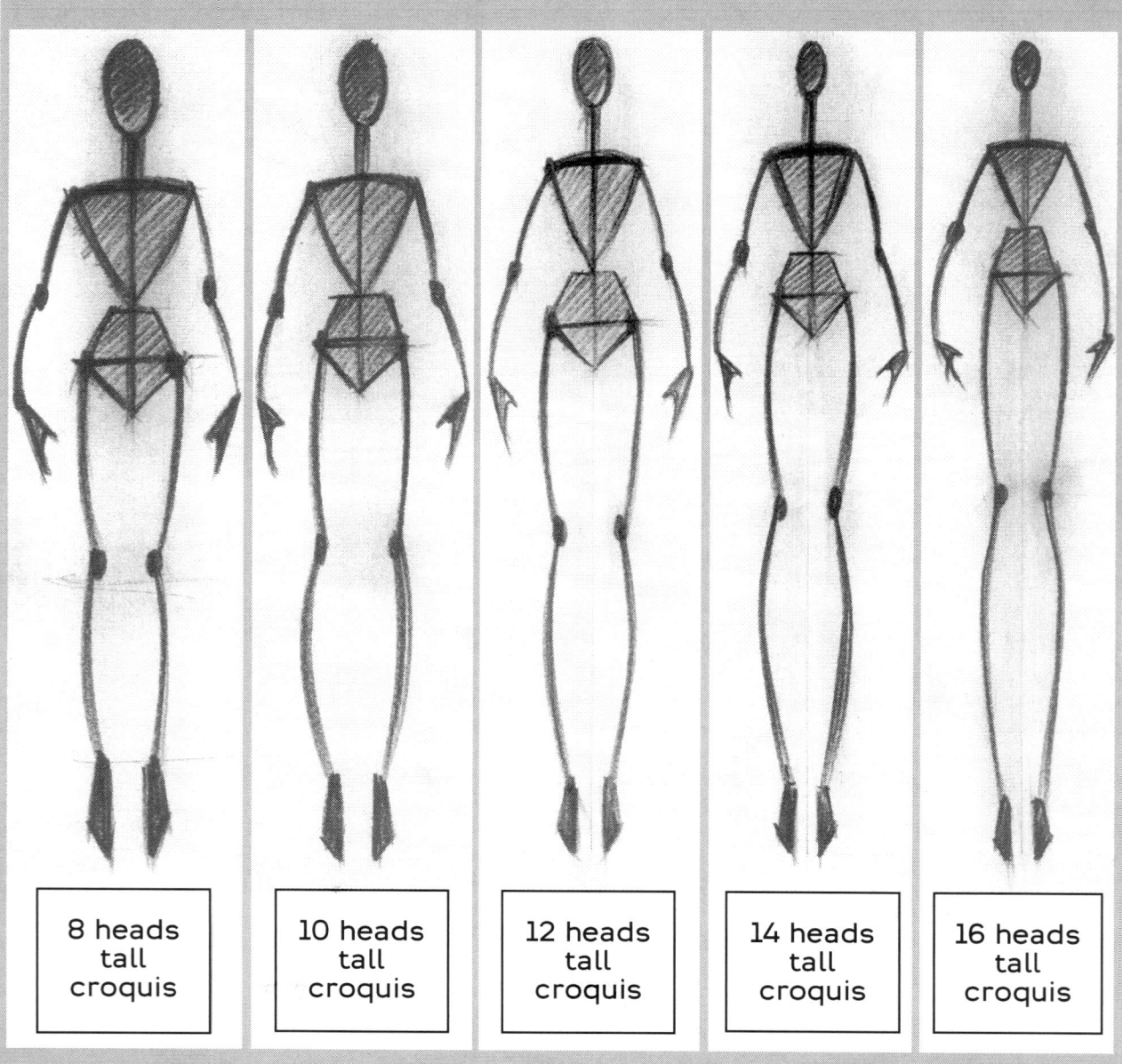

| 8 heads tall croquis | 10 heads tall croquis | 12 heads tall croquis | 14 heads tall croquis | 16 heads tall croquis |

Step #2. Choose the body style

Choose the body style for your croquis after you pick your head-body proportions.
Decide what kind of body type or body shape you want. It could depend on the style of garment collection, the demography of your customer, or maybe just on your artistic preferences.
See the below figures with the same head size, but different body shapes.

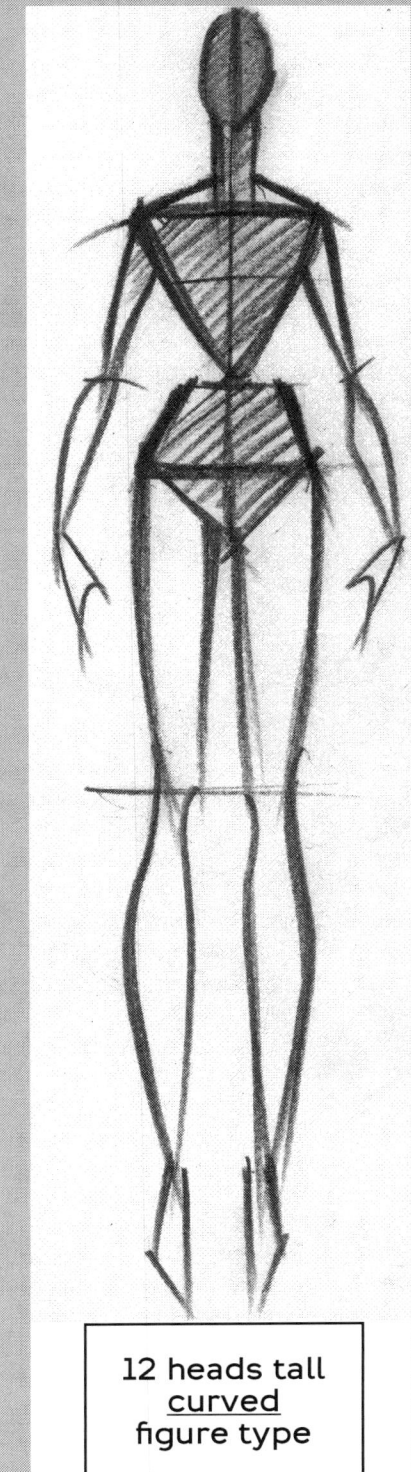

12 heads tall
<u>curved</u>
figure type

12 heads tall
<u>average</u>
figure type

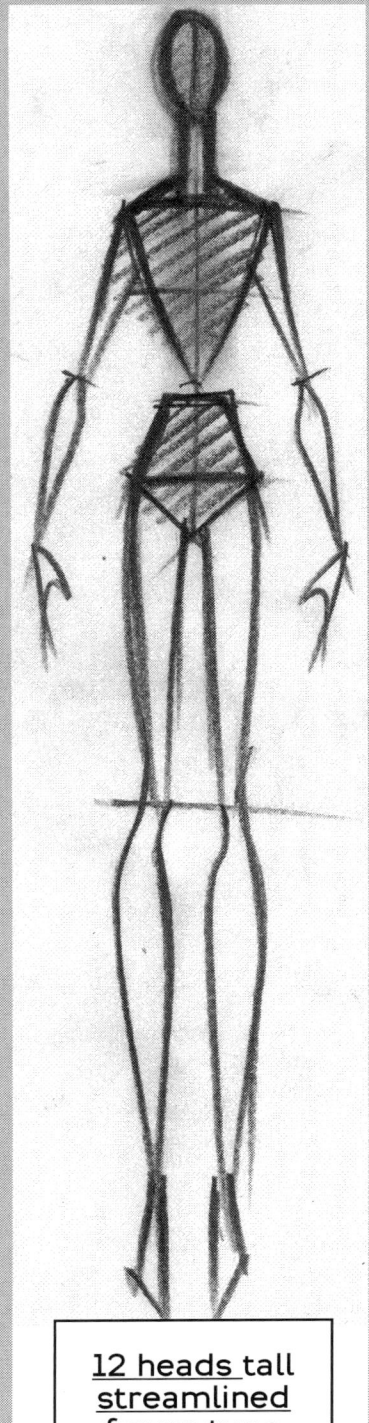

<u>12 heads</u> tall
<u>streamlined</u>
<u>figure type</u>

Step #3. Focus on the right body movement

Now focus on the **right body movement** for your croquis. An appropriate movement will show your garment in the best way, but the wrong movement may destroy it completely.

For a dress with train use side view croquis because it will be the only way to show the beauty of the train

Example #1

Dress with train

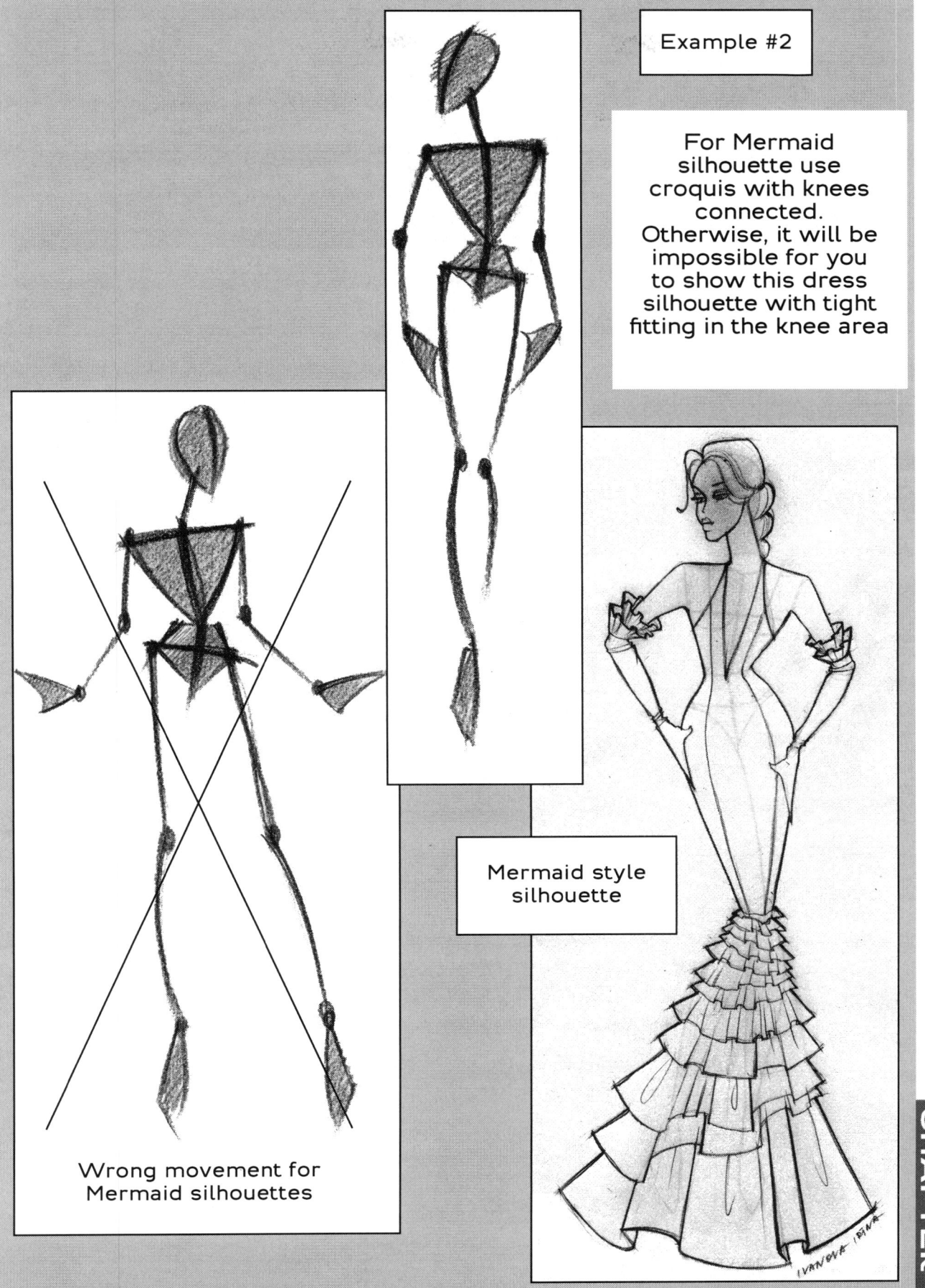

Example #2

For Mermaid silhouette use croquis with knees connected. Otherwise, it will be impossible for you to show this dress silhouette with tight fitting in the knee area

Mermaid style silhouette

Wrong movement for Mermaid silhouettes

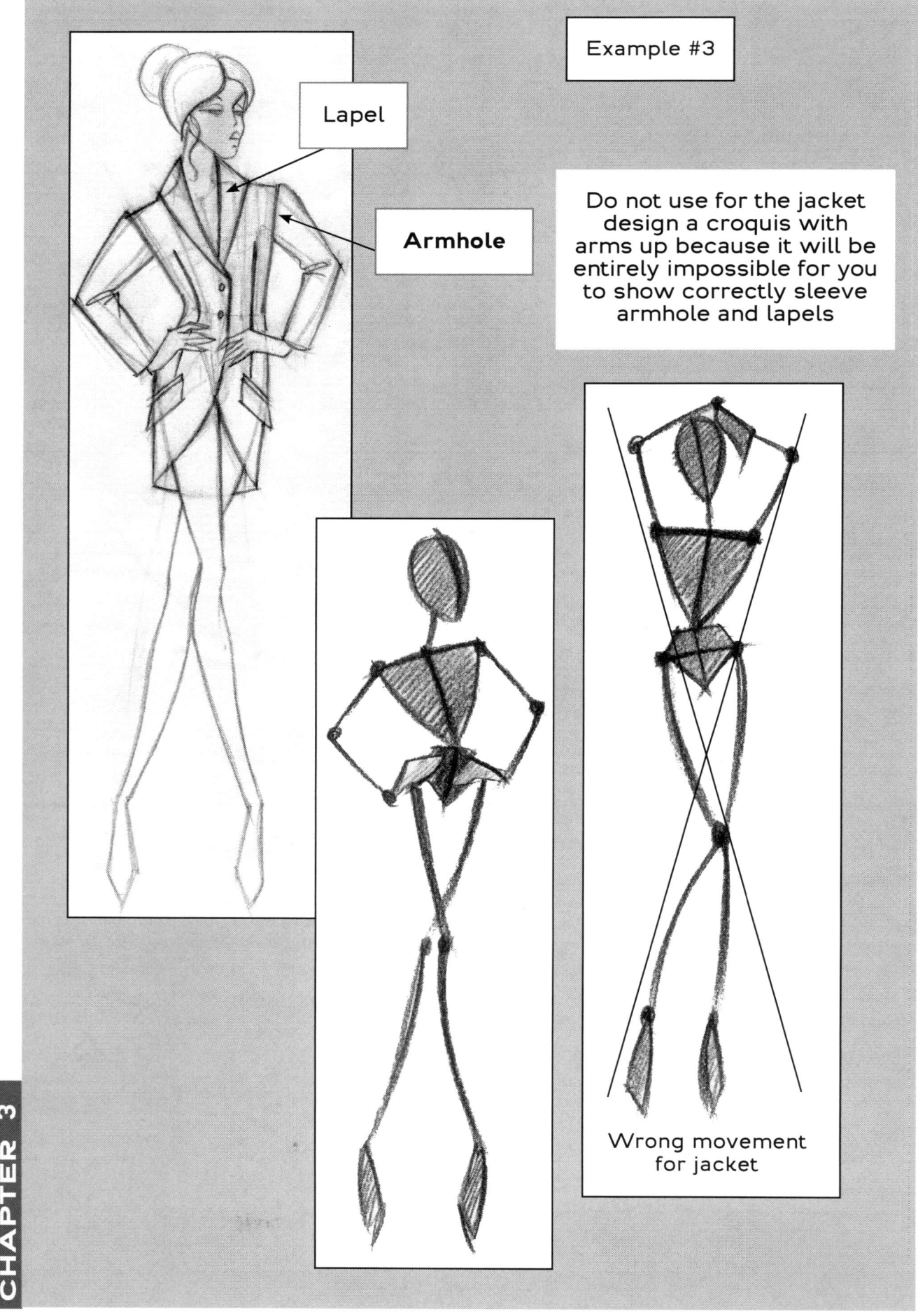

Example #3

Lapel

Armhole

Do not use for the jacket design a croquis with arms up because it will be entirely impossible for you to show correctly sleeve armhole and lapels

Wrong movement for jacket

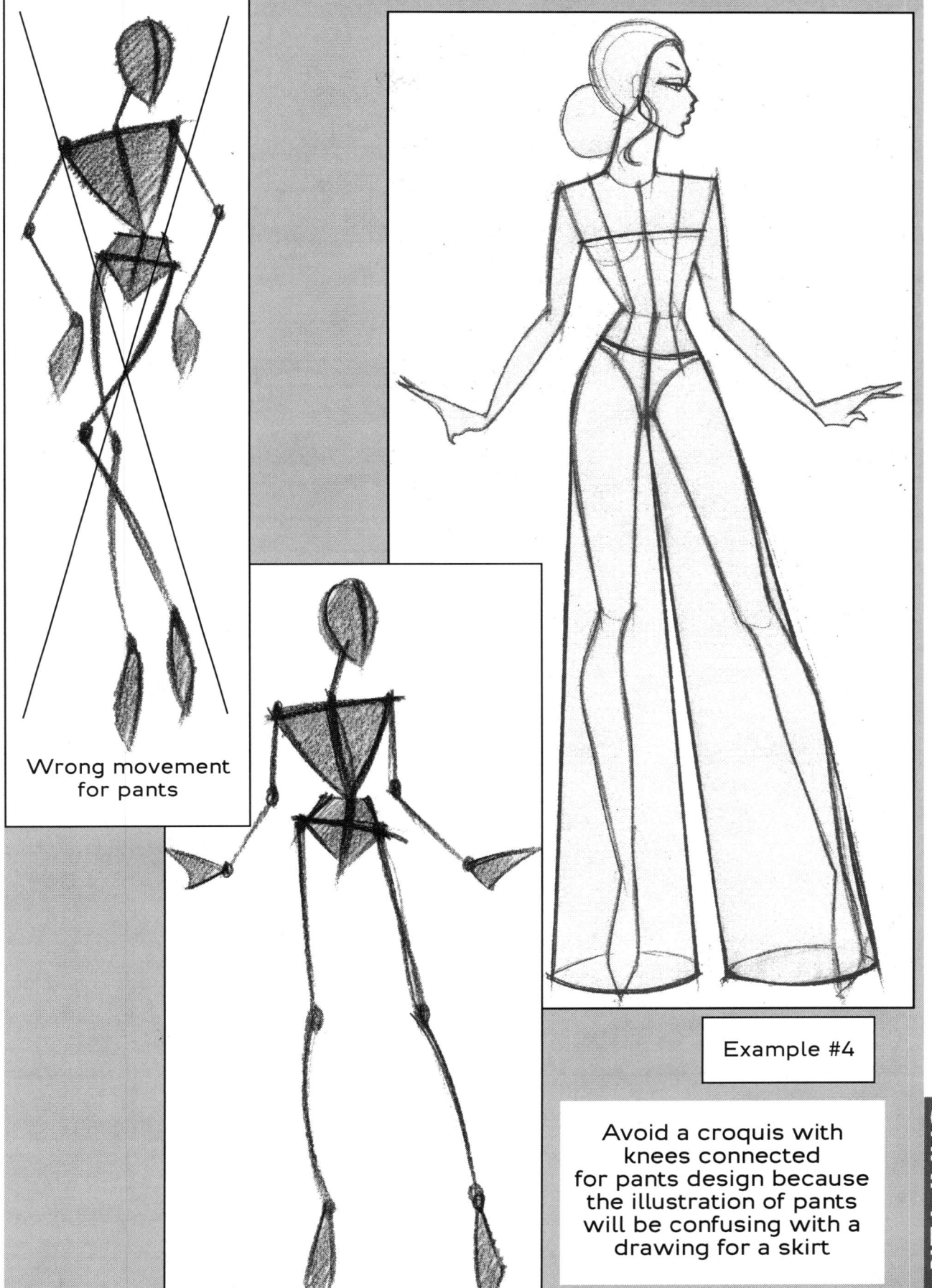

Wrong movement for pants

Example #4

Avoid a croquis with knees connected for pants design because the illustration of pants will be confusing with a drawing for a skirt

Step #4. Avoid sitting figure for fashion illustration

Do not draw **sitting figure** unless you are doing illustrations for an advertisement or editorial drawing. Use only standing or walking figures because it is the best way to show all garment design details.

Step #5. Do not use excessive body movement

Do not use **excessive body movement** in your illustration. Remember your goal is to show garment design but not a complex figure movement. Find the way to show movement without garment distraction.

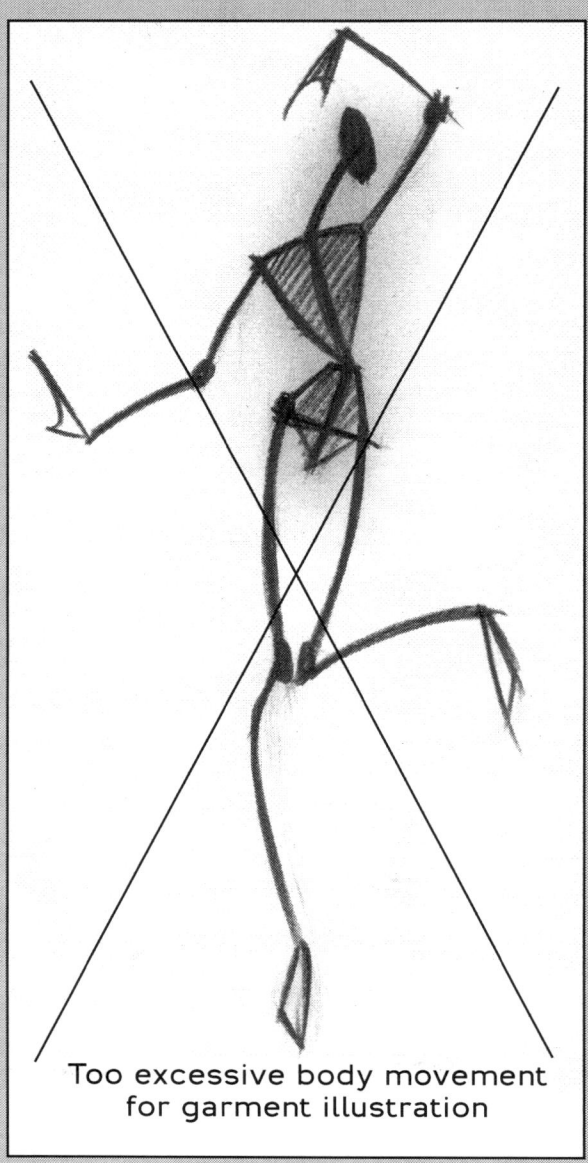

Too excessive body movement for garment illustration

Step #6. Avoid stiff static body poses

Try to avoid stiff static body poses. Use poses which add mood to your fashion illustration without distorting the garment.

Step #7. Make sure your figure drawing is accurate

Check and double check the accuracy of your croquis before you start using it for fashion illustration.

Step #8. Have strategy in place

Select body type, proportions and movement for your figure. Start with general outlining before you draw face and small details.

Step #9. Develop a set of croquis

Develop a set of croquis (a few figures in movement with the same body style and proportions).
Use your set to draw your garment collection. It will increase your productivity and let you focus on your primary goal – garment design.
You can always change body style and proportions of your croquis when you start a new project.
So, consider having a different set of croquis for different projects. For example, one set of croquis for a top model style and another set for women with curves.

Step #10. Be patient

At first, keep your figure drawing not detailed. Start slowly with lose, simple pencil line. Become comfortable with measuring and cultivate correct drawing habits. Make sure that all parts of the figure are correctly related and proportioned in the way you want. The drawing process will be more accurate and spontaneous after a while.

Step #11. Never be discouraged by mistakes!

Learn from your mistakes.
Each mistake can make you a better designer and illustrator.

Contents:

Chapter 1. Pages 9-25
Basics of body proportions

Chapter 2. Pages 27-35
Fashion figure schematics (wire skeleton study)

Chapter 3. Pages 37-45
Sketching strategy

Chapter 4. Pages 47-61
Freehand sketching for 10 heads tall fashion figure (front view)

Chapter 5. Pages 63-75
Freehand sketching for 10 heads tall fashion figure (side view)

Chapter 6. Pages 77-91
Cutting method for fashion figure croquis

Chapter 7. Pages 93-125
Figure croquis manipulations

Chapter 8. Pages 127-147
Faces and hands drawing

Index
Pages 148-149

About the author
Pages 150-151

Chapter 4

Freehand sketching for 10 heads tall fashion figure (front view)

Freehand sketching of front view croquis

Neck pit point

Tip

Start from wire skeleton!

Tip

Coordinate placement of the feet for correctly balanced body movement with balance line

Balance line

Step #1

- Use wire skeleton as an underdrawing for your future template with chosen head – body proportions (see page 38) and body style (see page 39)
- This underdrawing will be your visual guide for the whole sketching process till final steps
- Keep all lines very loose and light
- Do not forget about balance line (see page 28)!

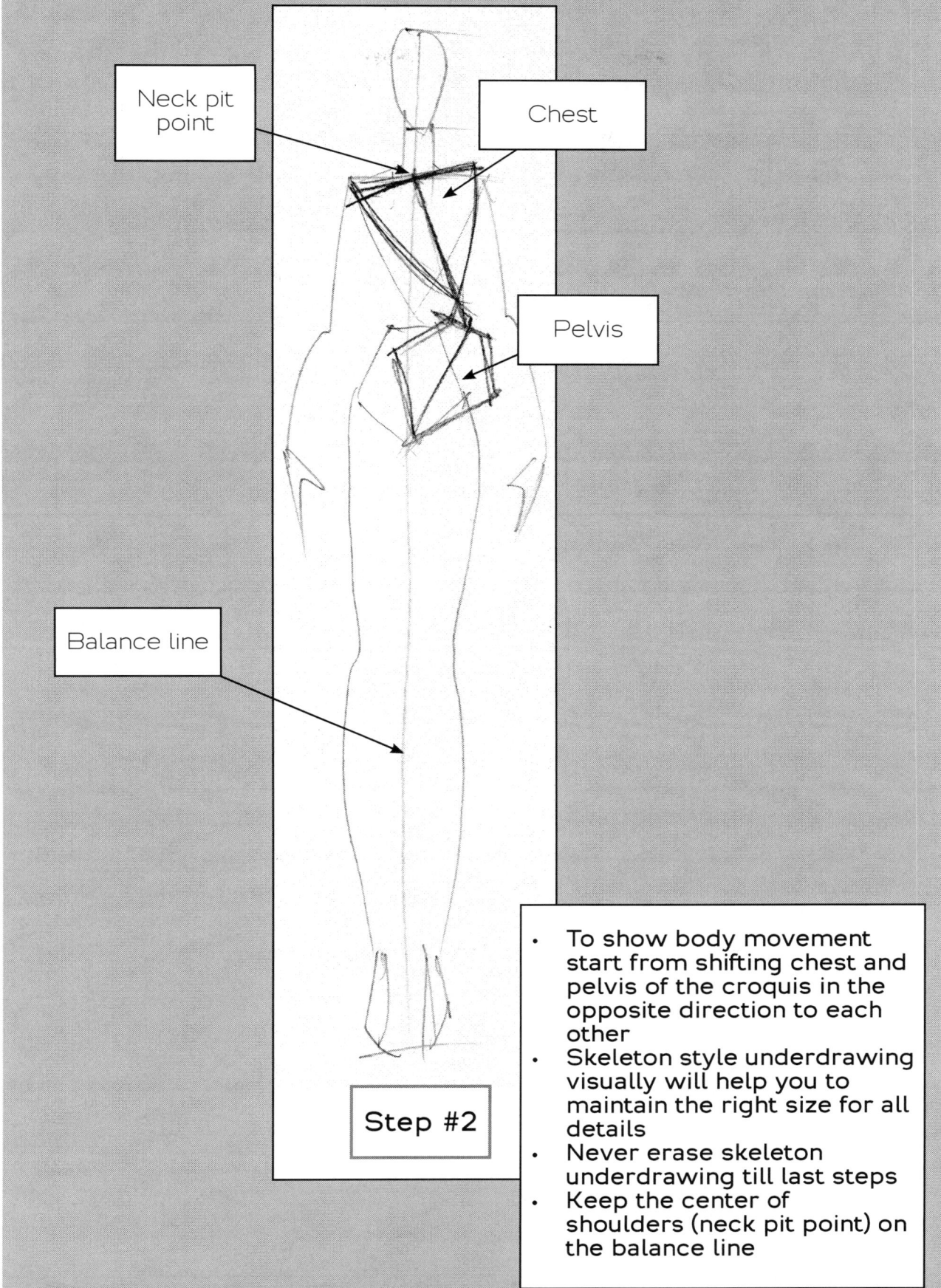

Freehand sketching of front view croquis (continued)

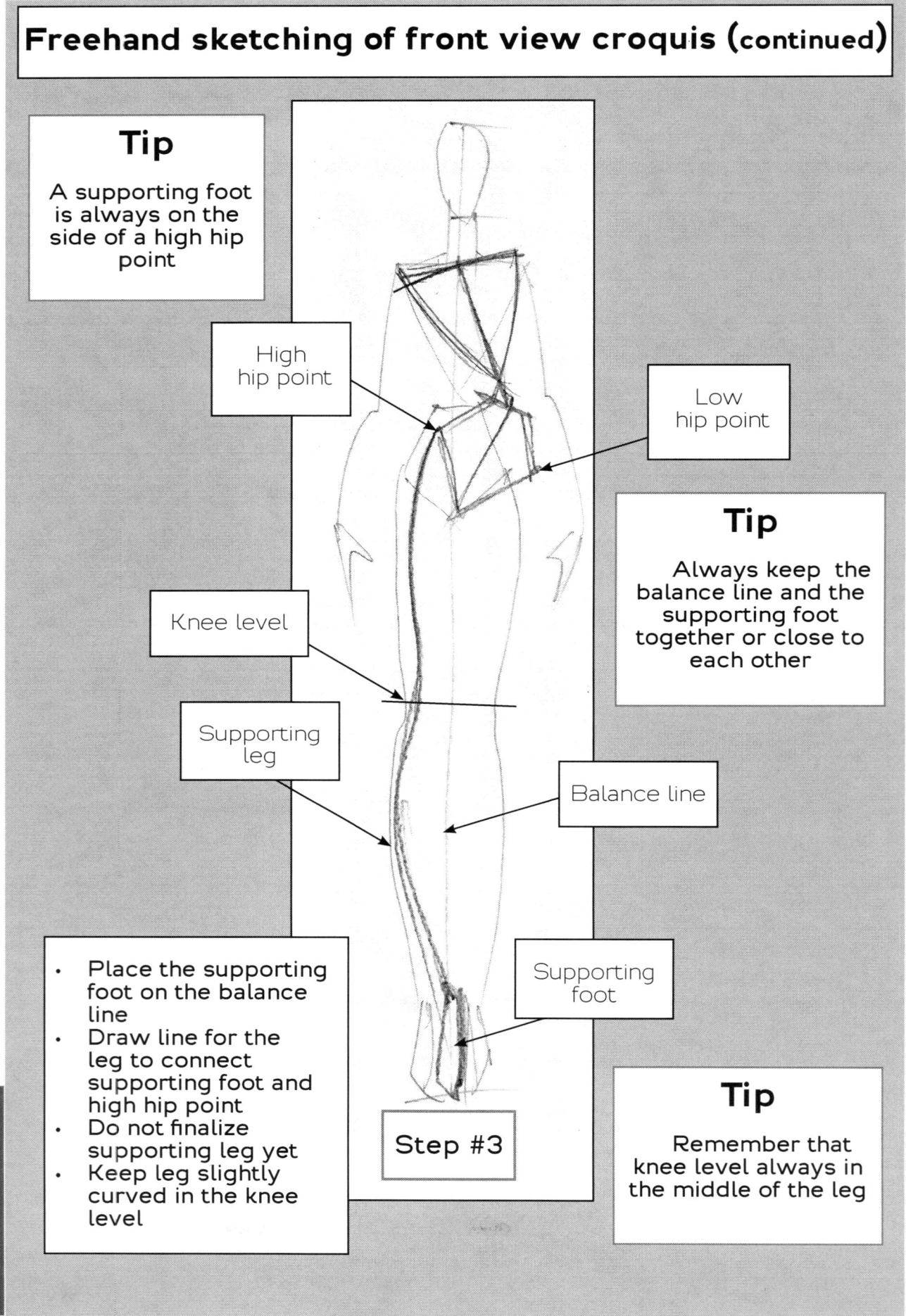

Tip

A supporting foot is always on the side of a high hip point

High hip point

Low hip point

Tip

Always keep the balance line and the supporting foot together or close to each other

Knee level

Supporting leg

Balance line

Supporting foot

- Place the supporting foot on the balance line
- Draw line for the leg to connect supporting foot and high hip point
- Do not finalize supporting leg yet
- Keep leg slightly curved in the knee level

Step #3

Tip

Remember that knee level always in the middle of the leg

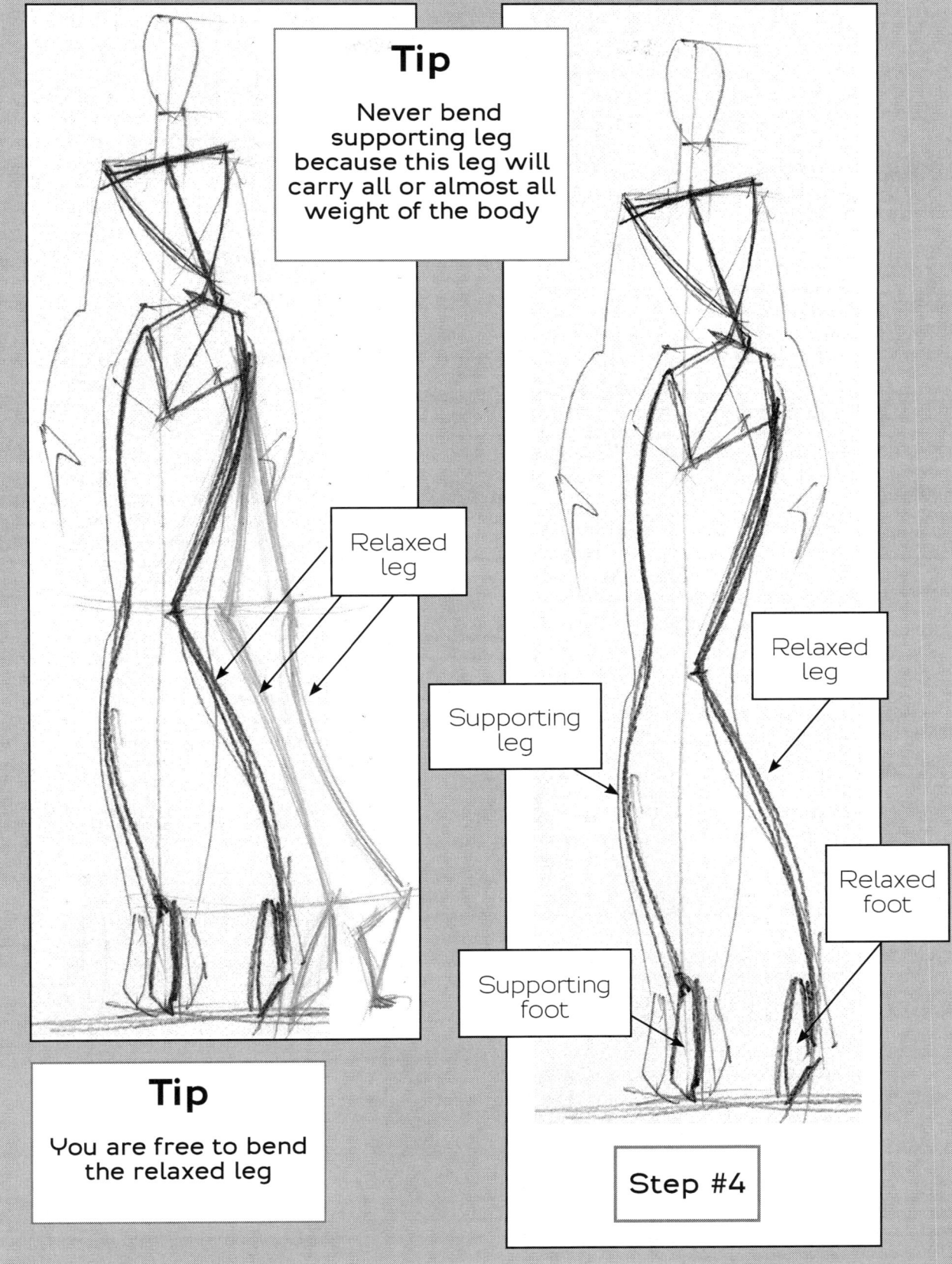

Tip

Never bend supporting leg because this leg will carry all or almost all weight of the body

Relaxed leg

Relaxed leg

Supporting leg

Relaxed foot

Supporting foot

Tip

You are free to bend the relaxed leg

Step #4

- Draw line for the relaxed leg to connect supporting foot and high hip point
- Do not finalize relaxed leg yet
- Keep both feet on the same horizontal level

Freehand sketching of front view croquis (continued)

Step #5

- Draw lines for both arms
- Outline simplified shape for both hands
- Do not finalize arms and hands drawing yet

Tip

With the same body and legs position you are free to draw any movement for arms and hands

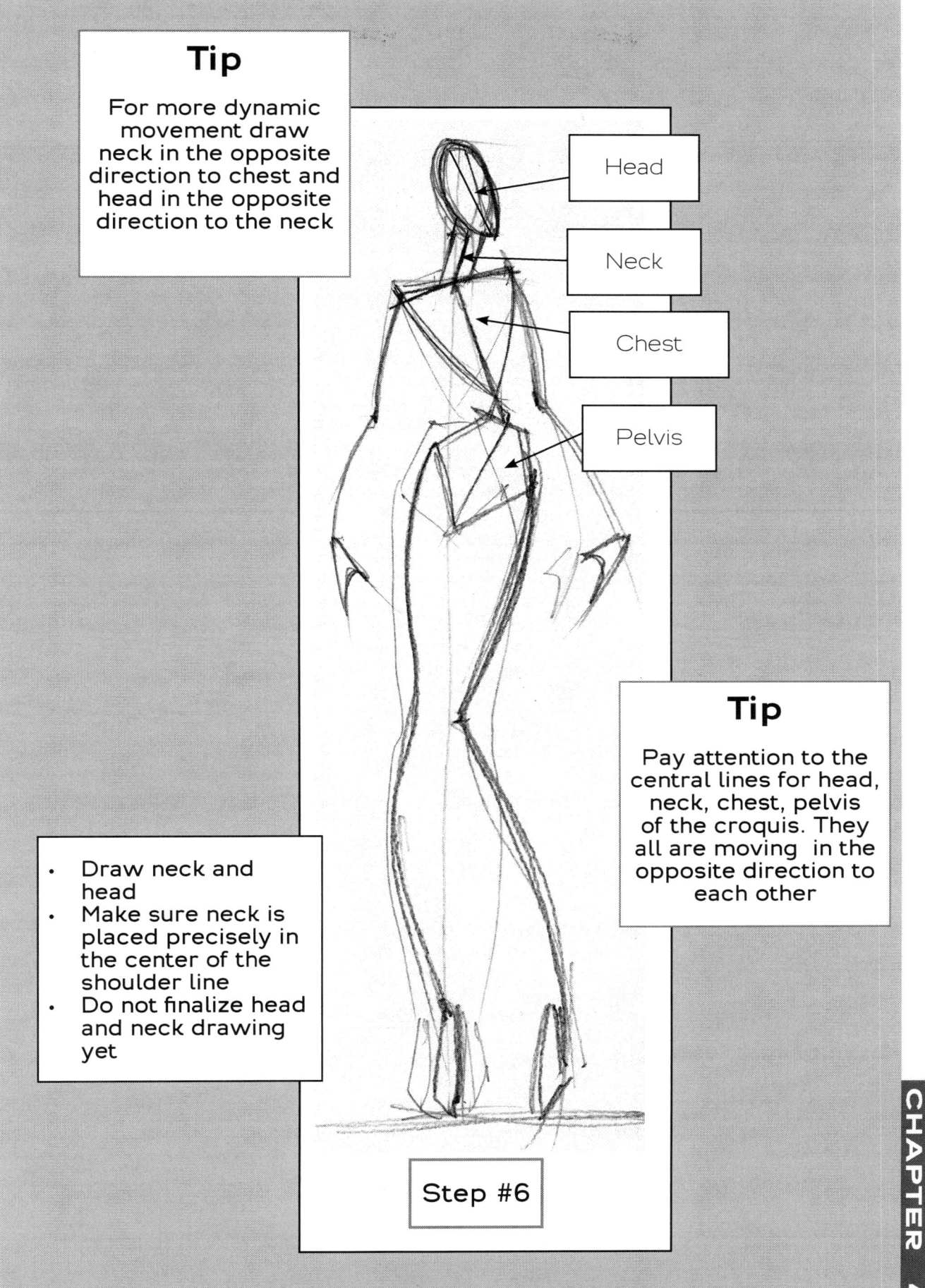

Tip

For more dynamic movement draw neck in the opposite direction to chest and head in the opposite direction to the neck

- Head
- Neck
- Chest
- Pelvis

Tip

Pay attention to the central lines for head, neck, chest, pelvis of the croquis. They all are moving in the opposite direction to each other

- Draw neck and head
- Make sure neck is placed precisely in the center of the shoulder line
- Do not finalize head and neck drawing yet

Step #6

Freehand sketching of front view croquis (continued)

Step #7

- Connect shoulders and waistline for outlining of the upper body shape

Step #8

- Add shape to connect neck and shoulders smoothly

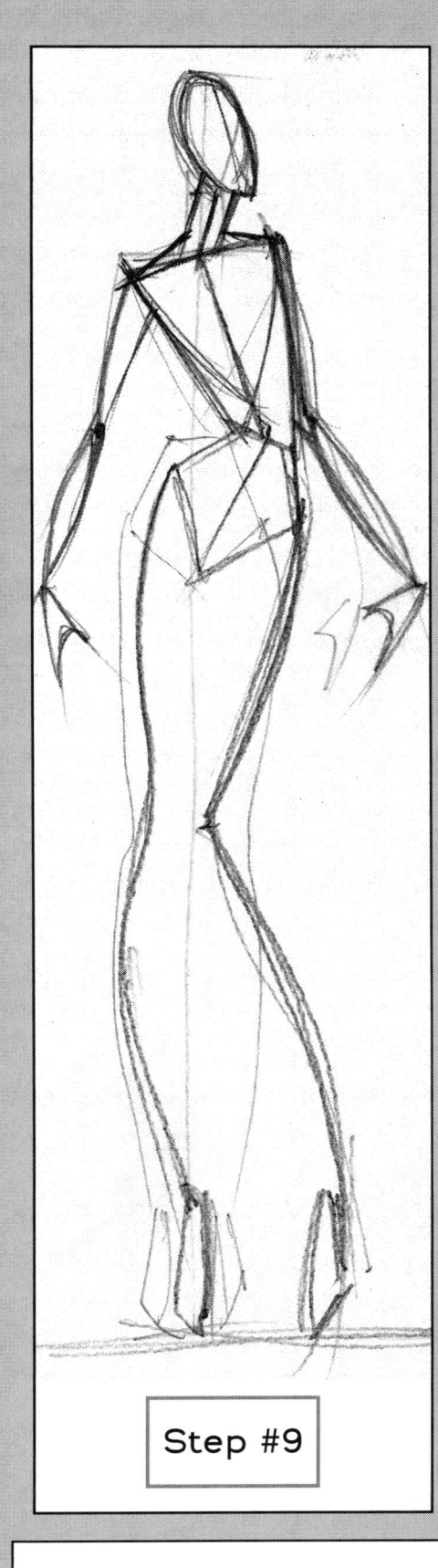

Step #9
- Add volume to arms

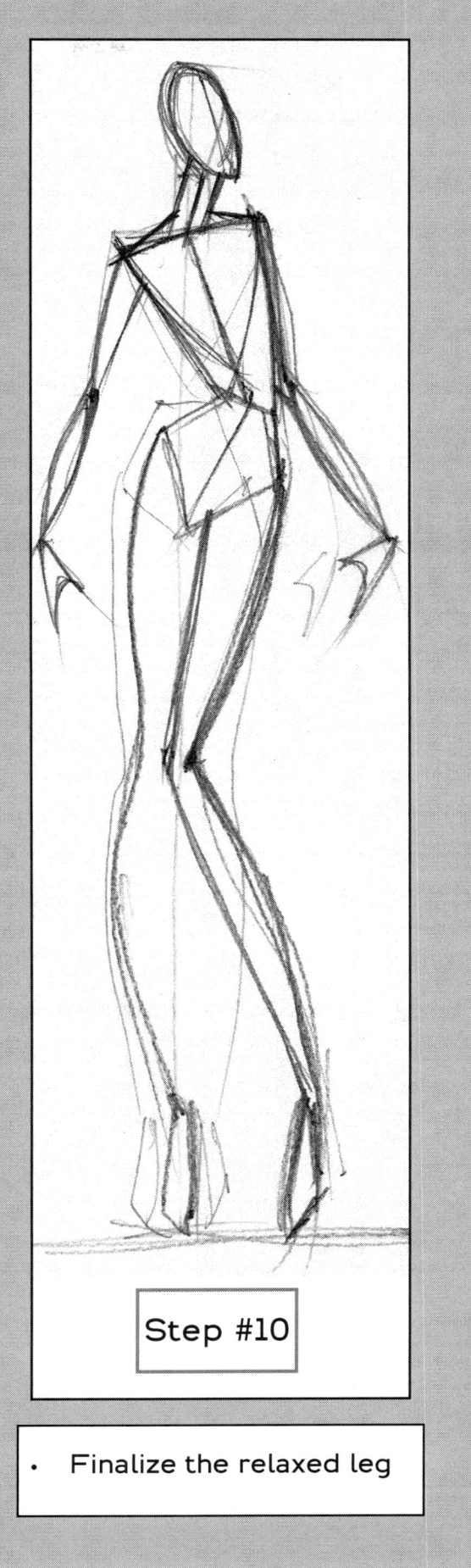

Step #10
- Finalize the relaxed leg

Freehand sketching of front view croquis (continued)

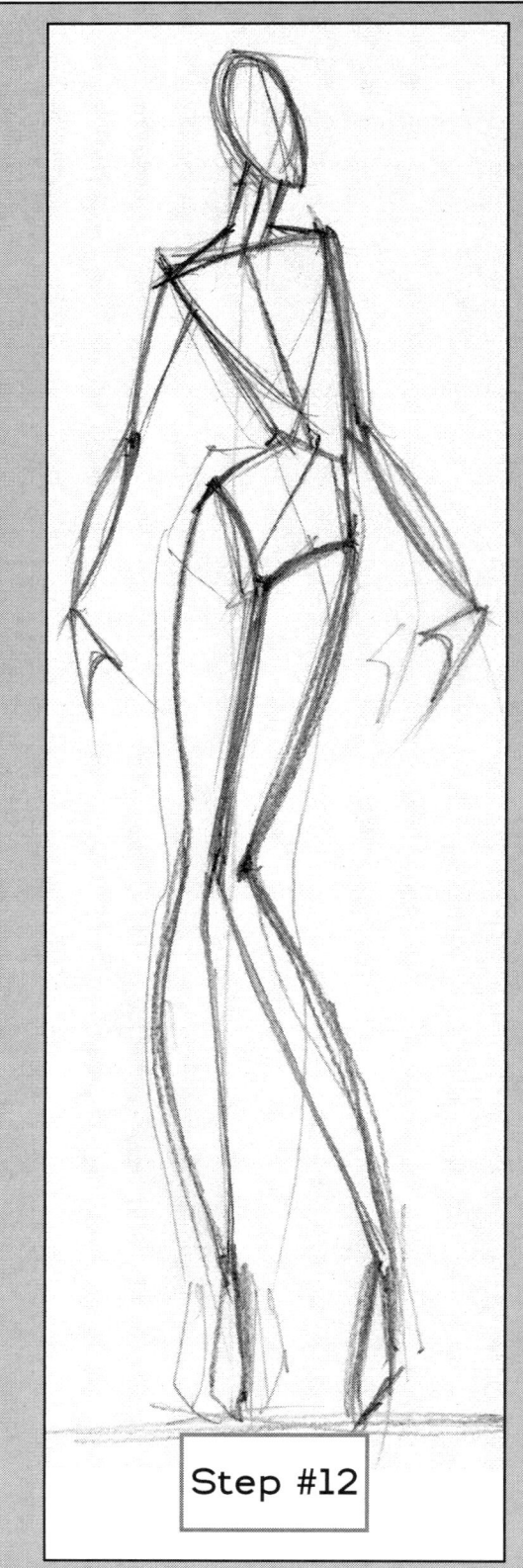

Step #11

Step #12

- Finalize the supporting leg
- Add curve lines to show the connection between pelvis and legs

Step #13

Step #14

- Soften connections between all body parts
- Show basic shape for hair
- Draw more detailed face outlining

- Show essential placement for face details

Freehand sketching of front view croquis (continued)

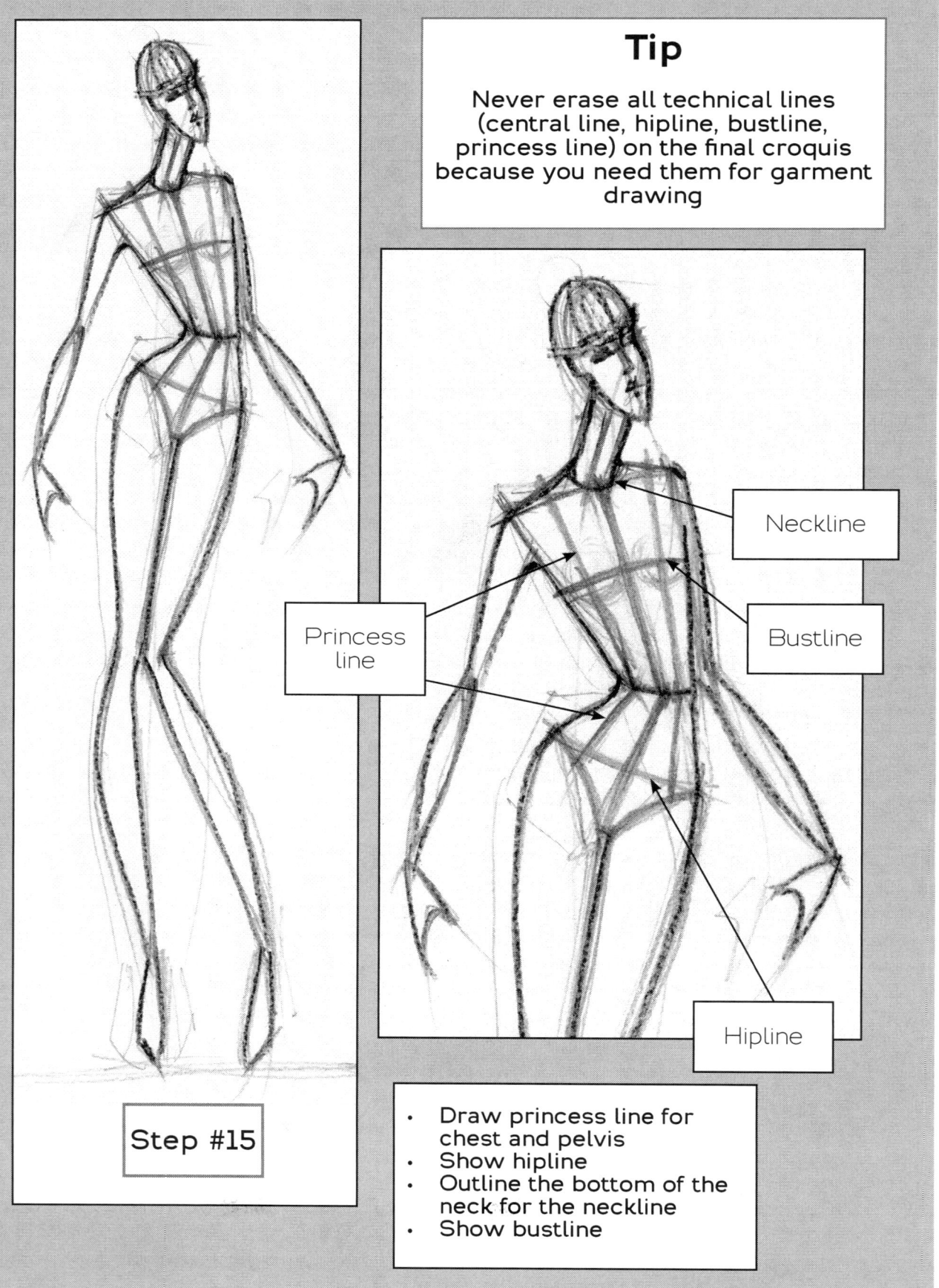

Tip

Never erase all technical lines (central line, hipline, bustline, princess line) on the final croquis because you need them for garment drawing

Step #15

- Draw princess line for chest and pelvis
- Show hipline
- Outline the bottom of the neck for the neckline
- Show bustline

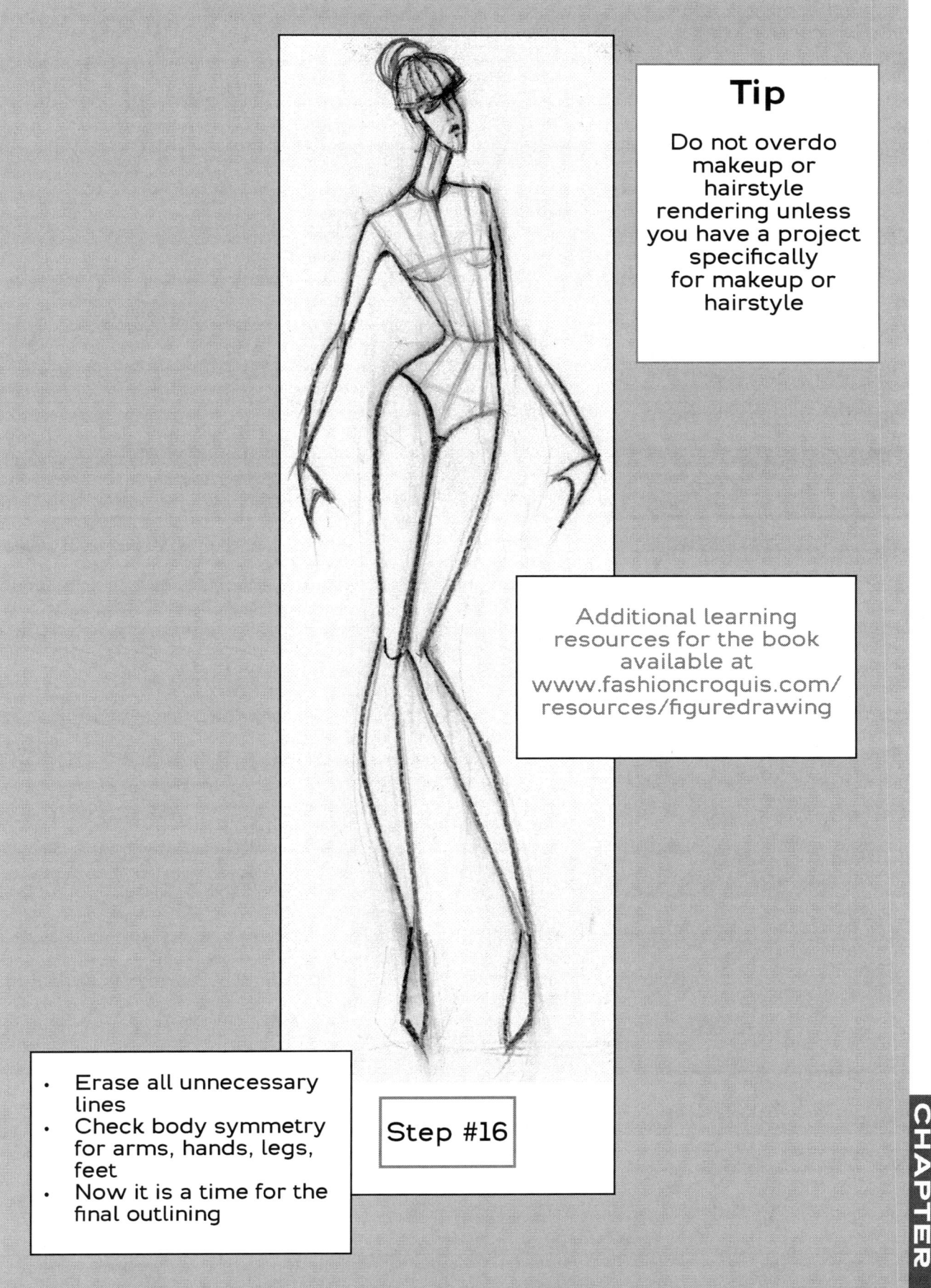

Tip

Do not overdo makeup or hairstyle rendering unless you have a project specifically for makeup or hairstyle

Additional learning resources for the book available at www.fashioncroquis.com/resources/figuredrawing

- Erase all unnecessary lines
- Check body symmetry for arms, hands, legs, feet
- Now it is a time for the final outlining

Step #16

Freehand sketching of front view croquis at a glance

| Step #1 | Step #2 | Step #3 | Step #4 |
| See page 48 | See page 49 | See page 50 | See page 51 |

| Step #5 | Step #6 | Step #7 | Step #8 |
| See page 52 | See page 53 | See page 54 | See page 54 |

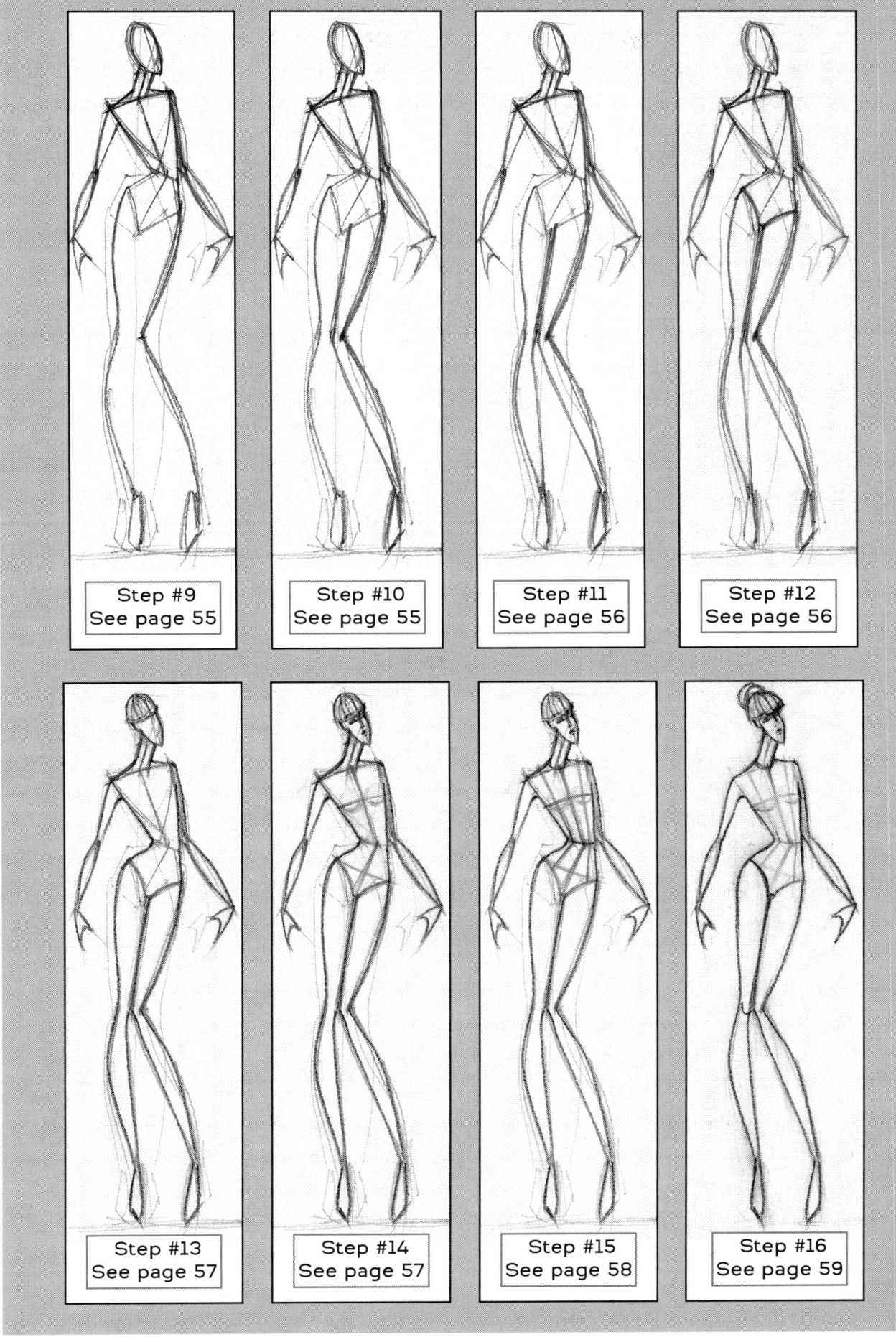

Contents:

Chapter 1. Pages 9-25
Basics of body proportions

Chapter 2. Pages 27-35
Fashion figure schematics (wire skeleton study)

Chapter 3. Pages 37-45
Sketching strategy

Chapter 4. Pages 47-61
Freehand sketching for 10 heads tall fashion figure (front view)

Chapter 5. Pages 63-75
Freehand sketching for 10 heads tall fashion figure (side view)

Chapter 6. Pages 77-91
Cutting method for fashion figure croquis

Chapter 7. Pages 93-125
Figure croquis manipulations

Chapter 8. Pages 127-147
Faces and hands drawing

Index
Pages 148-149

About the author
Pages 150-151

Chapter 5

Freehand sketching for 10 heads tall fashion figure (side view)

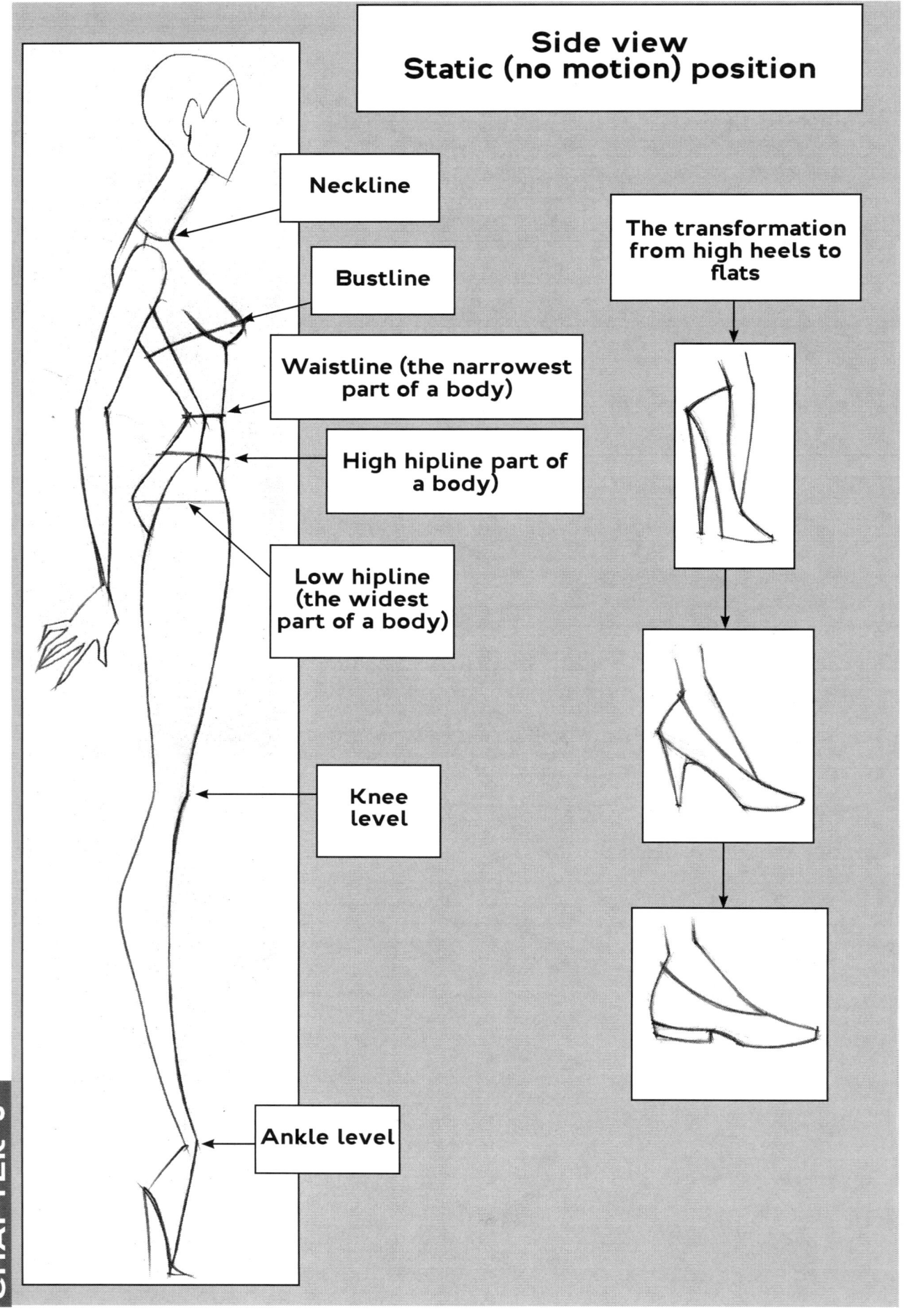

Templates with the different heel height

How to Draw Fashion Figure Essential figure drawing techniques by Irina V. Ivanova

CHAPTER 5

Freehand sketching of side view croquis

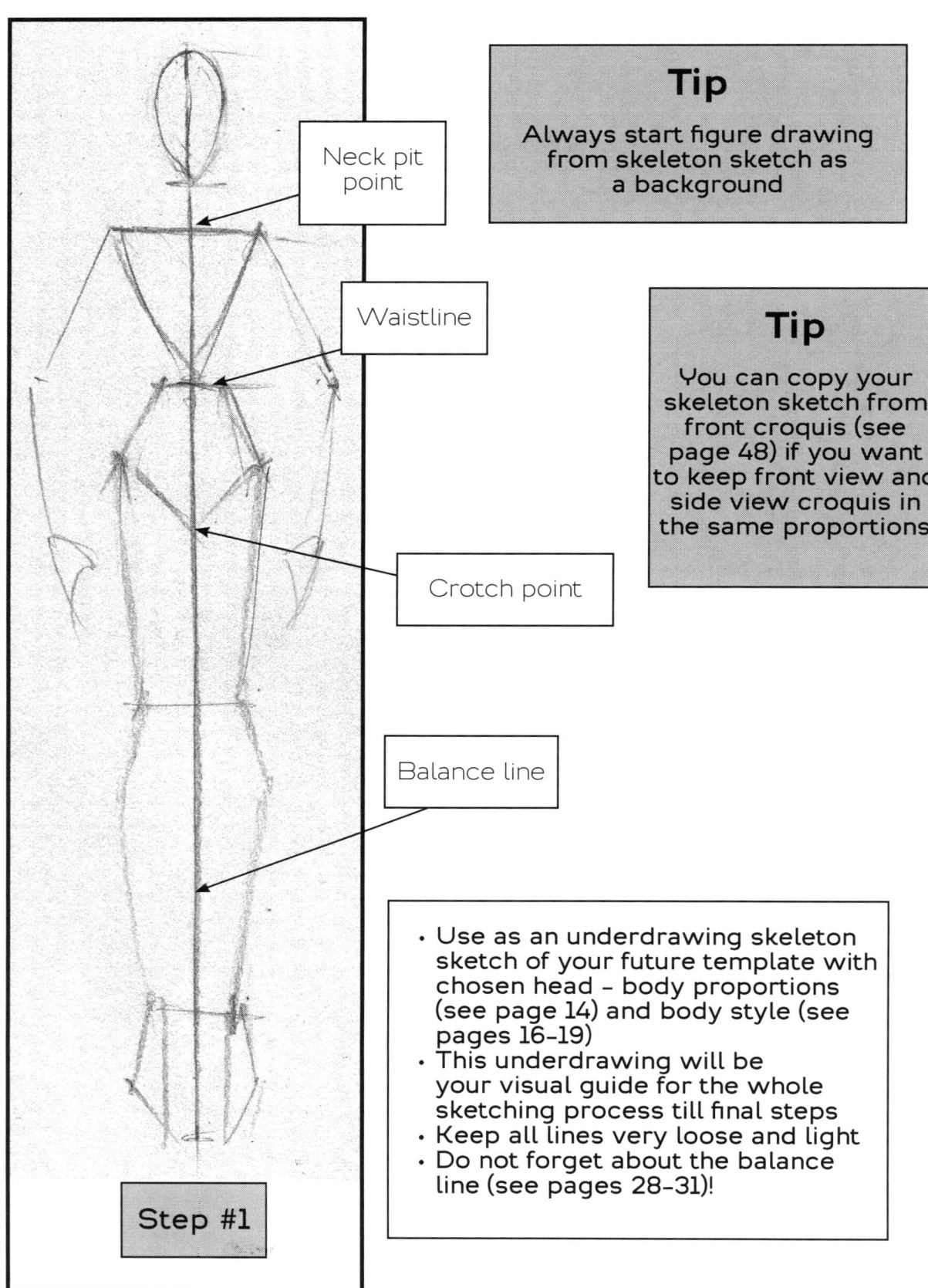

Step #1

- Neck pit point
- Waistline
- Crotch point
- Balance line

Tip

Always start figure drawing from skeleton sketch as a background

Tip

You can copy your skeleton sketch from front croquis (see page 48) if you want to keep front view and side view croquis in the same proportions

- Use as an underdrawing skeleton sketch of your future template with chosen head – body proportions (see page 14) and body style (see pages 16-19)
- This underdrawing will be your visual guide for the whole sketching process till final steps
- Keep all lines very loose and light
- Do not forget about the balance line (see pages 28-31)!

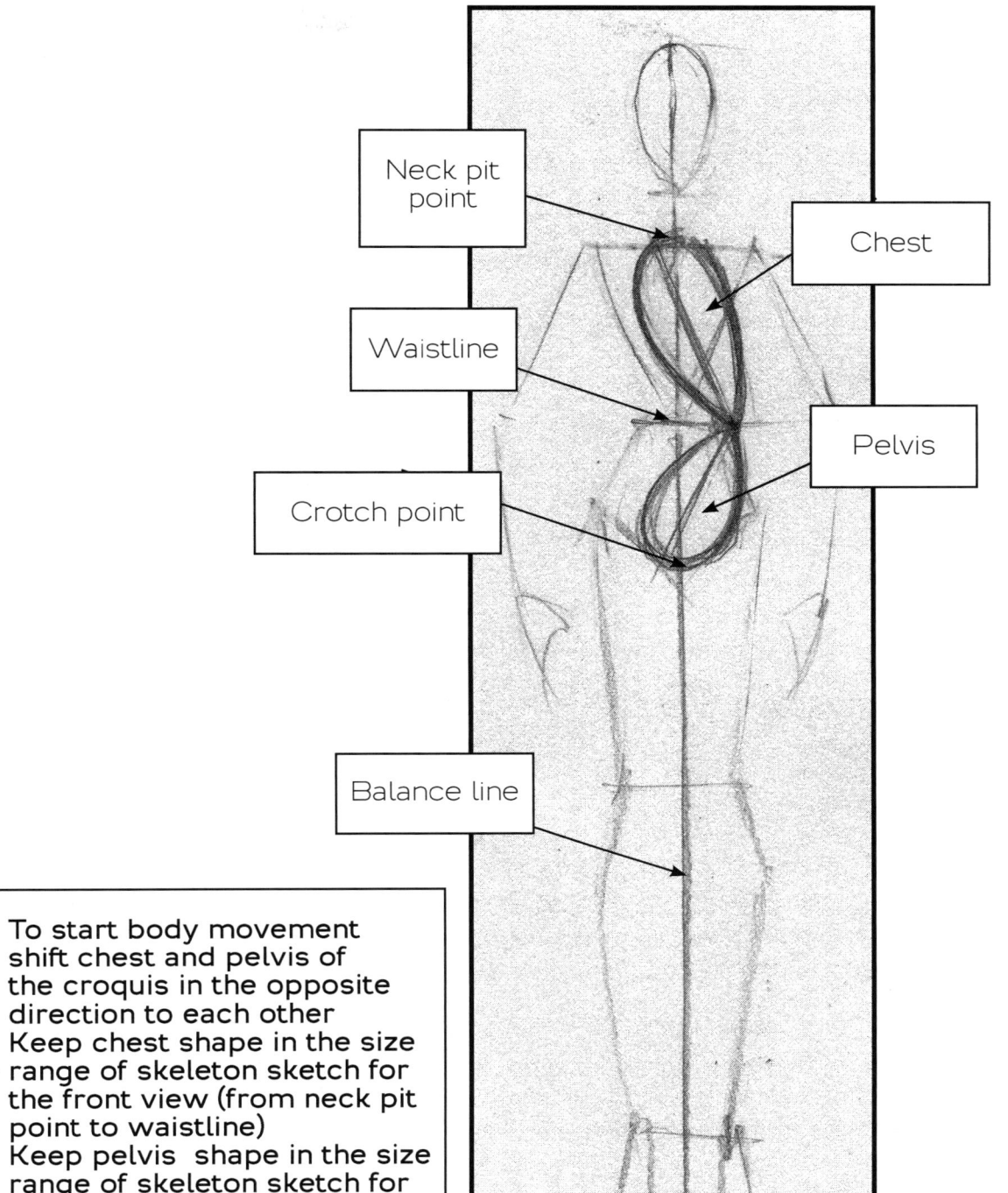

- To start body movement shift chest and pelvis of the croquis in the opposite direction to each other
- Keep chest shape in the size range of skeleton sketch for the front view (from neck pit point to waistline)
- Keep pelvis shape in the size range of skeleton sketch for the front view (from waistline to crotch point)
- Skeleton style underdrawing visually will help you to maintain the correct size of chest and pelvis
- Never erase skeleton underdrawing till last steps
- Keep the center of shoulders (neck pit point) on the balance line

Step #2

Freehand sketching of side view croquis (continued)

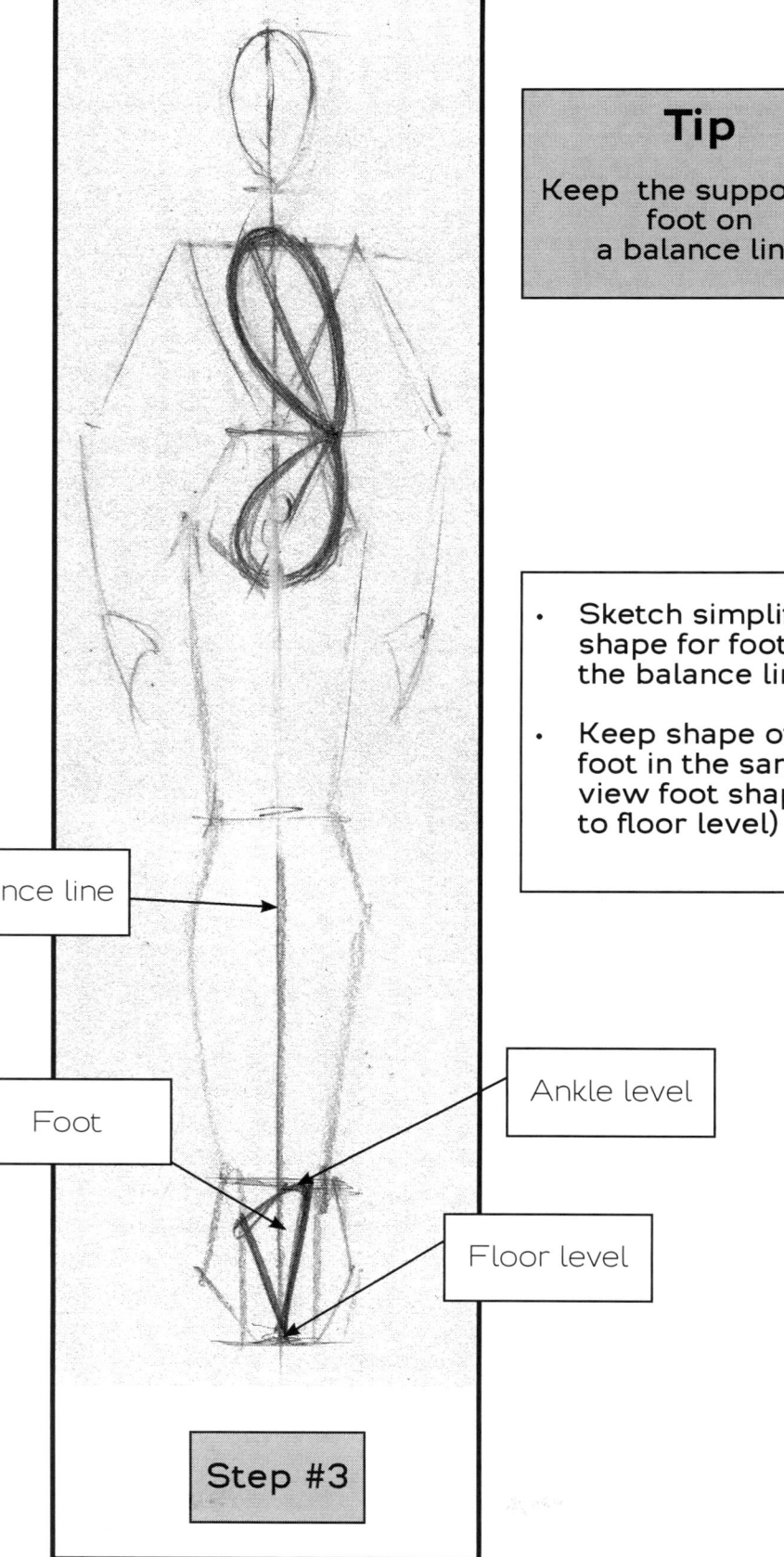

Tip
Keep the supporting foot on a balance line

- Sketch simplified triangle shape for foot precisely on the balance line
- Keep shape of the side view foot in the same size as front view foot shape (from ankle to floor level)

Balance line

Ankle level

Foot

Floor level

Step #3

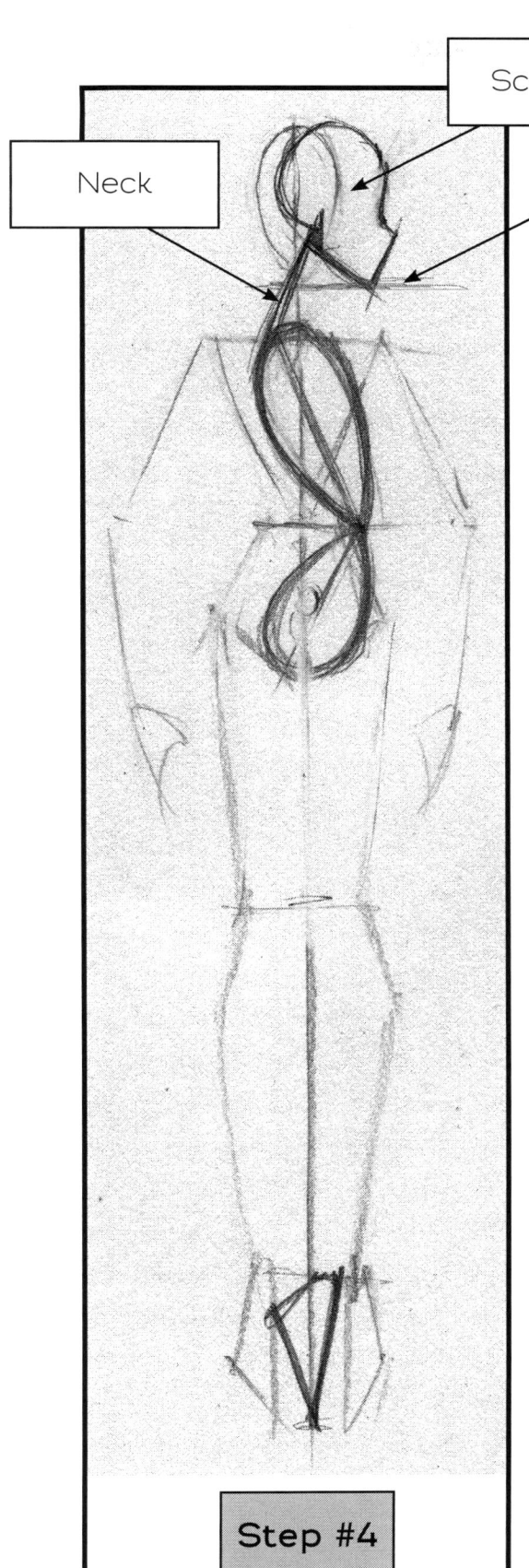

- Sketch the side view of the scalp

- Keep the shape of side view scalp in the same size as front view scalp shape (from top of the head to chin level)

- Draw the line for neck

- Make sure you move the neck in the opposite direction to the chest

- Make sure you move the chest in the opposite direction to the pelvis

Step #4

Freehand sketching of side view croquis (continued)

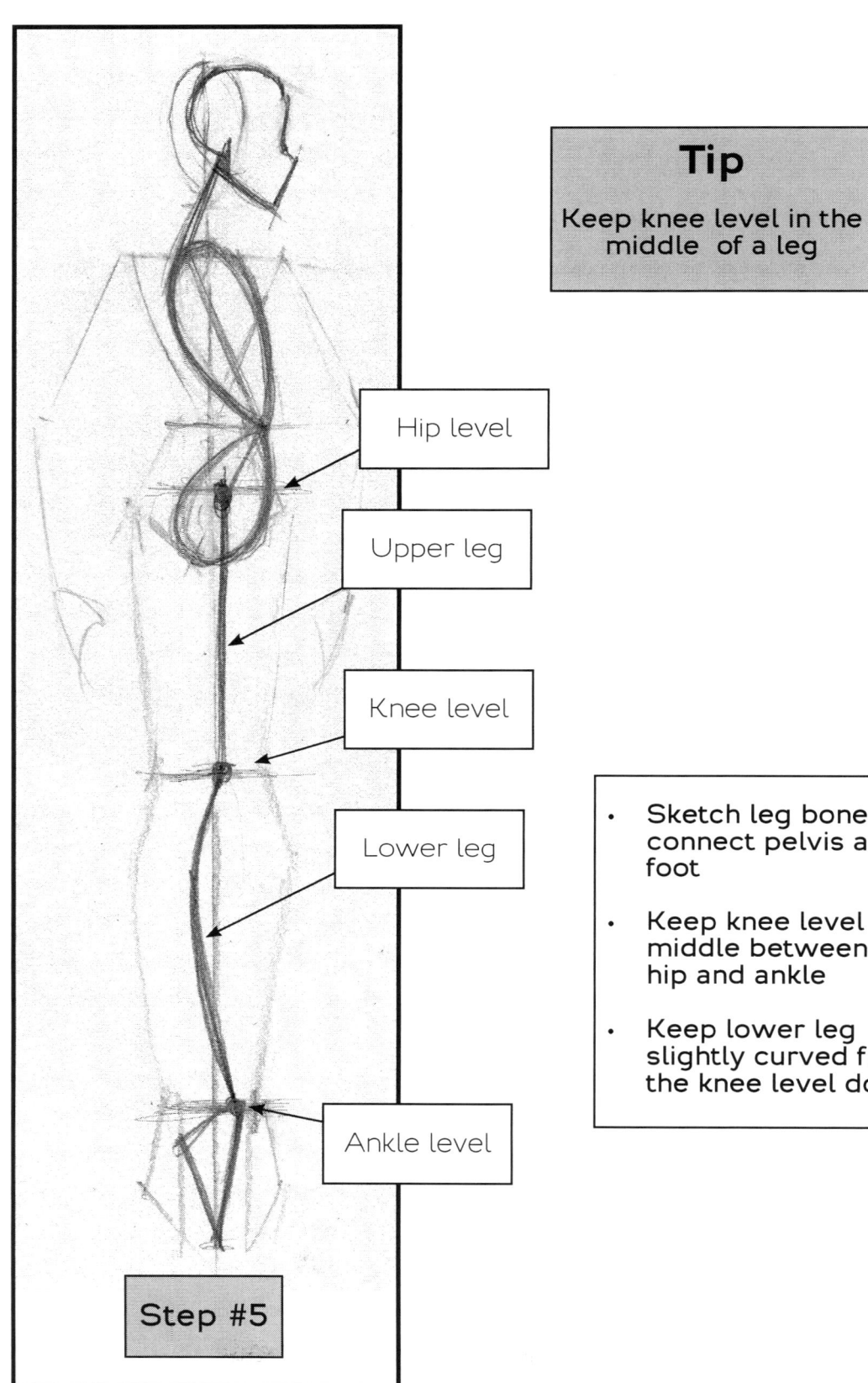

Step #5

Tip

Keep knee level in the middle of a leg

- Hip level
- Upper leg
- Knee level
- Lower leg
- Ankle level

- Sketch leg bones to connect pelvis and foot
- Keep knee level in the middle between the hip and ankle
- Keep lower leg slightly curved from the knee level down

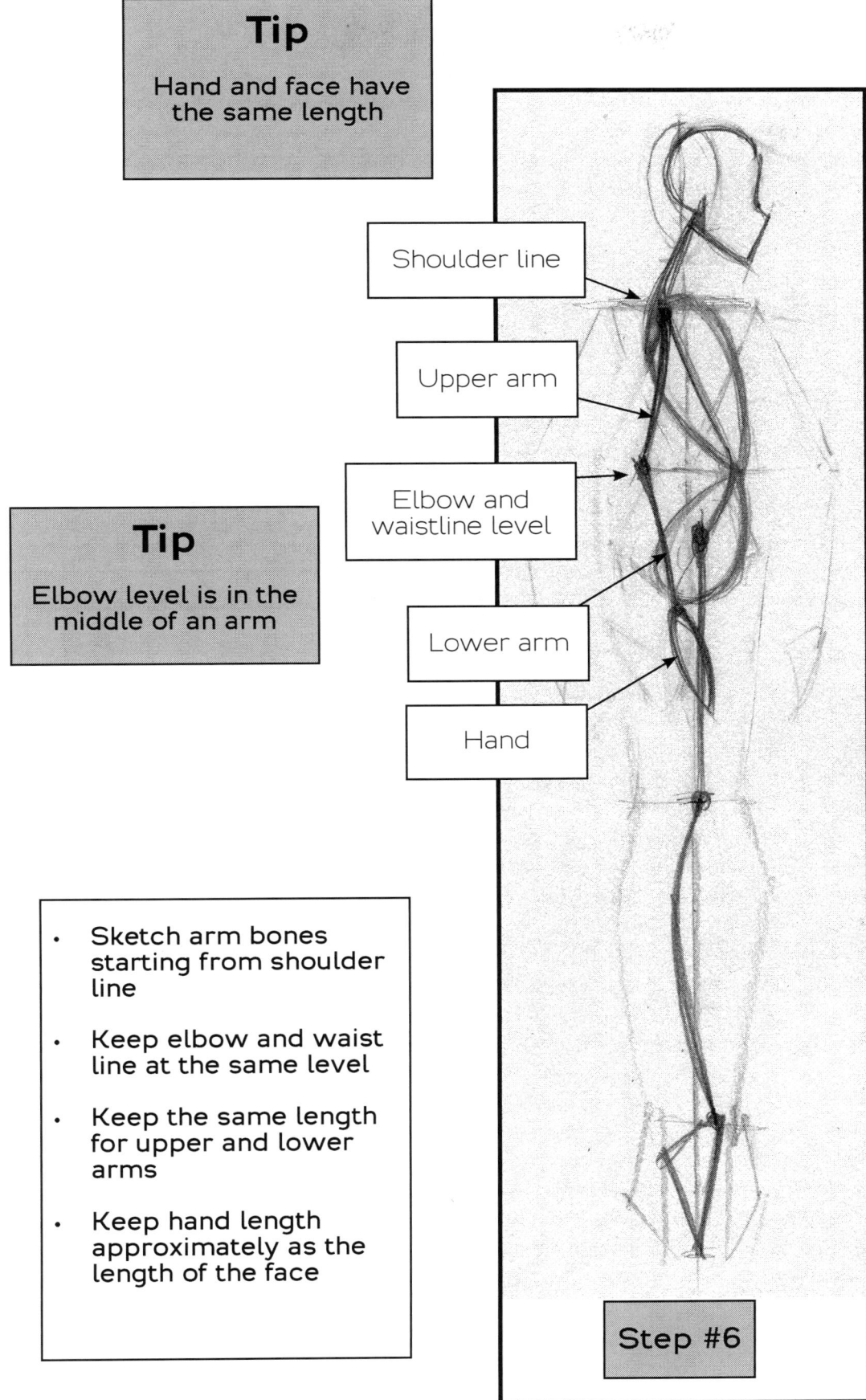

Tip
Hand and face have the same length

Tip
Elbow level is in the middle of an arm

- Sketch arm bones starting from shoulder line
- Keep elbow and waist line at the same level
- Keep the same length for upper and lower arms
- Keep hand length approximately as the length of the face

Step #6

Freehand sketching of side view croquis (continued)

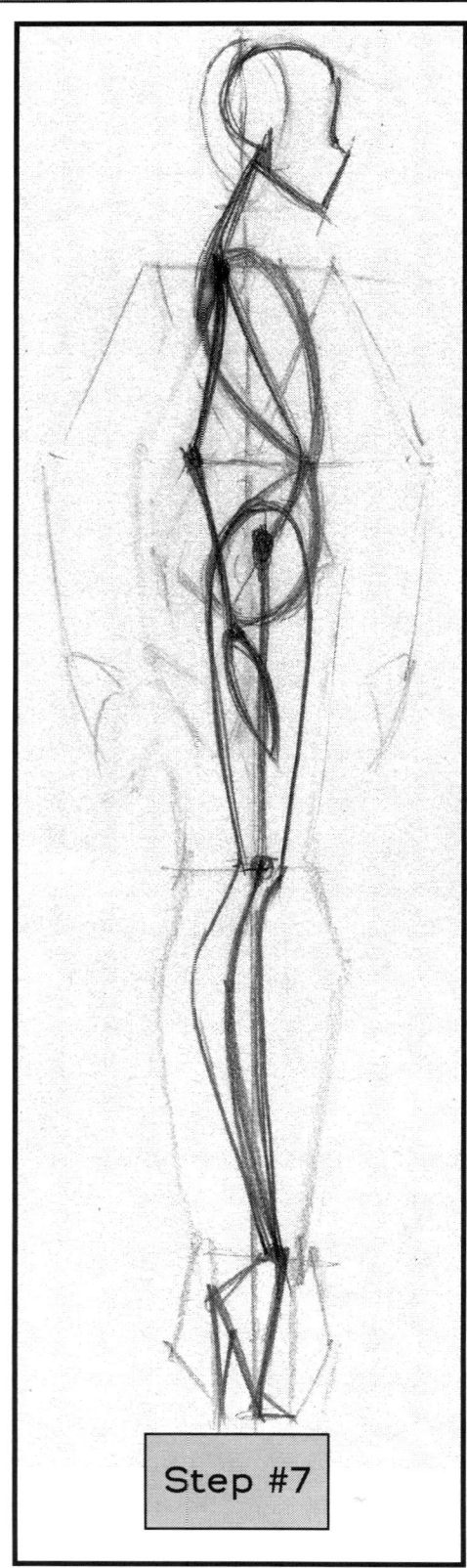

Step #7

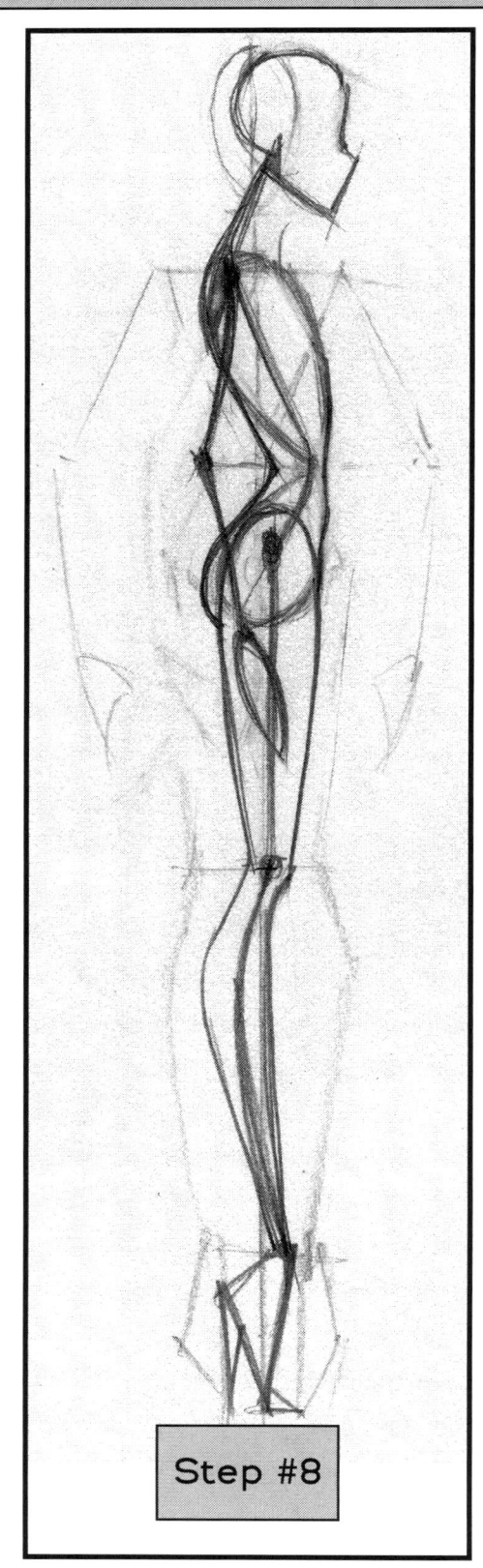

Step #8

- Finalize the leg outlining

- Add more body to buttocks
- Show outlining of back in waist area

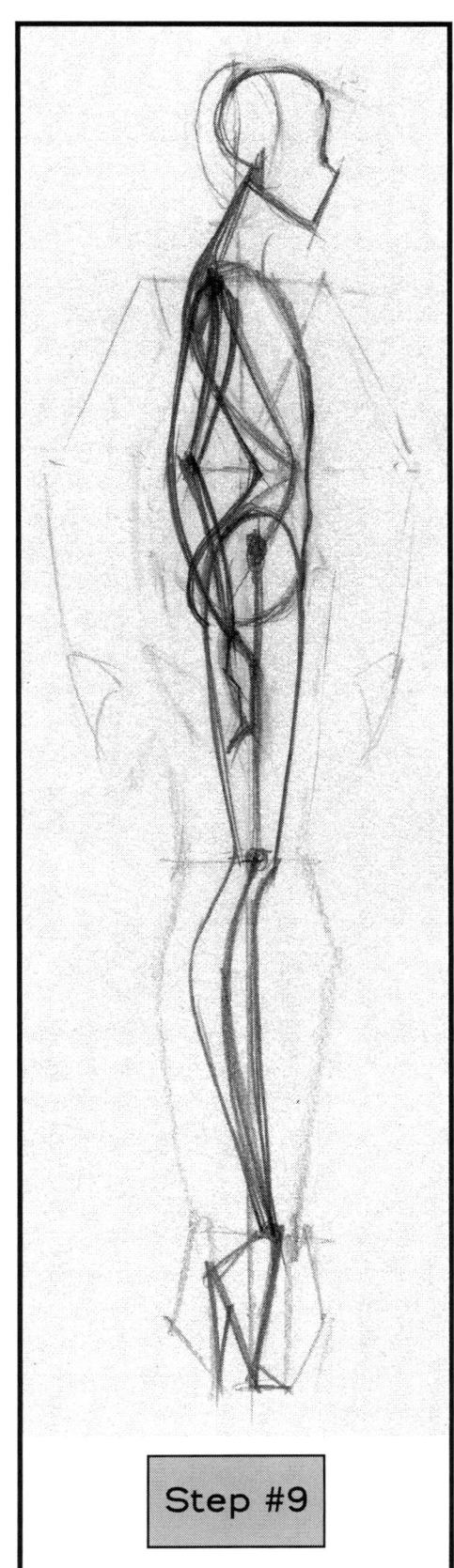

Step #9

- Finalize the arm outlining

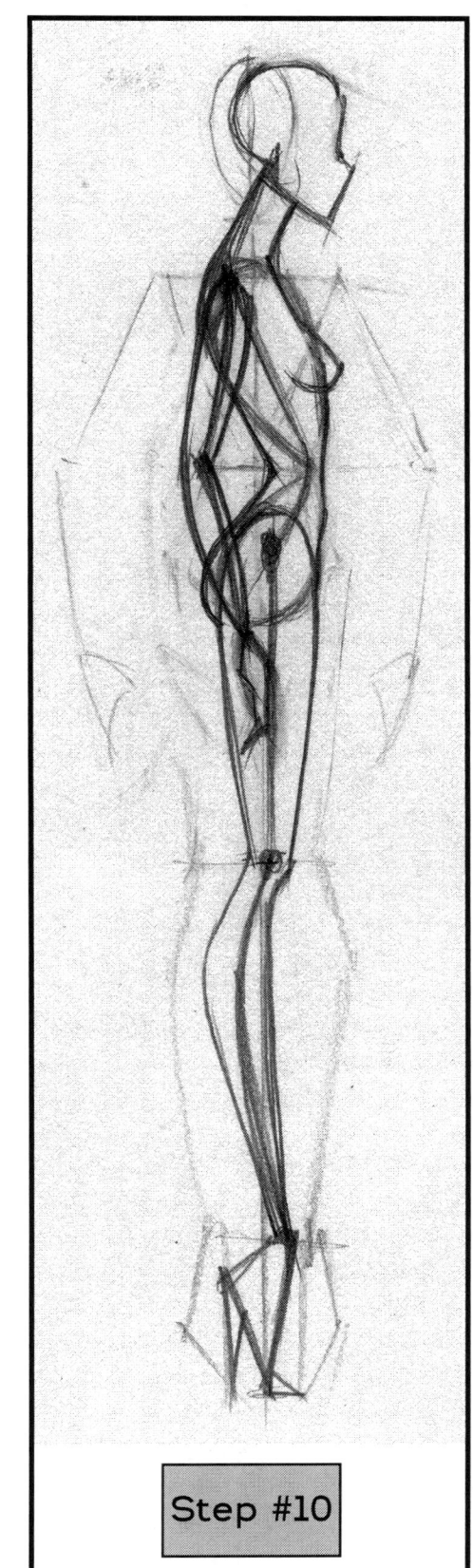

Step #10

- Add shape to the breast area
- Finalize the neck outlining

Freehand sketching of side view croquis (continued)

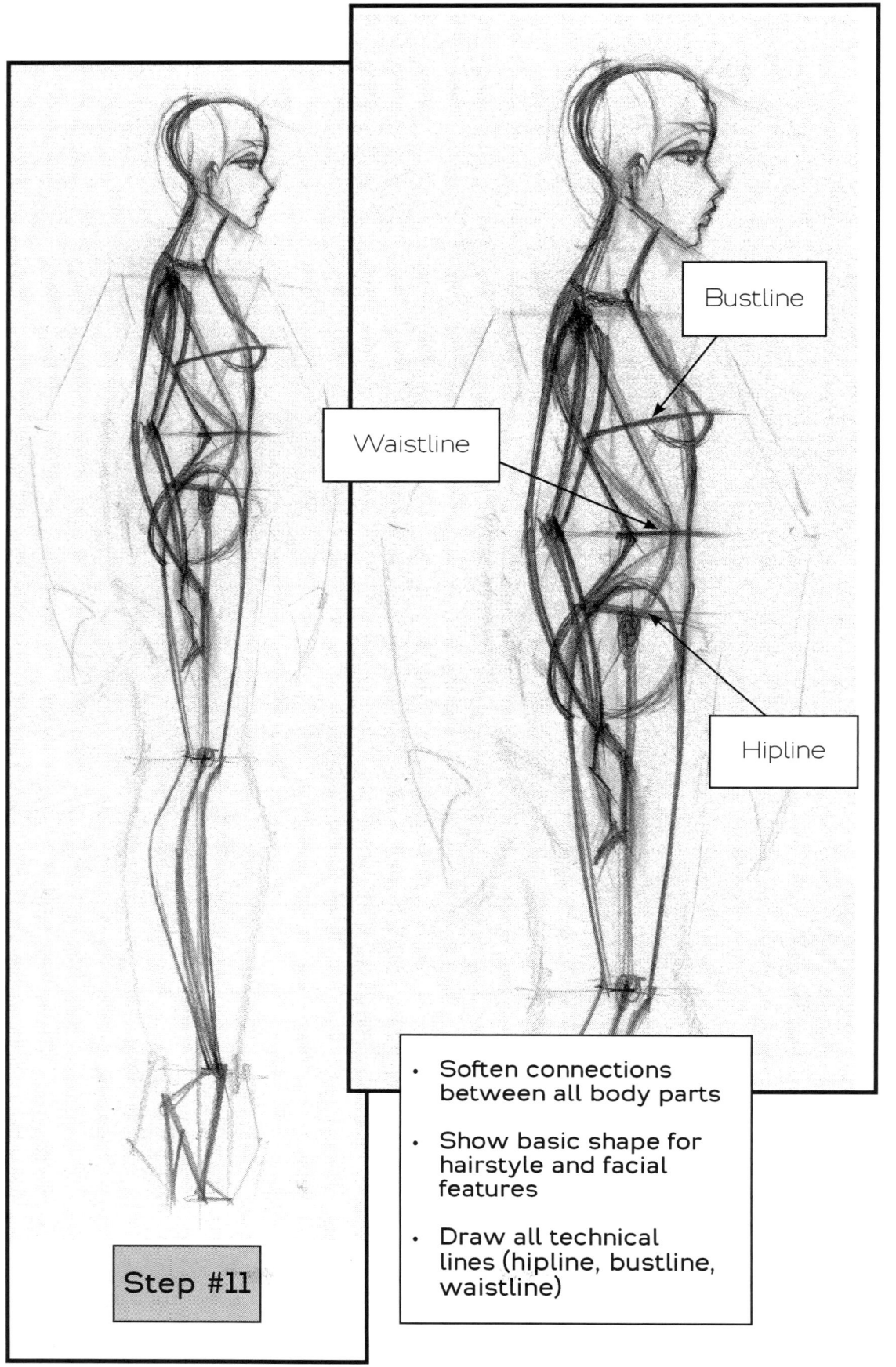

Step #11

- Soften connections between all body parts
- Show basic shape for hairstyle and facial features
- Draw all technical lines (hipline, bustline, waistline)

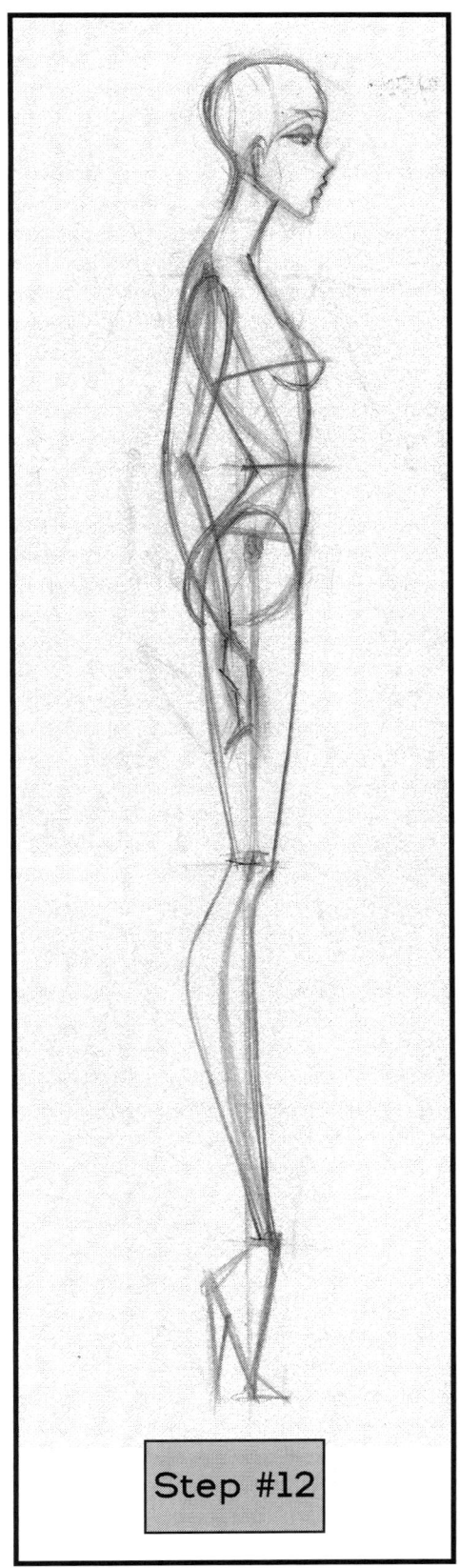

Step #12

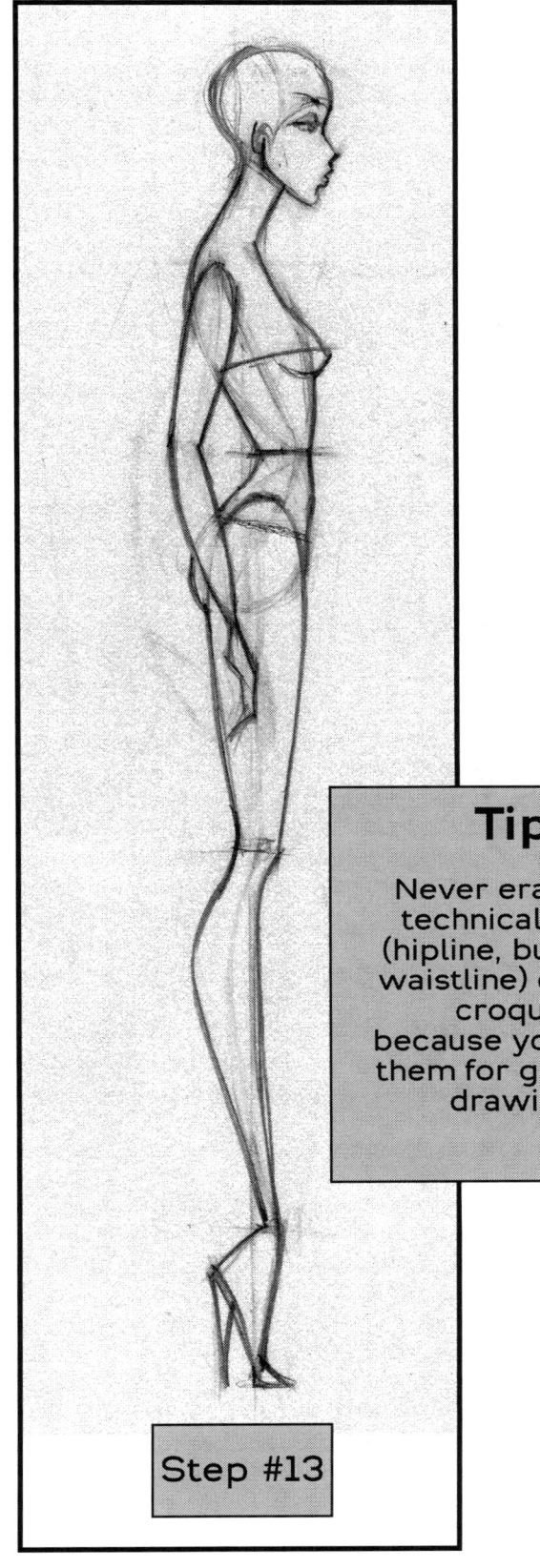

Step #13

Tip

Never erase all technical lines (hipline, bustline, waistline) on final croquis because you need them for garment drawing

- Erase all unnecessary lines
- Check everything before final outlining

- Do final outlining

Contents:

Chapter 1. Pages 9-25
Basics of body proportions

Chapter 2. Pages 27-35
Fashion figure schematics (wire skeleton study)

Chapter 3. Pages 37-45
Sketching strategy

Chapter 4. Pages 47-61
Freehand sketching for 10 heads tall fashion figure (front view)

Chapter 5. Pages 63-75
Freehand sketching for 10 heads tall fashion figure (side view)

Chapter 6. Pages 77-91
Cutting method for fashion figure croquis

Chapter 7. Pages 93-125
Figure croquis manipulations

Chapter 8. Pages 127-147
Faces and hands drawing

Index
Pages 148-149

About the author
Pages 150-151

Chapter 6

Cutting method for fashion figure croquis

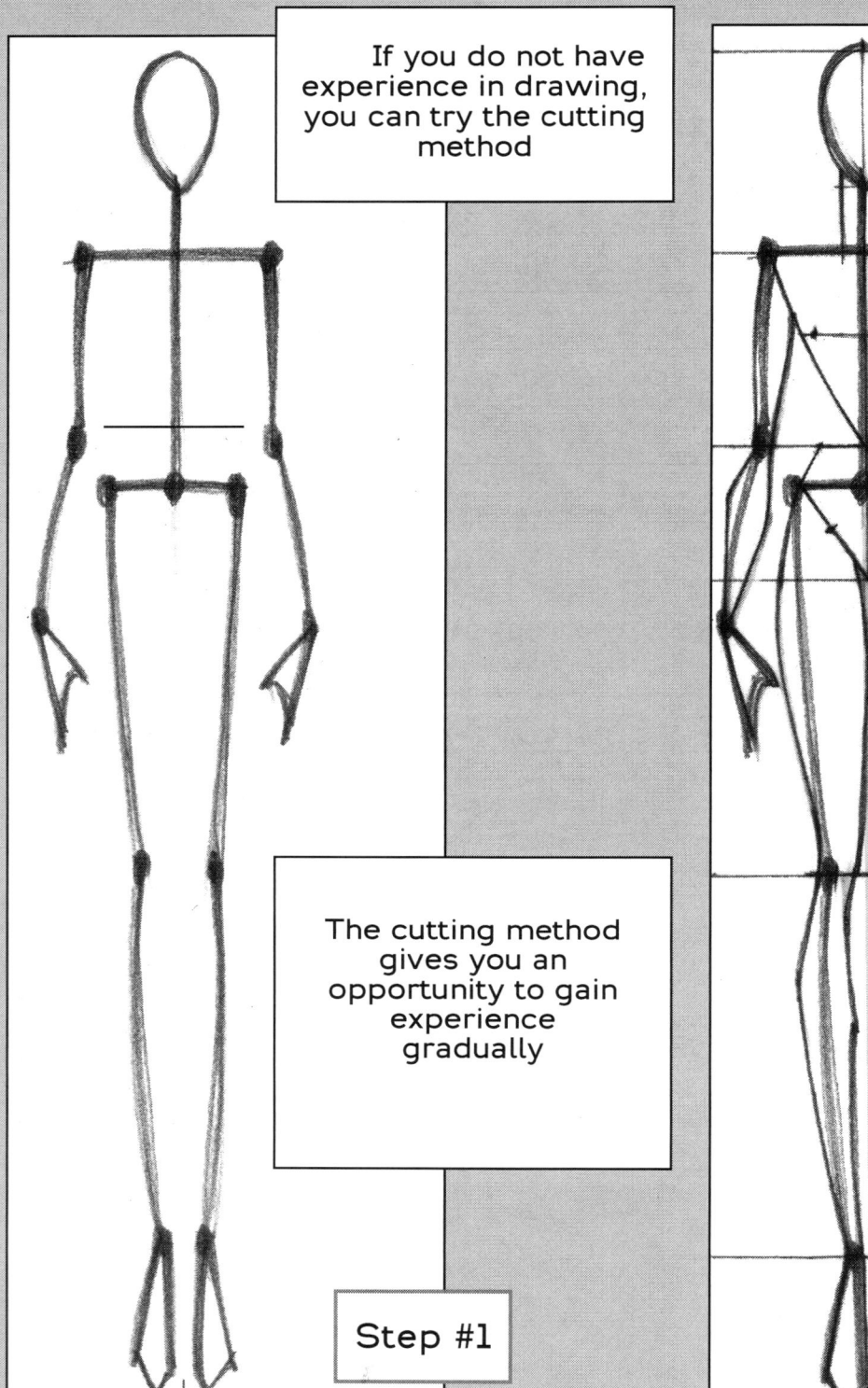

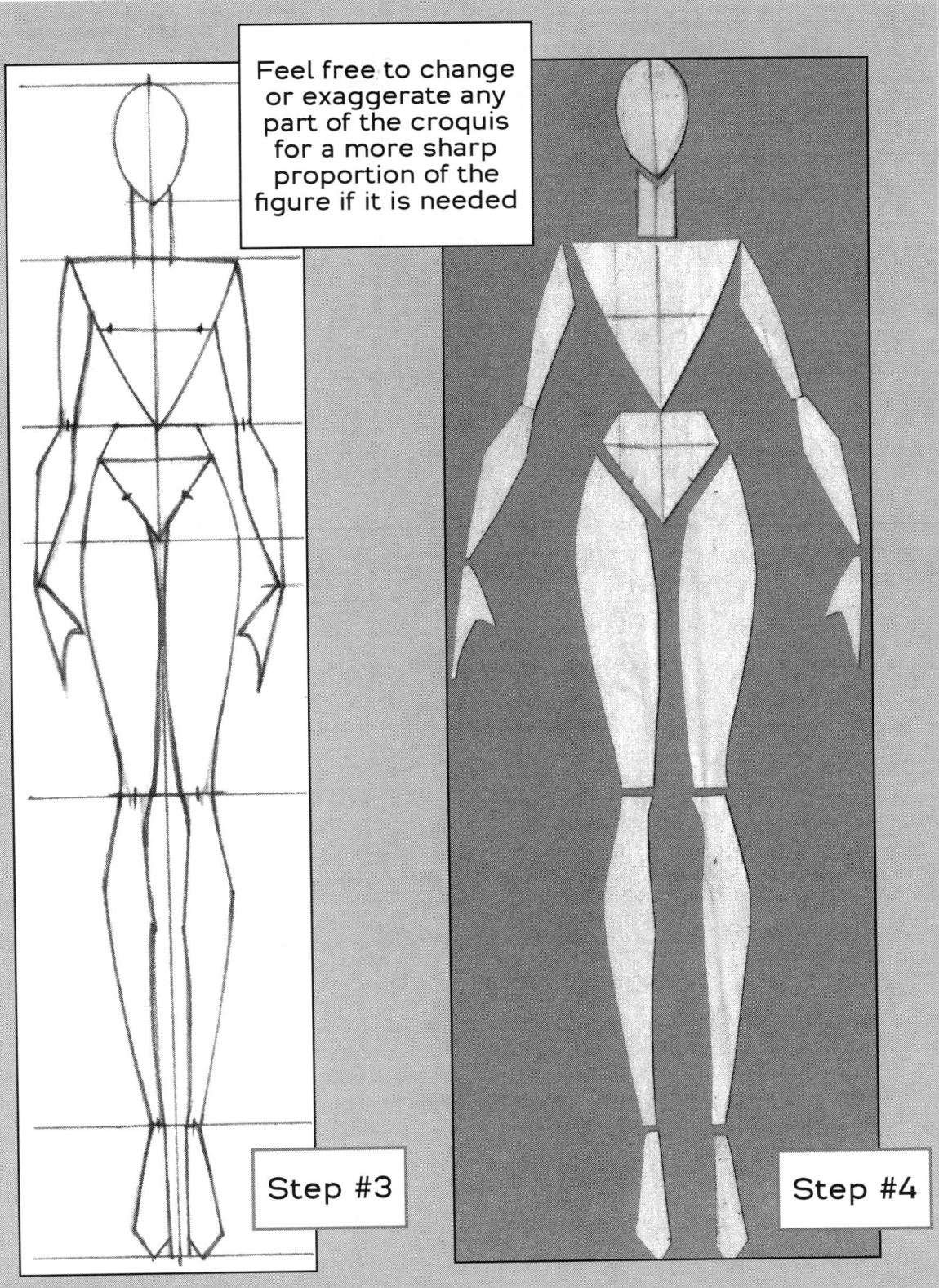

Feel free to change or exaggerate any part of the croquis for a more sharp proportion of the figure if it is needed

Step #3

Step #4

- Erase all unnecessary line
- Croquis is ready to use
- You can laminate the croquis before cutting to make it lasts longer

- Cut your croquis into separate pieces: head, chest, pelvis, upper arms, and legs, lower arms and legs, hands, feet

Cutting method for front view croquis (continued)

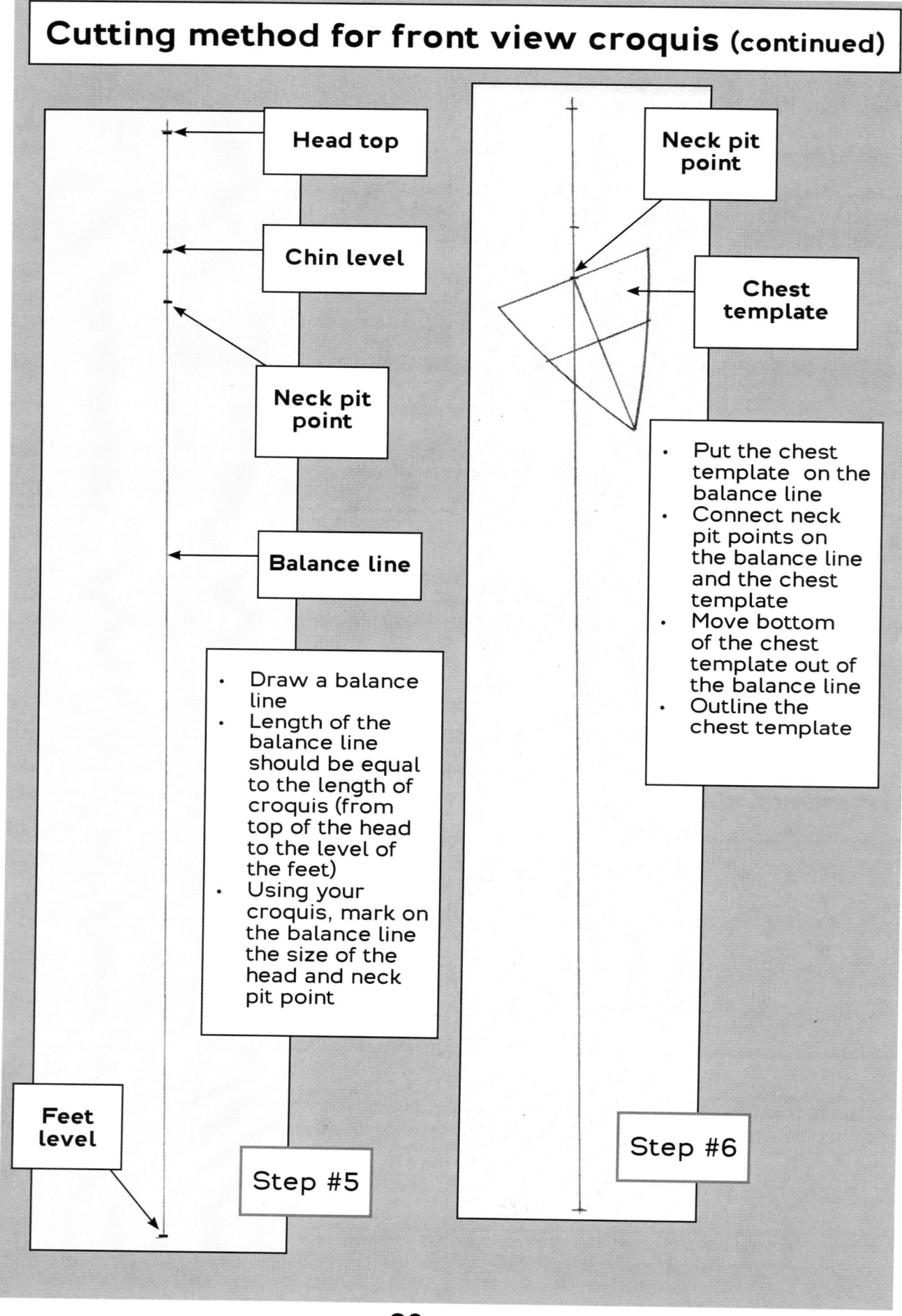

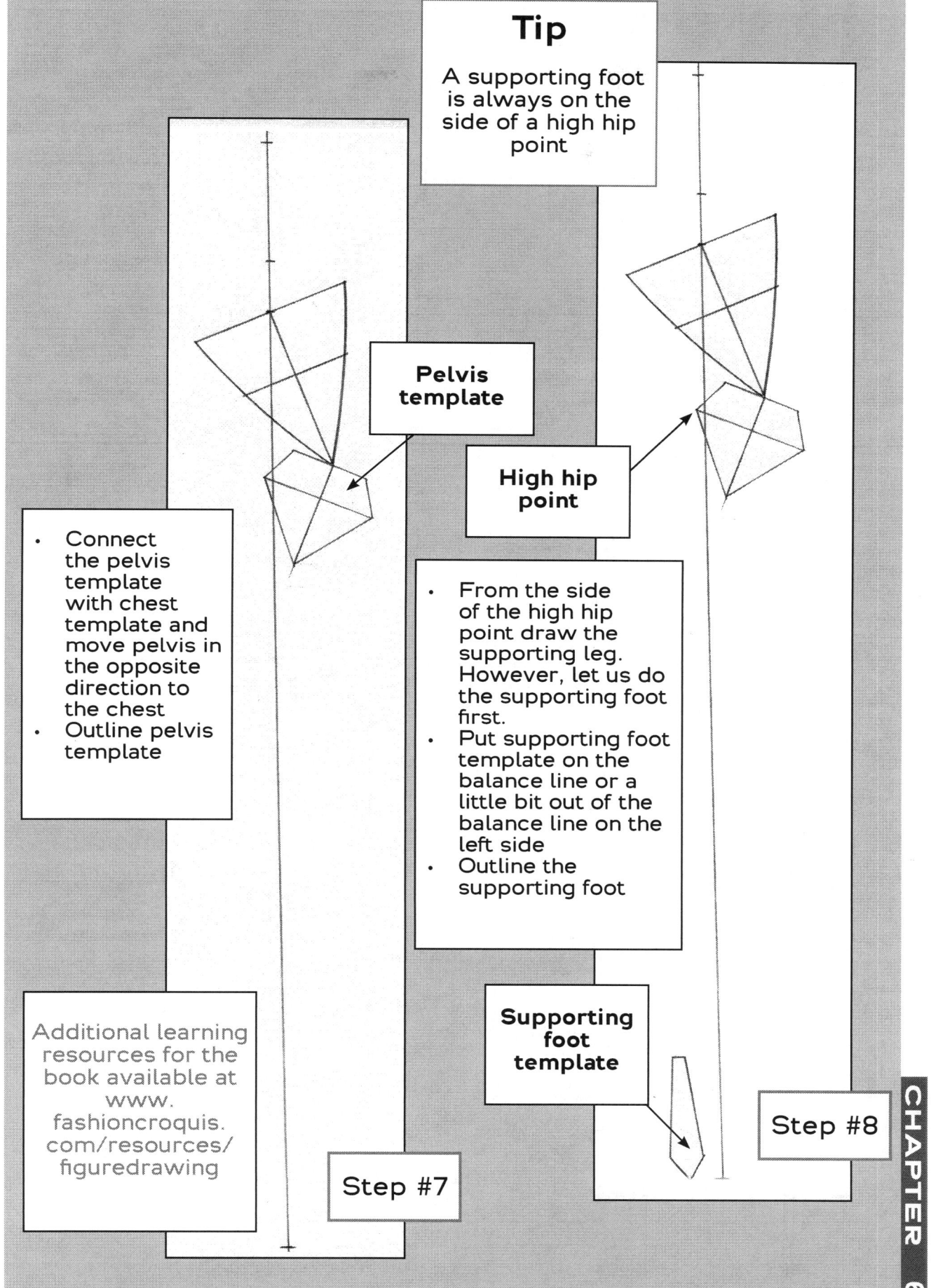

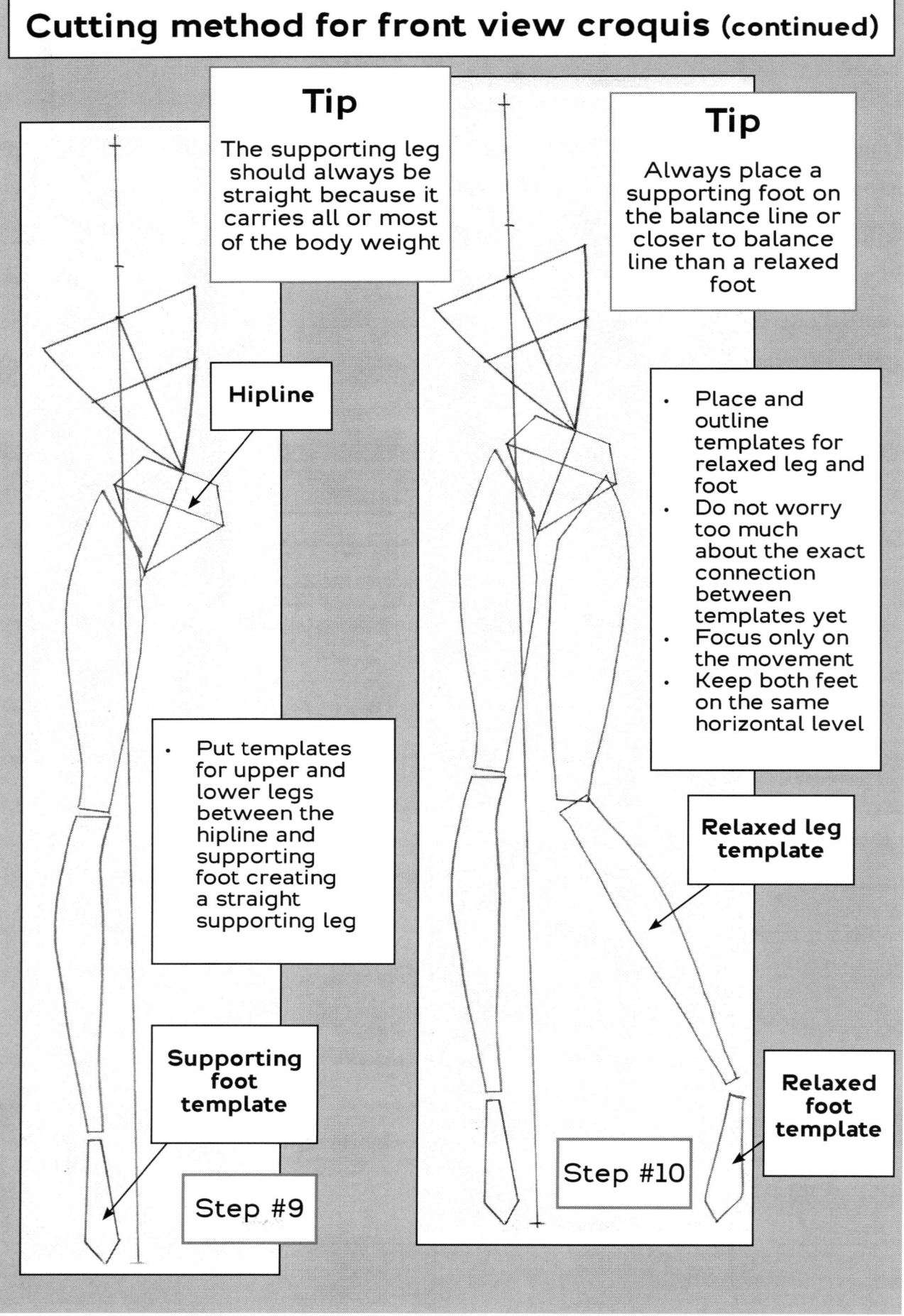

- Now, complete the drawing
- Outline arms, hands, head templates

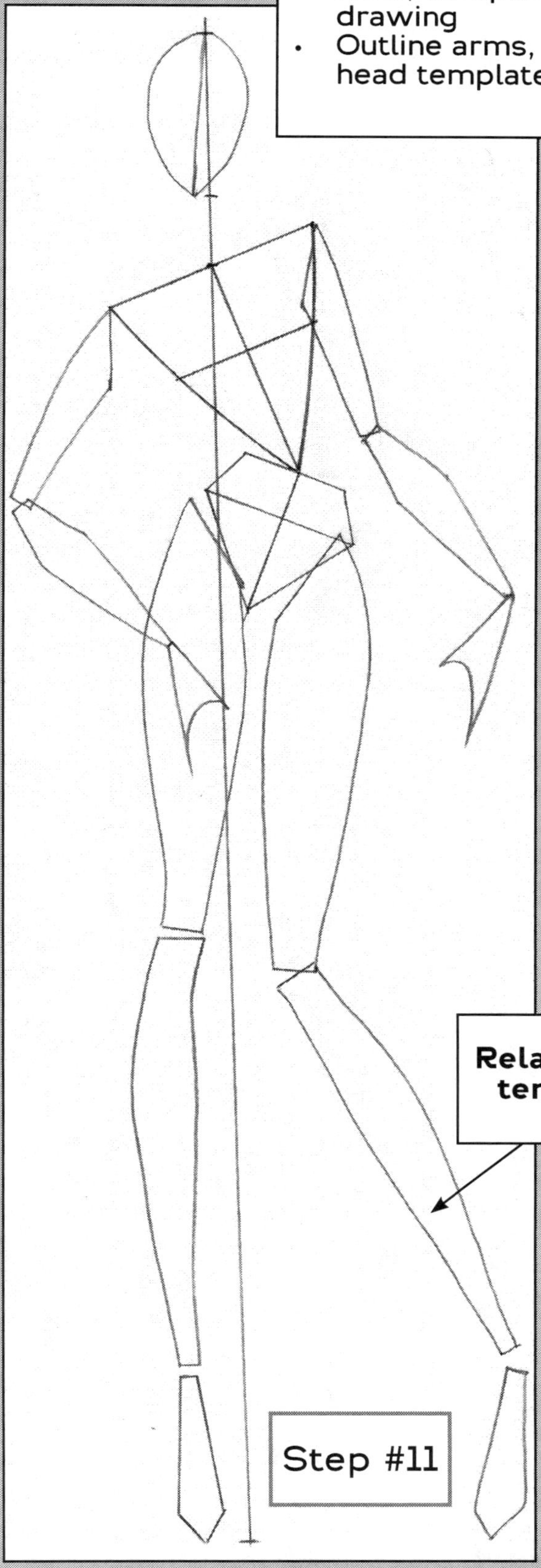

Shoulder line

Waistline

Relaxed leg template

Step #11

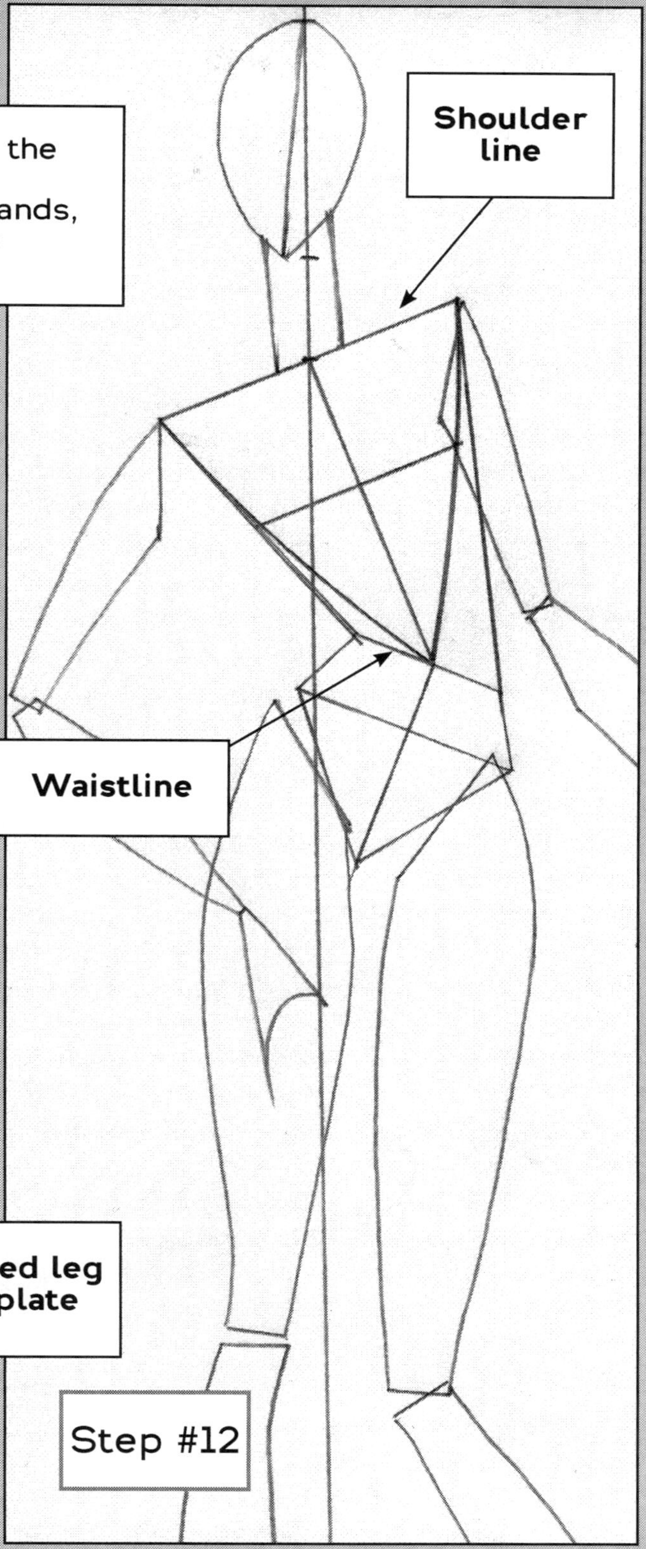

Step #12

- Connect shoulder line and waistline
- For neck outlining draw two parallel lines between head and shoulder line

How to Draw Fashion Figure Essential figure drawing techniques by Irina V. Ivanova

CHAPTER 6

© 2019 Irina V. Ivanova

Cutting method for front view croquis (continued)

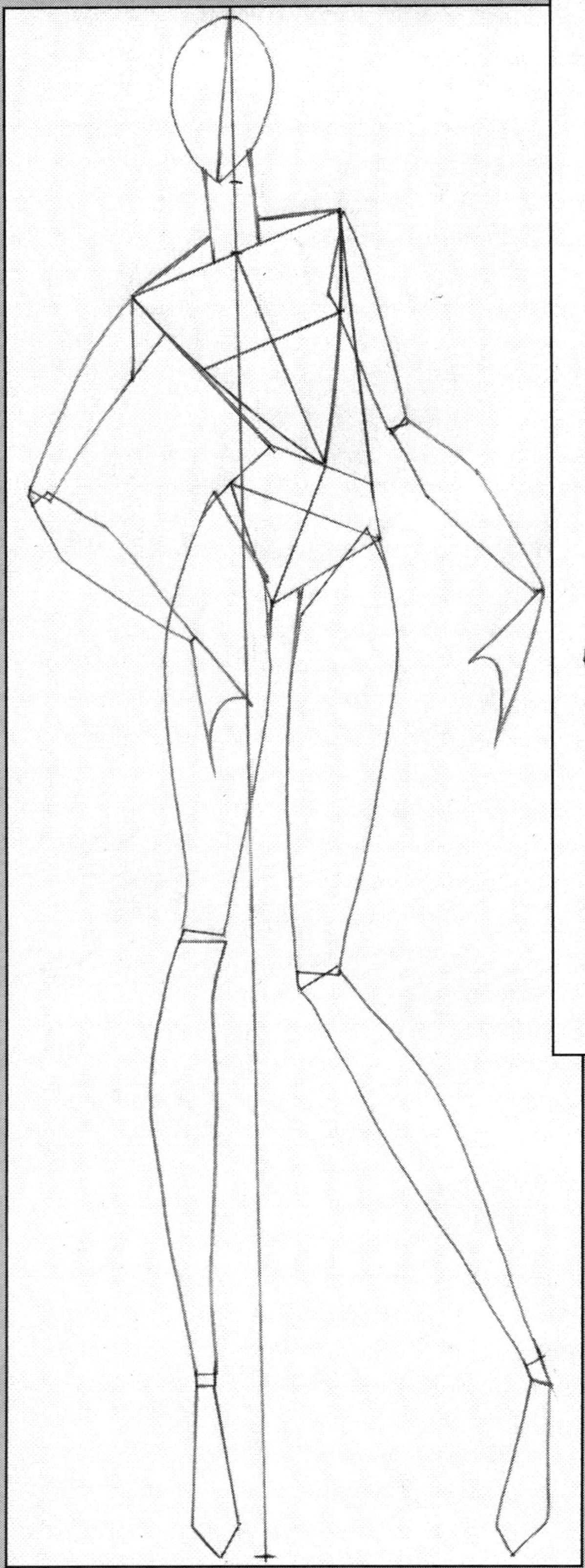

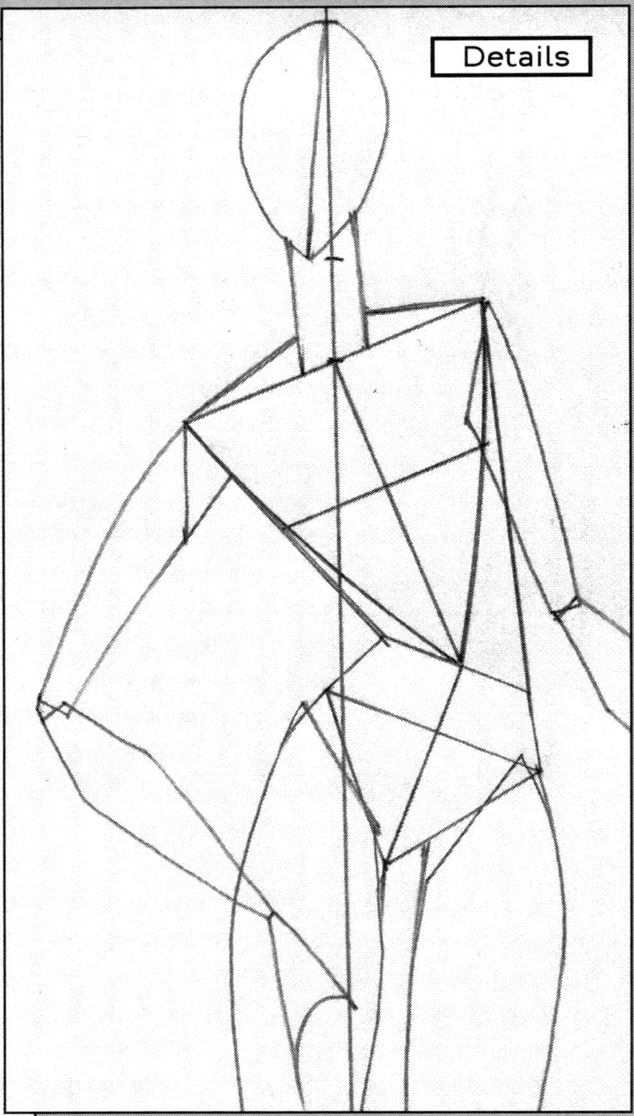

Details

- Add extra shape to the shoulder area
- Connect upper legs and pelvis
- Connect lower legs and upper legs
- Connect lower legs and feet
- Connect upper arms and lower arms

Step #13

Details

Step #14

- Erase all unnecessary lines
- Finalize pelvis outlining
- Check all details

How to Draw Fashion Figure Essential figure drawing techniques by Irina V. Ivanova

CHAPTER 6

Cutting method for front view croquis (final steps)

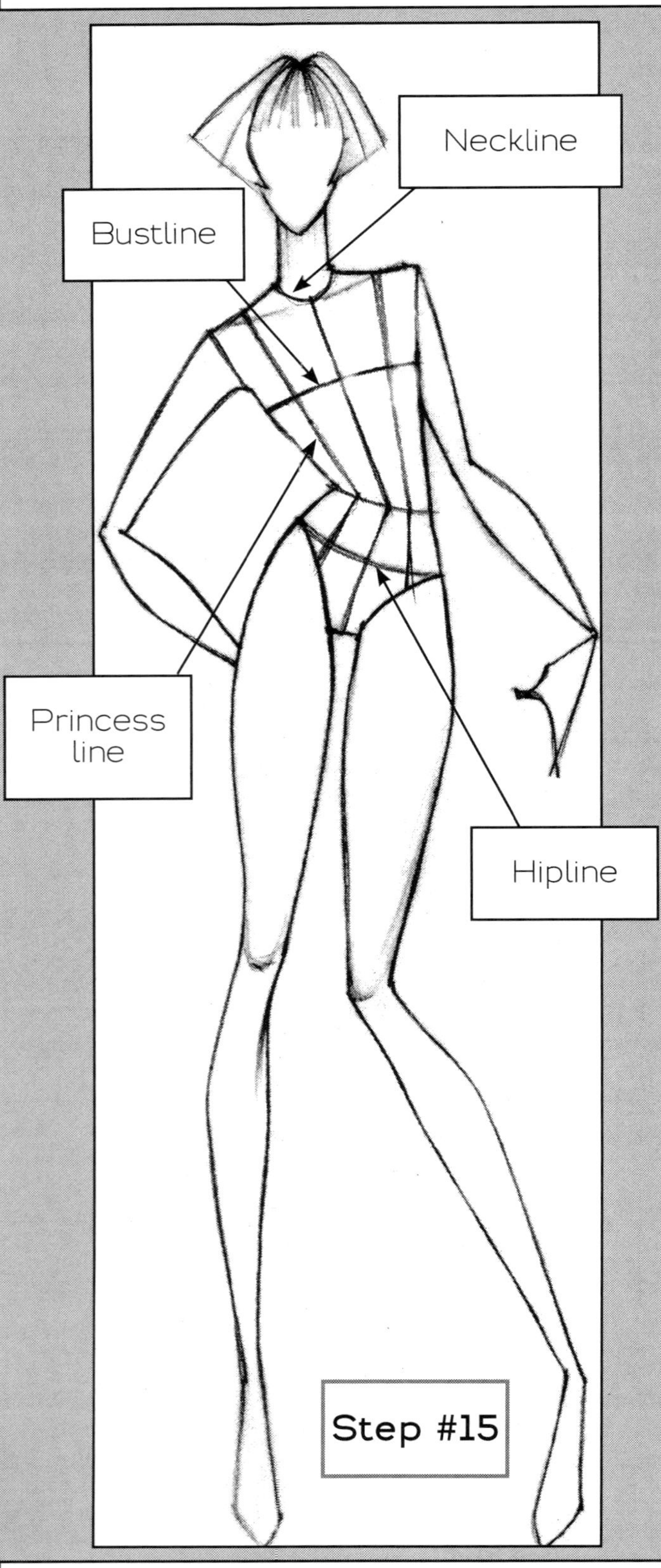

Labels on Step #15: Neckline, Bustline, Princess line, Hipline

Step #15

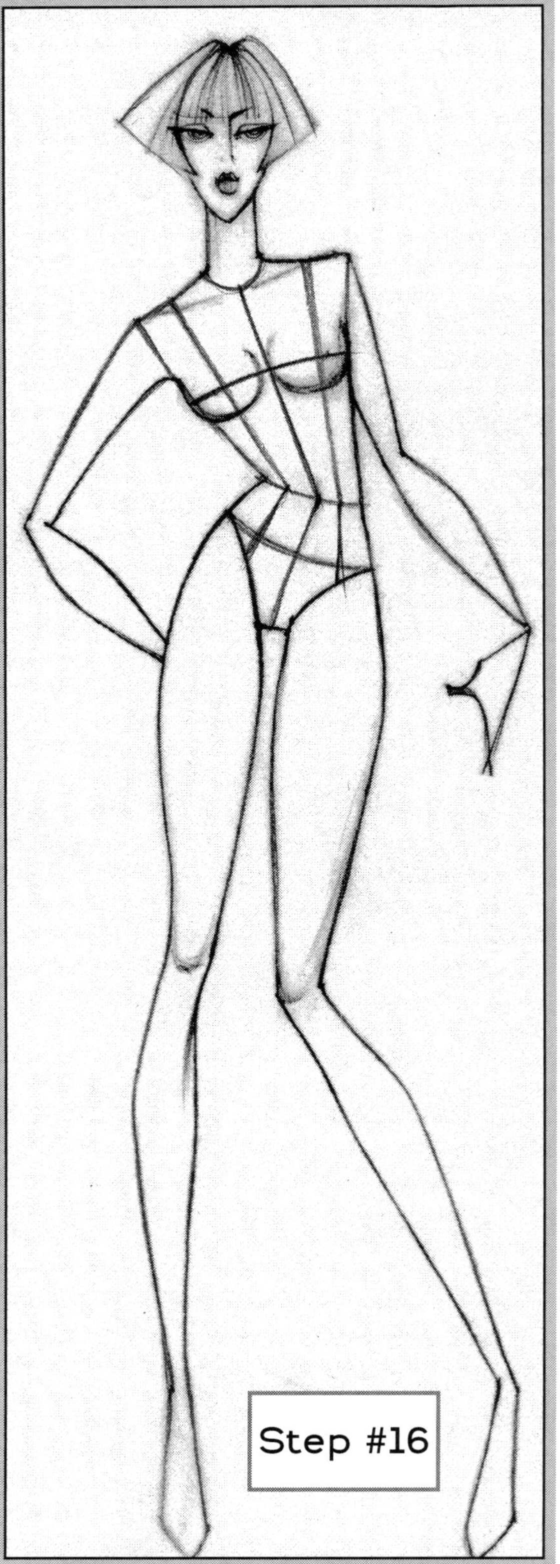

Step #16

- Draw princess line for chest and pelvis
- Show hipline, bustline and neckline
- Check everything before final outlining
- Show basic shape for hairstyle

- Do final outlining
- Draw face features

More croquis by cutting method

Example #1

More croquis by cutting method (continued)

Example #2

Example #3

How to Draw Fashion Figure Essential figure drawing techniques **by Irina V. Ivanova**

CHAPTER 6

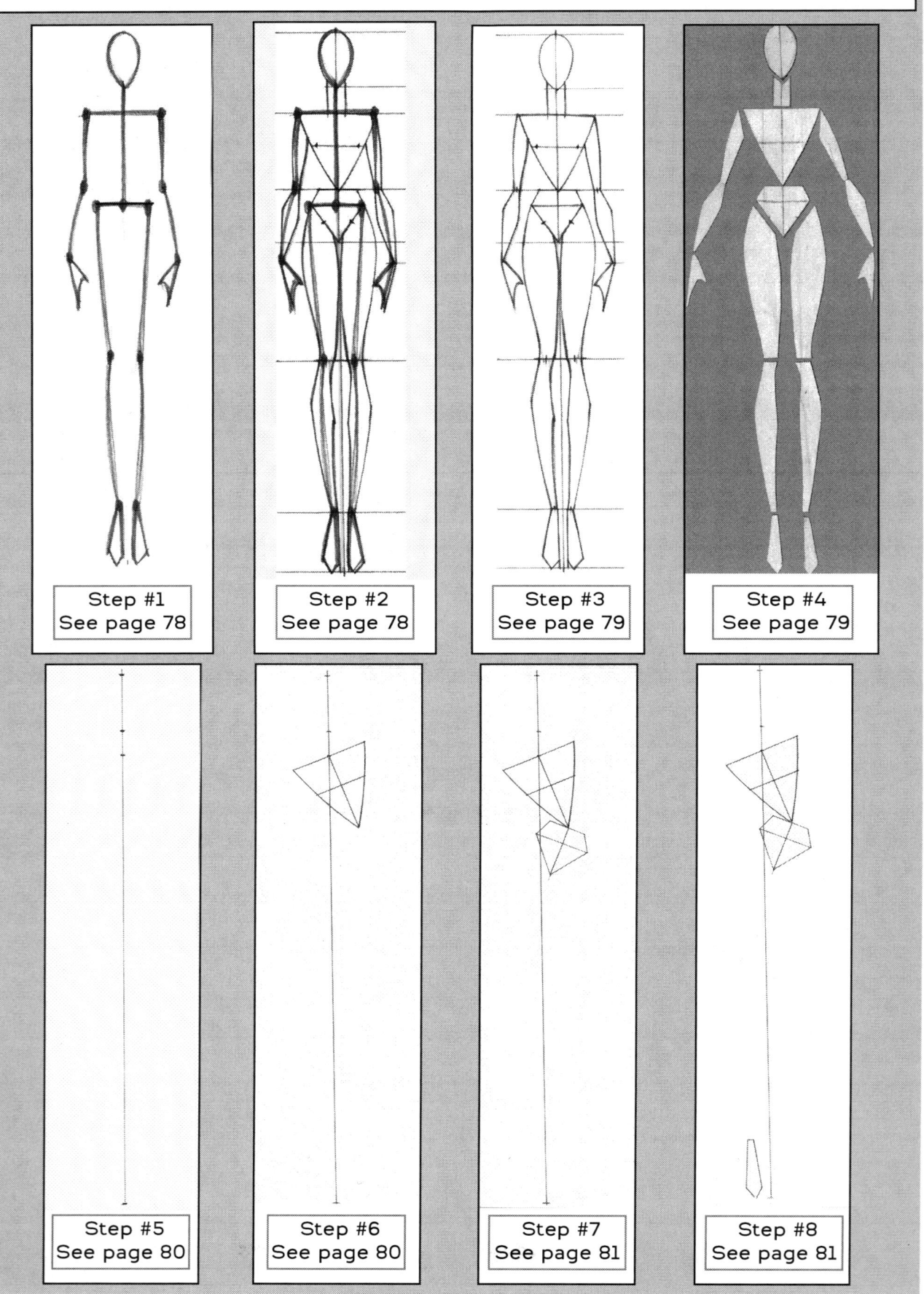

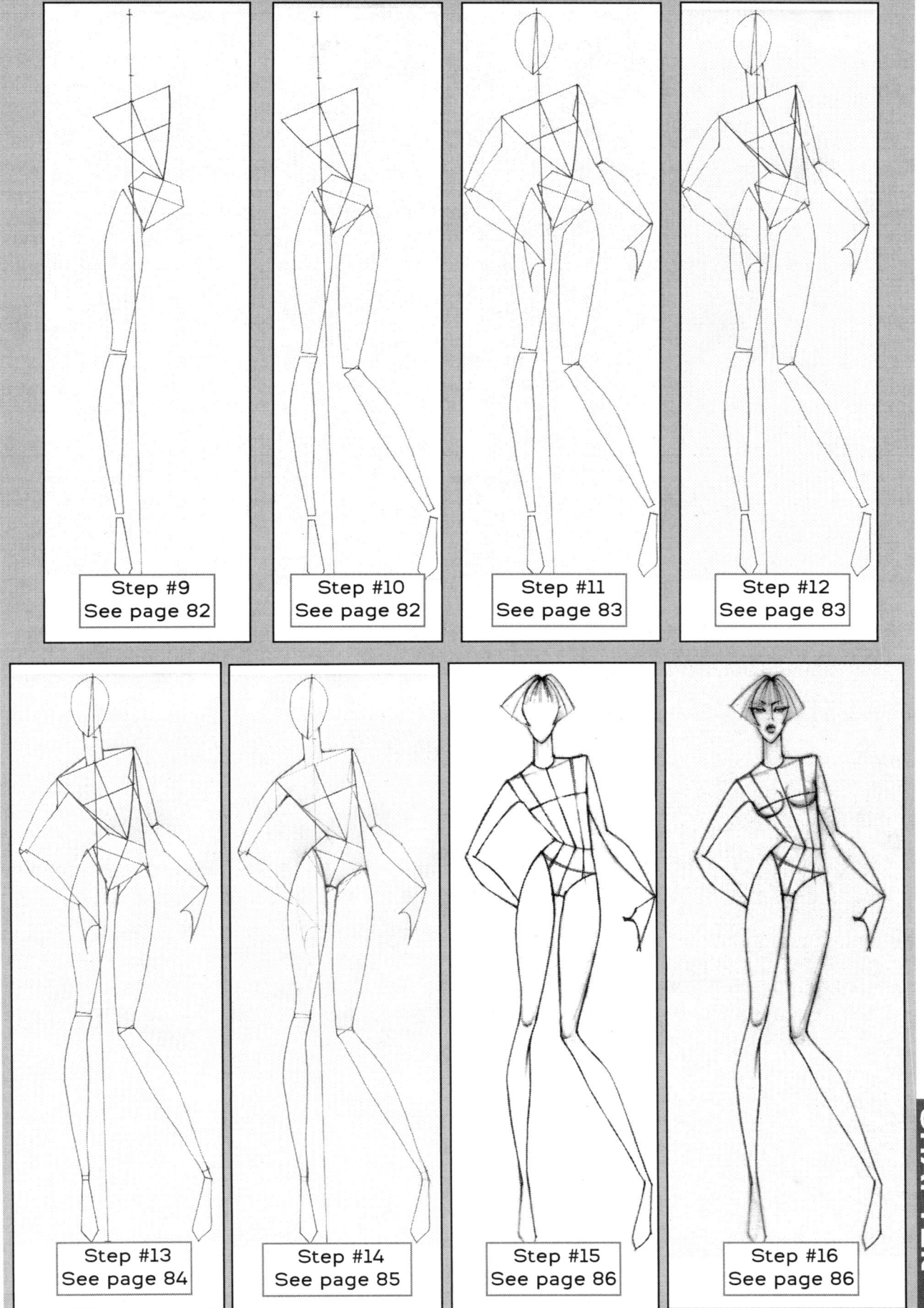

Contents:

Chapter 1. Pages 9-25
Basics of body proportions

Chapter 2. Pages 27-35
Fashion figure schematics (wire skeleton study)

Chapter 3. Pages 37-45
Sketching strategy

Chapter 4. Pages 47-61
Freehand sketching for 10 heads tall fashion figure (front view)

Chapter 5. Pages 63-75
Freehand sketching for 10 heads tall fashion figure (side view)

Chapter 6. Pages 77-91
Cutting method for fashion figure croquis

Chapter 7. Pages 93-125
Figure croquis manipulations

Chapter 8. Pages 127-147
Faces and hands drawing

Index
Pages 148-149

About the author
Pages 150-151

Chapter 7

Figure croquis manipulations

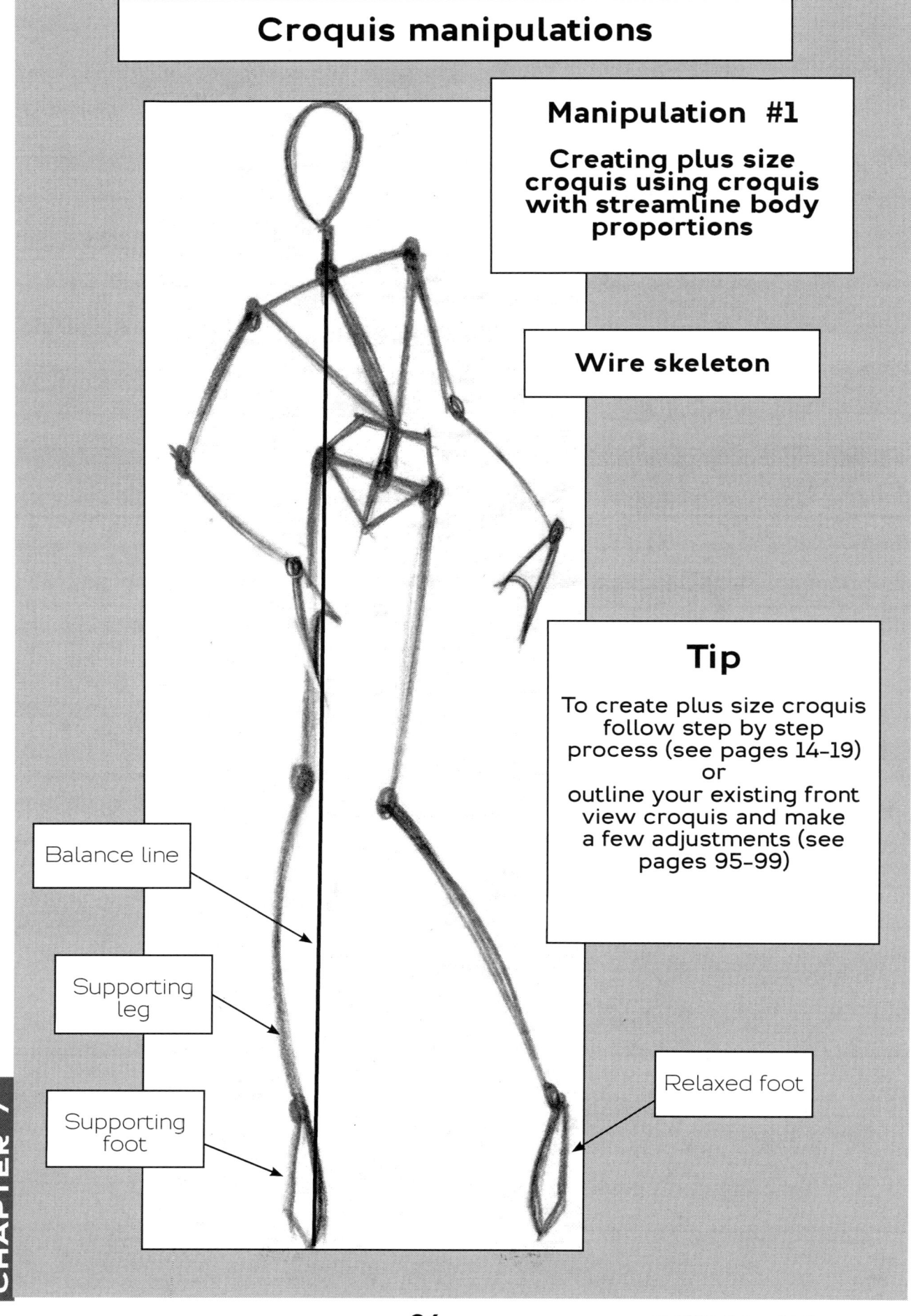

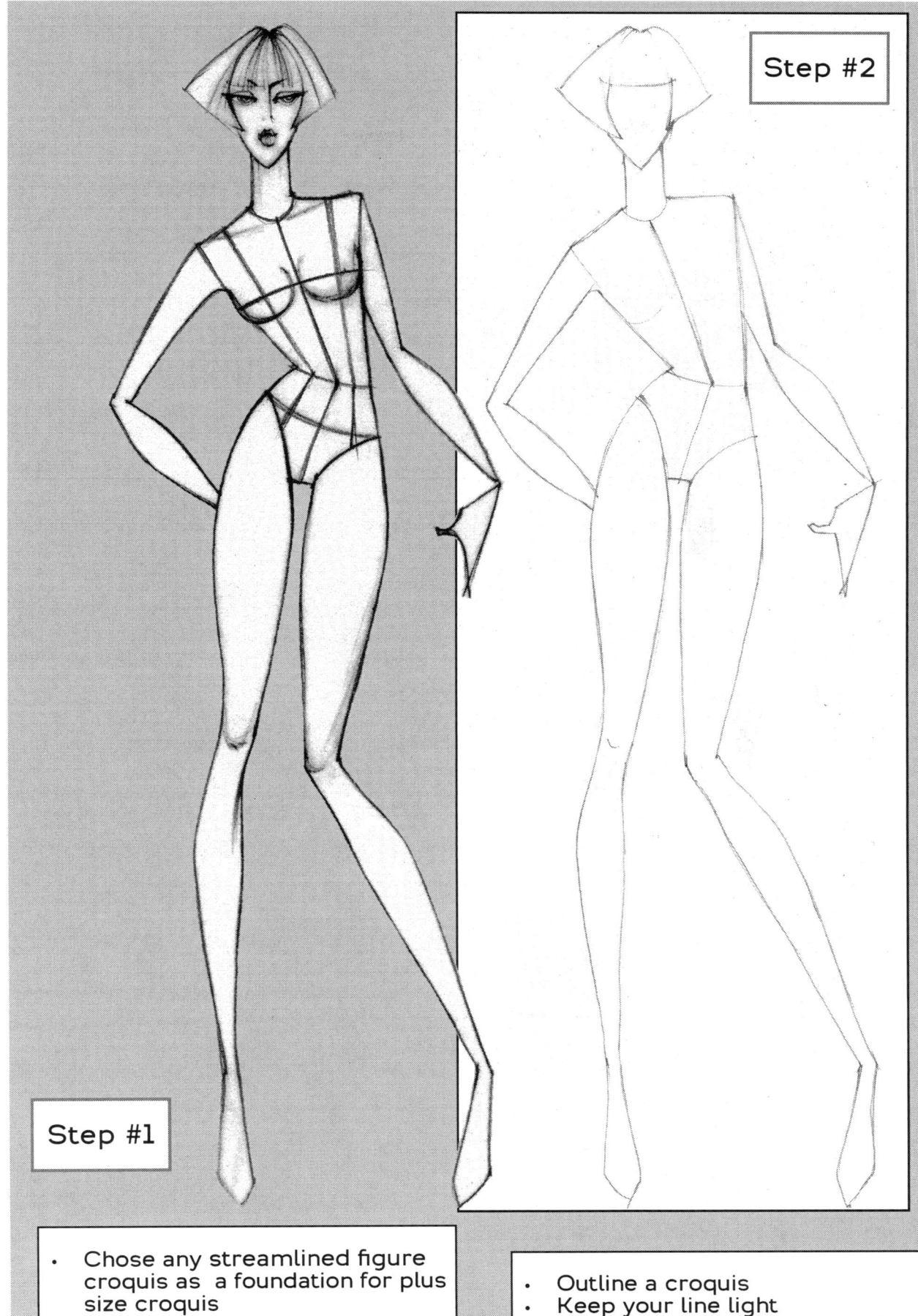

Step #2

Step #1

- Chose any streamlined figure croquis as a foundation for plus size croquis

- Outline a croquis
- Keep your line light
- Do not trace any small details

How to Draw Fashion Figure Essential figure drawing techniques by Irina V. Ivanova

CHAPTER 7

Croquis manipulations (continued)

Step #3

Step #4

Manipulation #1

Creating plus size croquis using croquis with streamline body proportions (continued)

- Add extra volume to face, neck, and chest

- Add extra volume to the legs

Step #5

Step #6

- Add additional extra volume to the legs if necessary
- Add extra volume to arms and hands

Croquis manipulations (continued)

Step #7

Step #8

Manipulation #1

Creating plus size croquis using croquis with streamline body proportions (continued)

- Erase all unnecessary lines (preliminary outlining)
- Show face features

- Check all details and overall body proportions
- Show center, waist, upper hip, bust, and neck lines

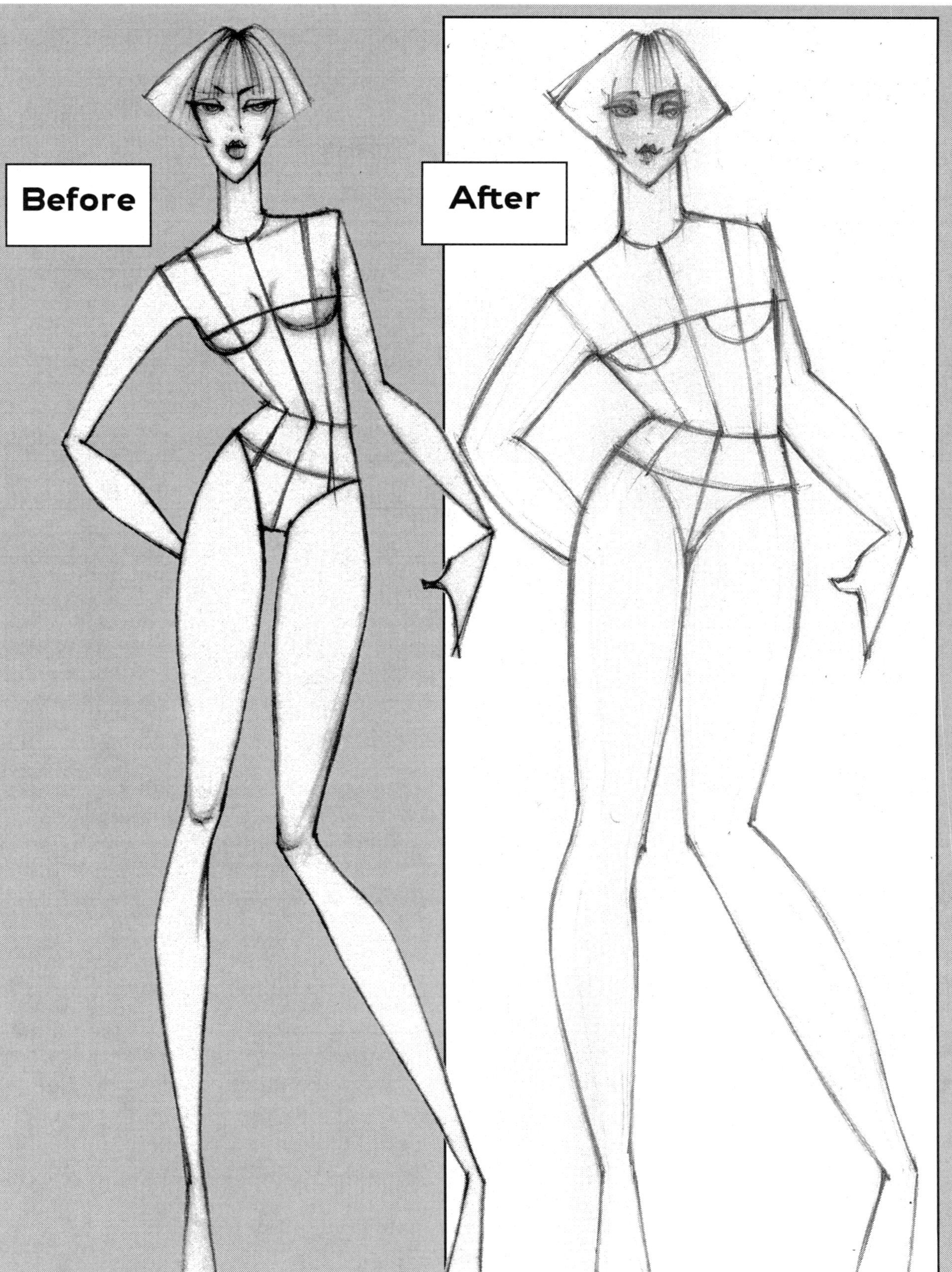

Before

After

Final comparison for Manipulation #1

99

Croquis manipulations (continued)

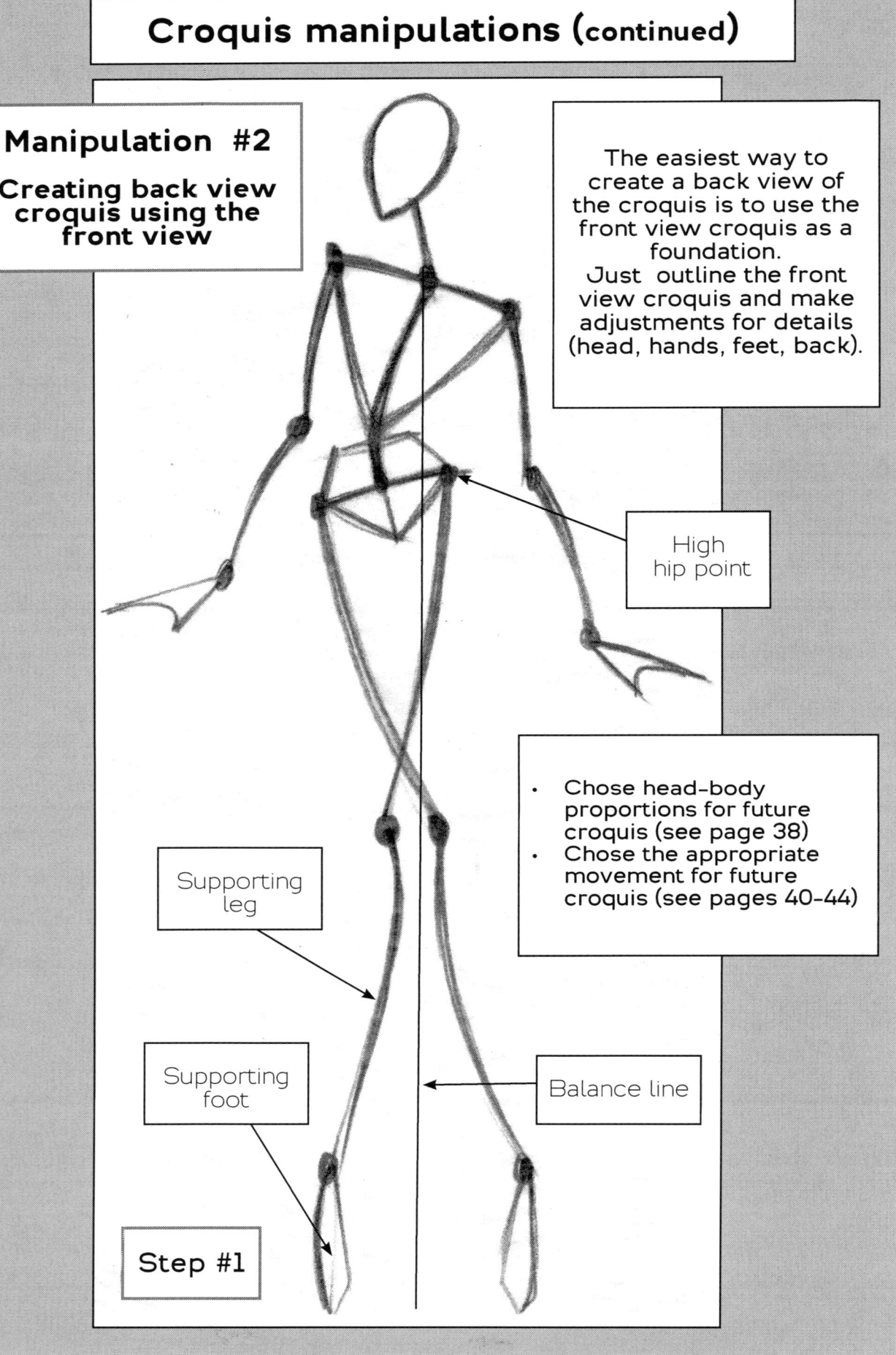

Manipulation #2

Creating back view croquis using the front view

The easiest way to create a back view of the croquis is to use the front view croquis as a foundation.
Just outline the front view croquis and make adjustments for details (head, hands, feet, back).

High hip point

- Chose head-body proportions for future croquis (see page 38)
- Chose the appropriate movement for future croquis (see pages 40-44)

Supporting leg

Supporting foot

Balance line

Step #1

- Follow step by step process (see pages 48-59) and create your front view croquis
- Make sure you have no mistakes in the movement and proportions
- Draw all details

Step #2

How to Draw Fashion Figure Essential figure drawing techniques **by Irina V. Ivanova**

CHAPTER 7

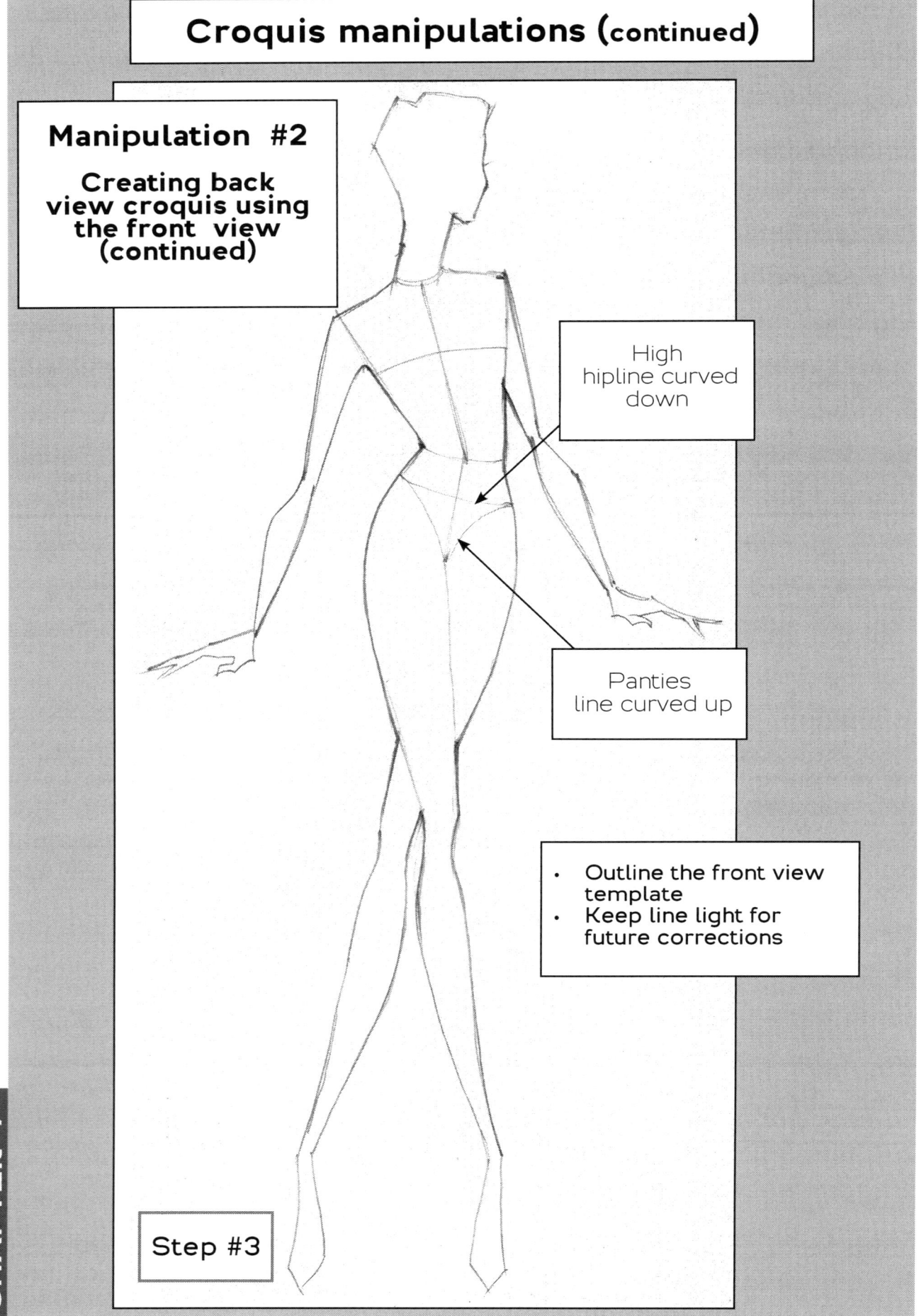

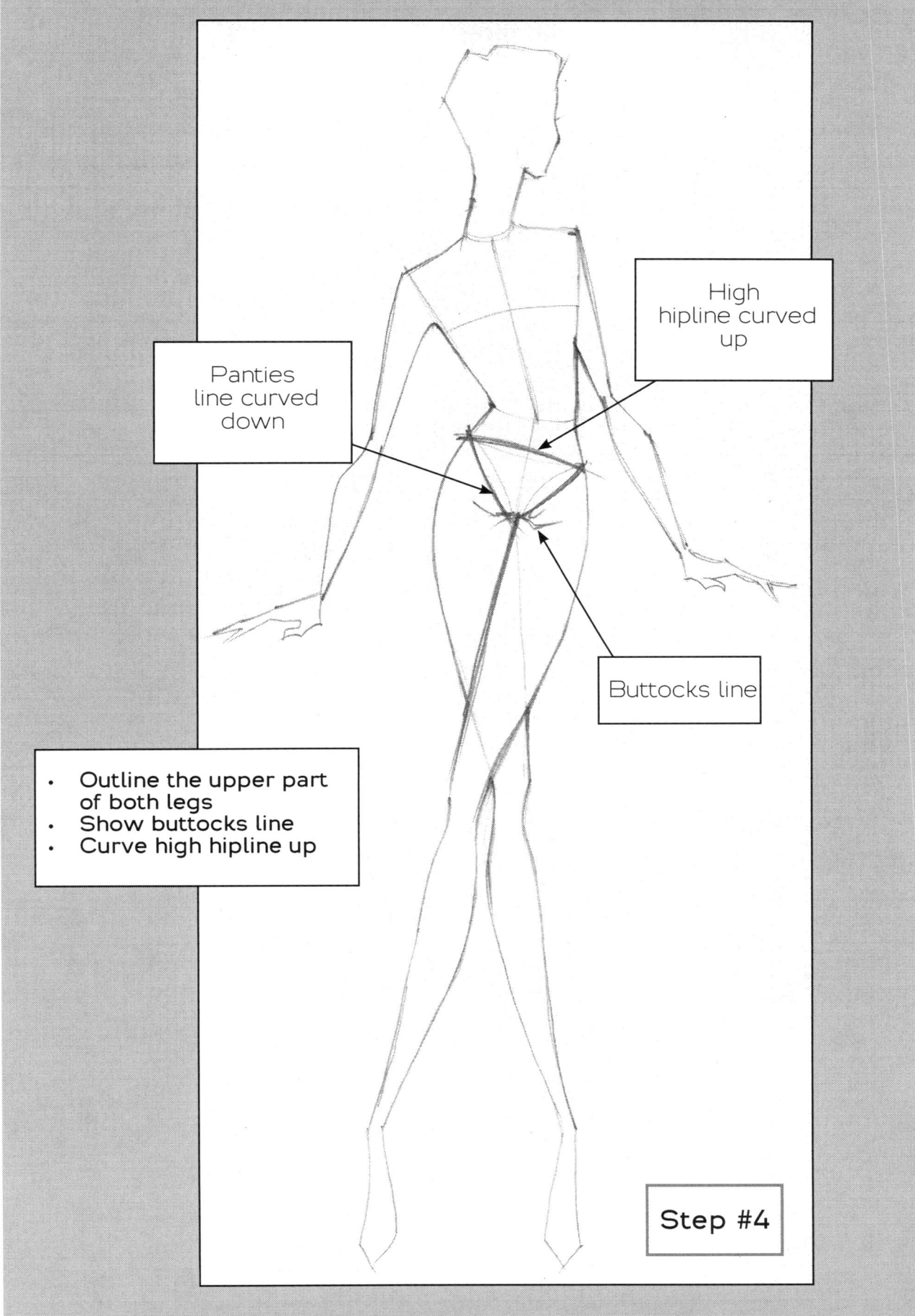

Croquis manipulations (continued)

Manipulation #2
Creating back view croquis using the front view (continued)

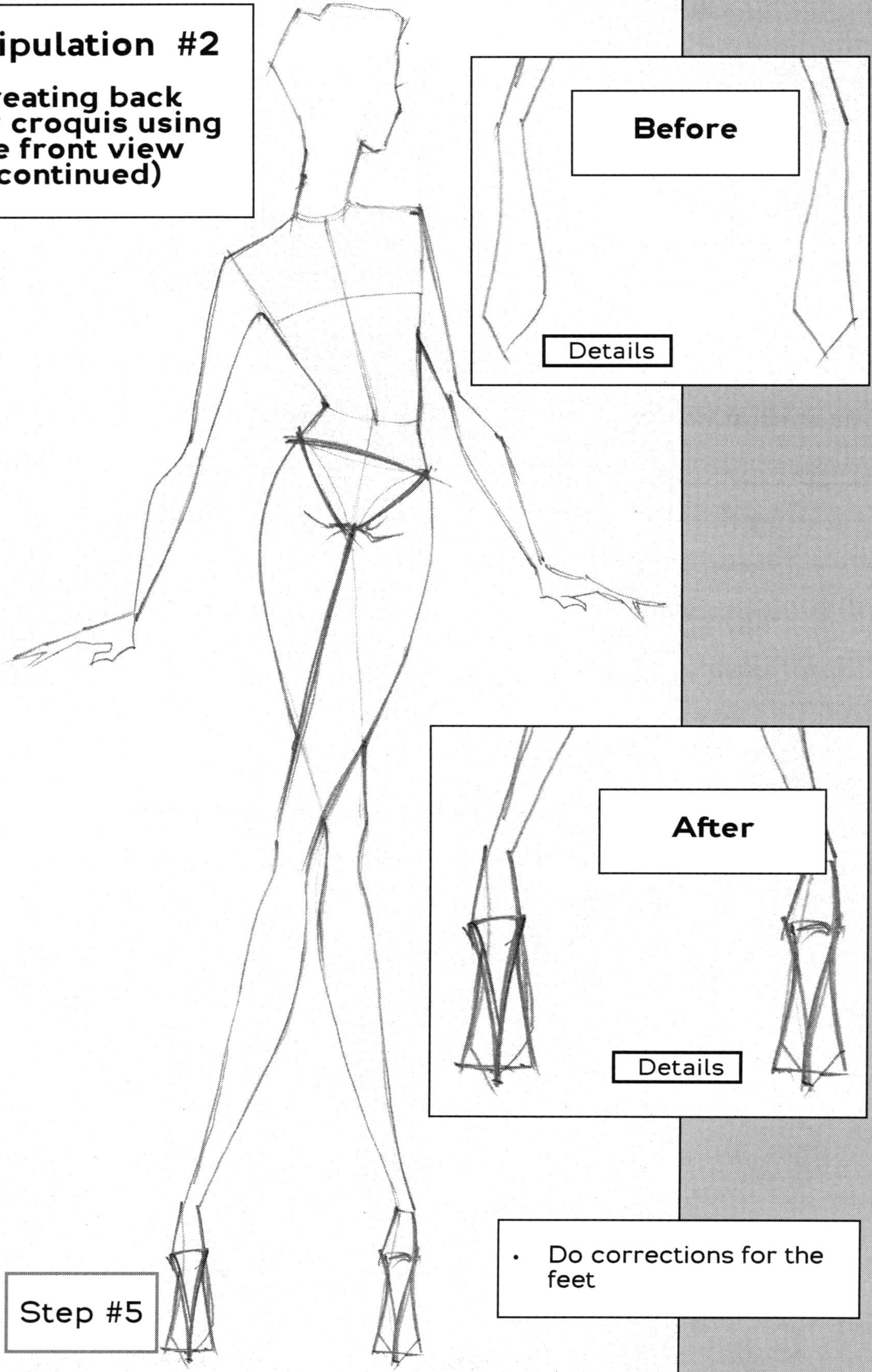

Before

Details

After

Details

- Do corrections for the feet

Step #5

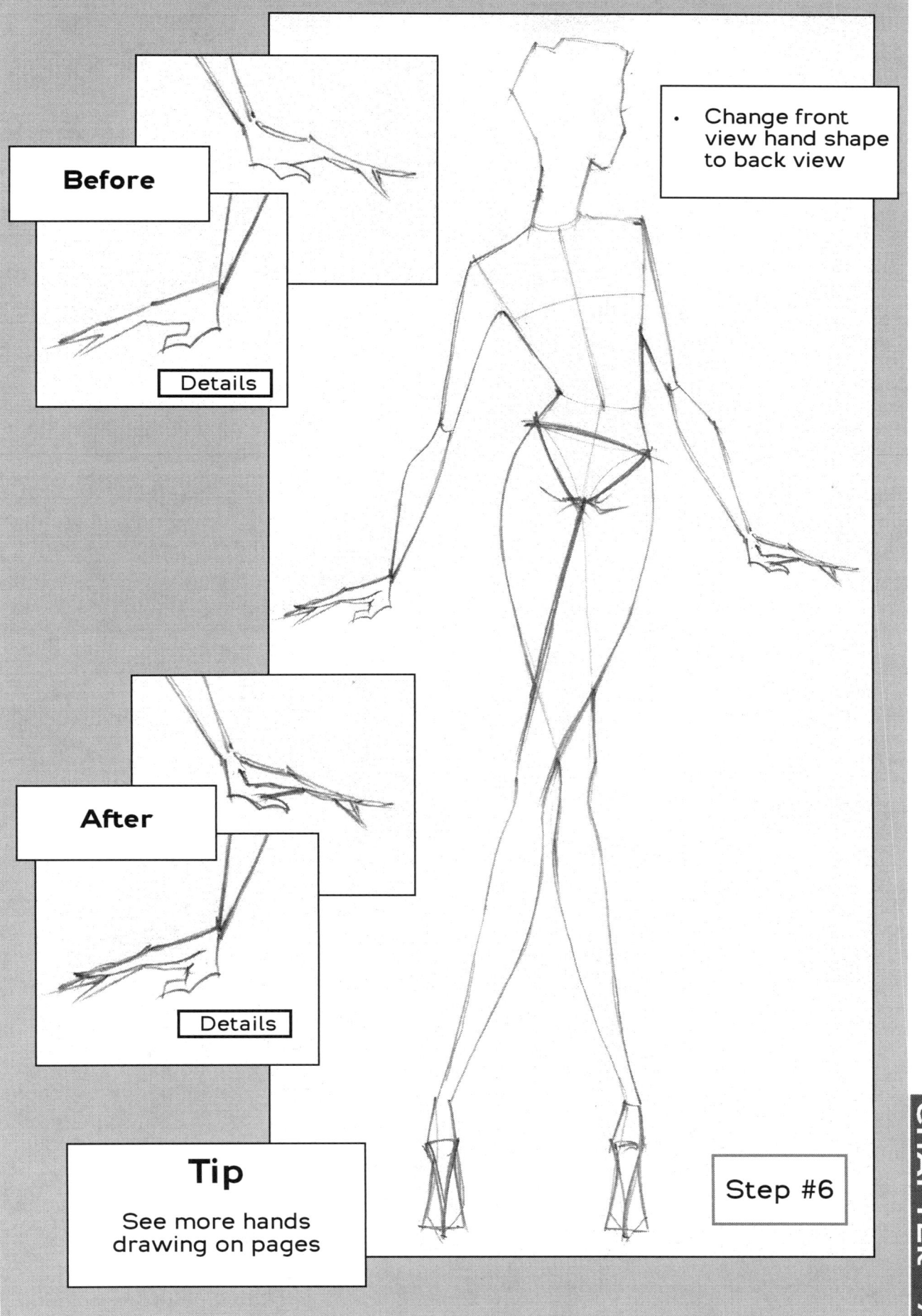

Croquis manipulations (continued)

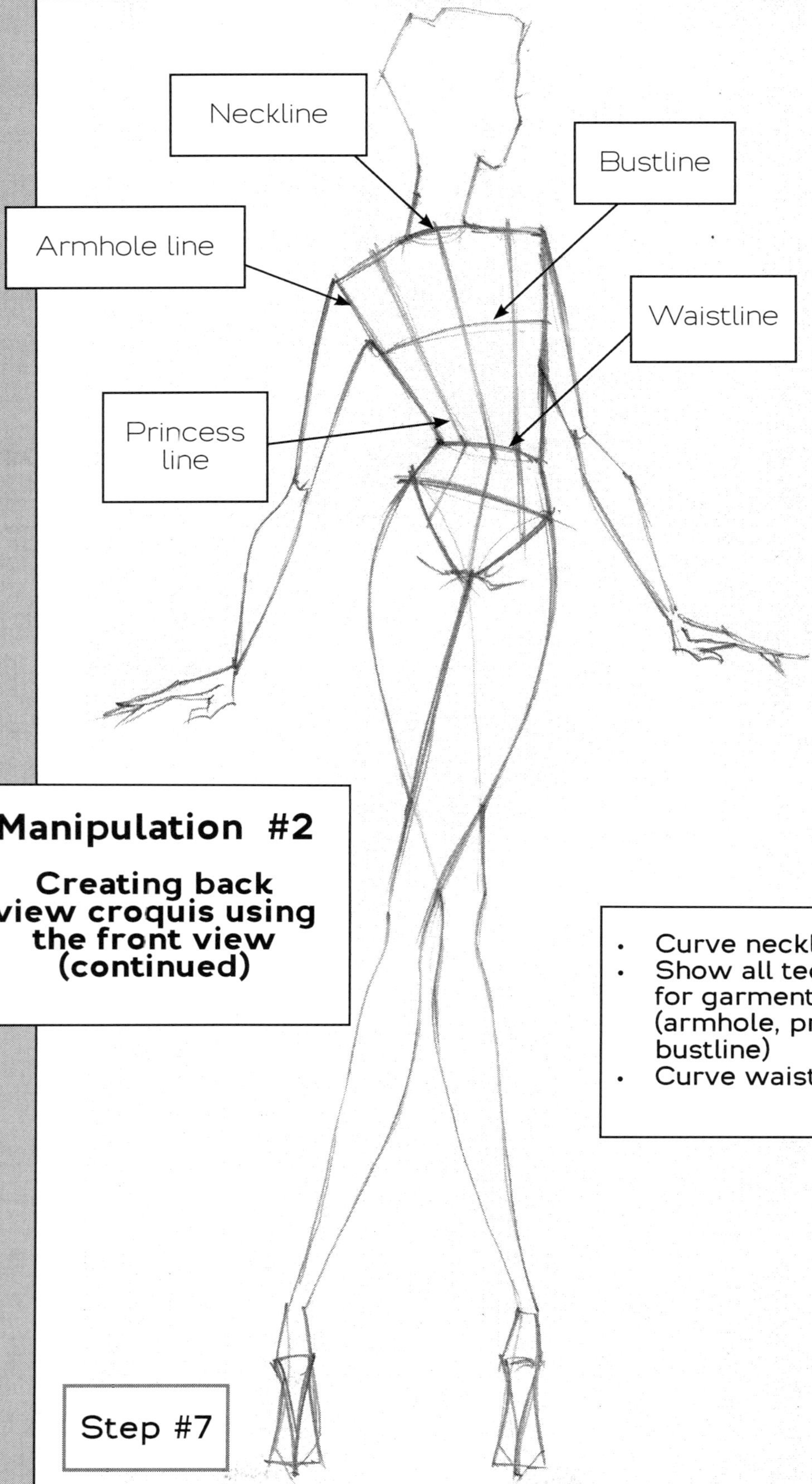

- Neckline
- Bustline
- Armhole line
- Waistline
- Princess line

Manipulation #2
Creating back view croquis using the front view (continued)

- Curve neckline up
- Show all technical lines for garment drawing (armhole, princess, bustline)
- Curve waistline up

Step #7

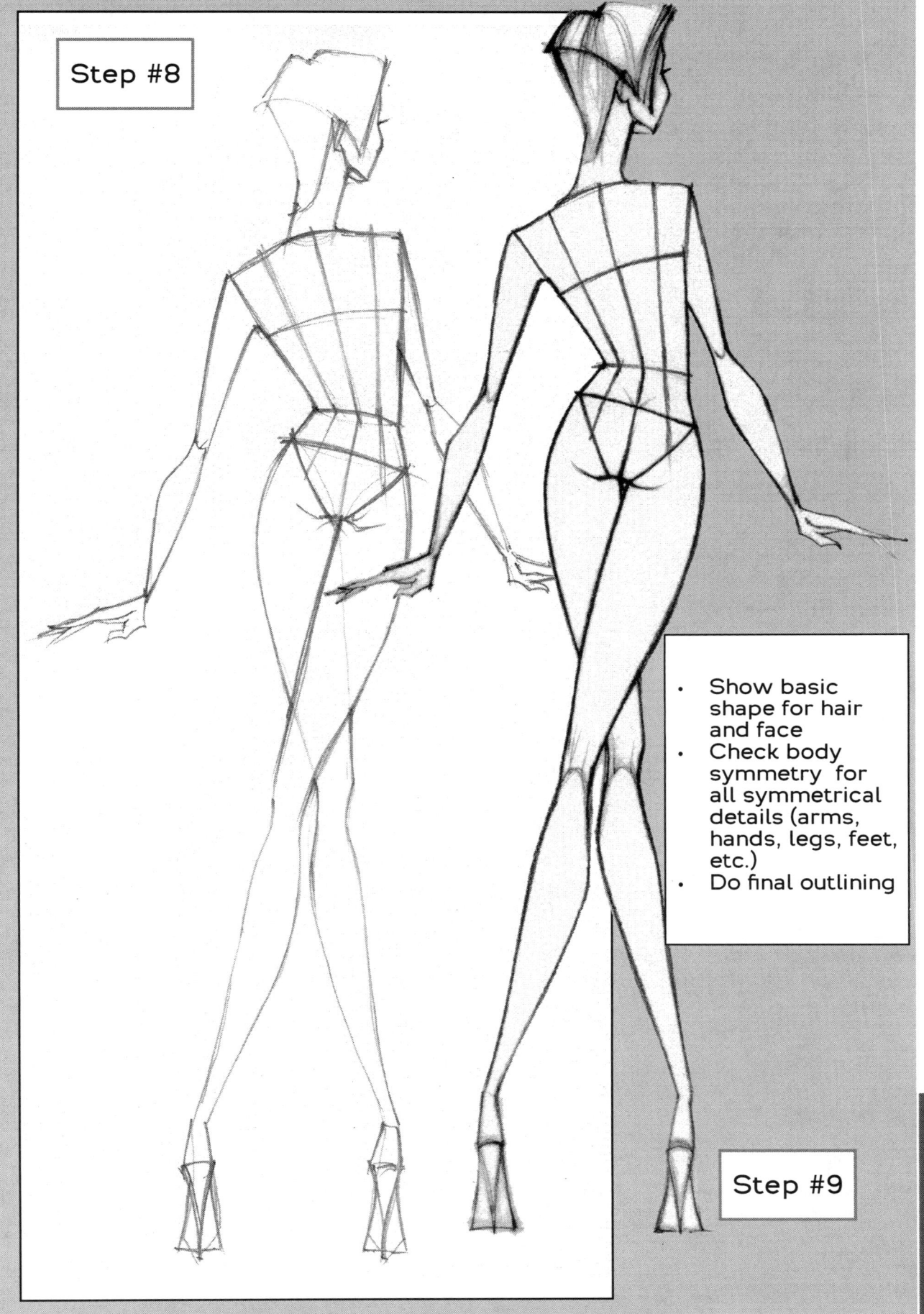

Croquis manipulations (continued)

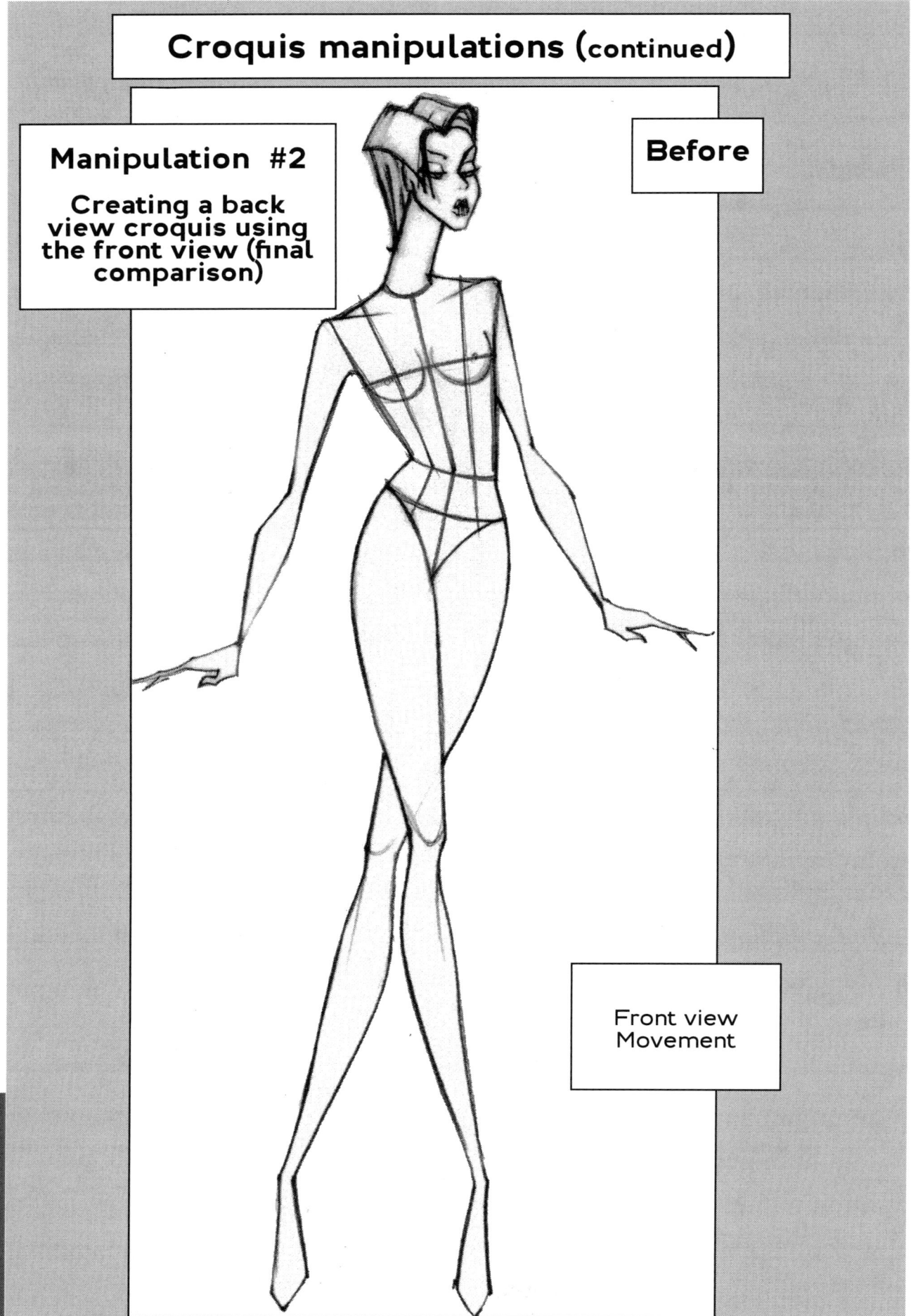

Manipulation #2

Creating a back view croquis using the front view (final comparison)

Before

Front view Movement

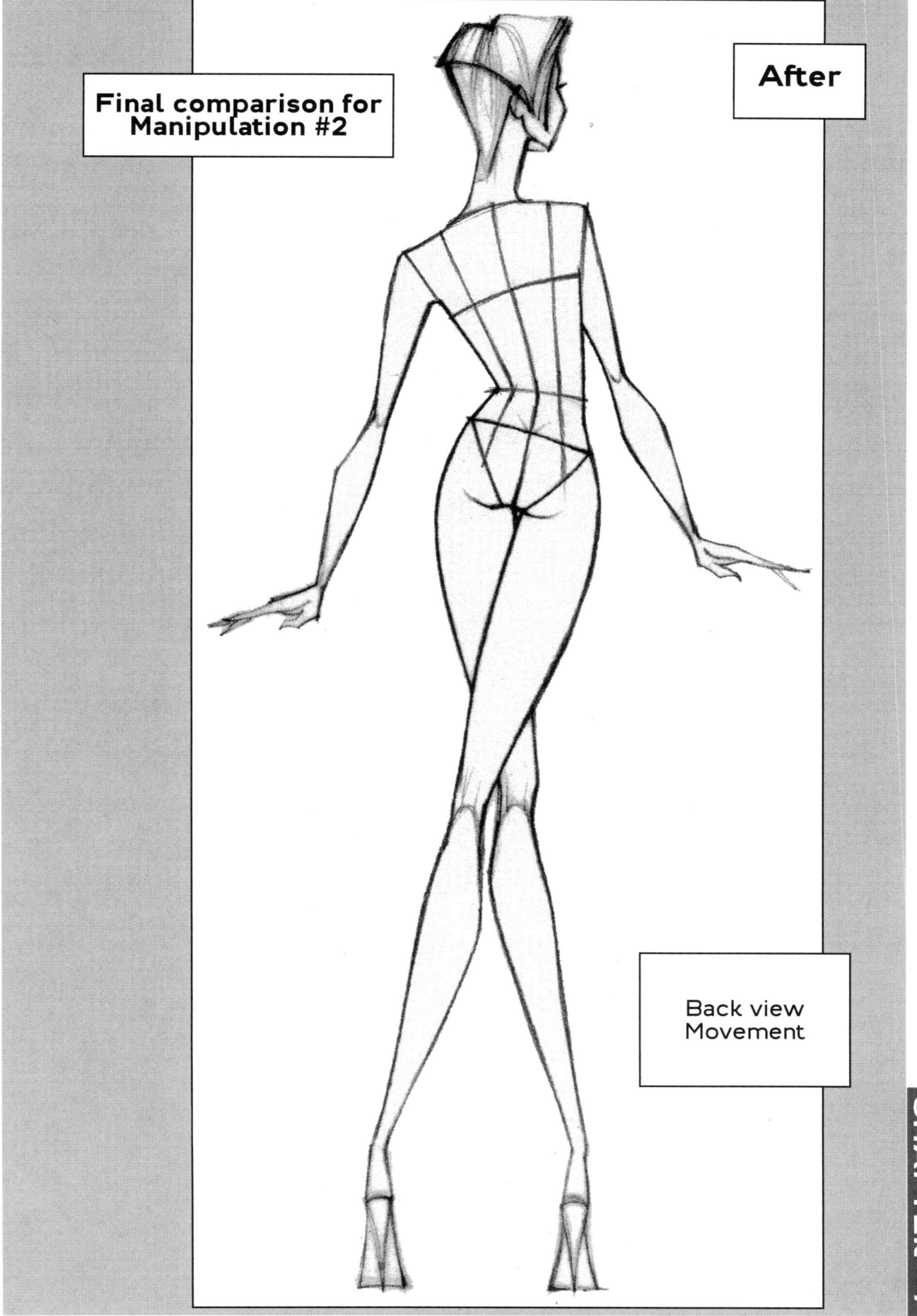

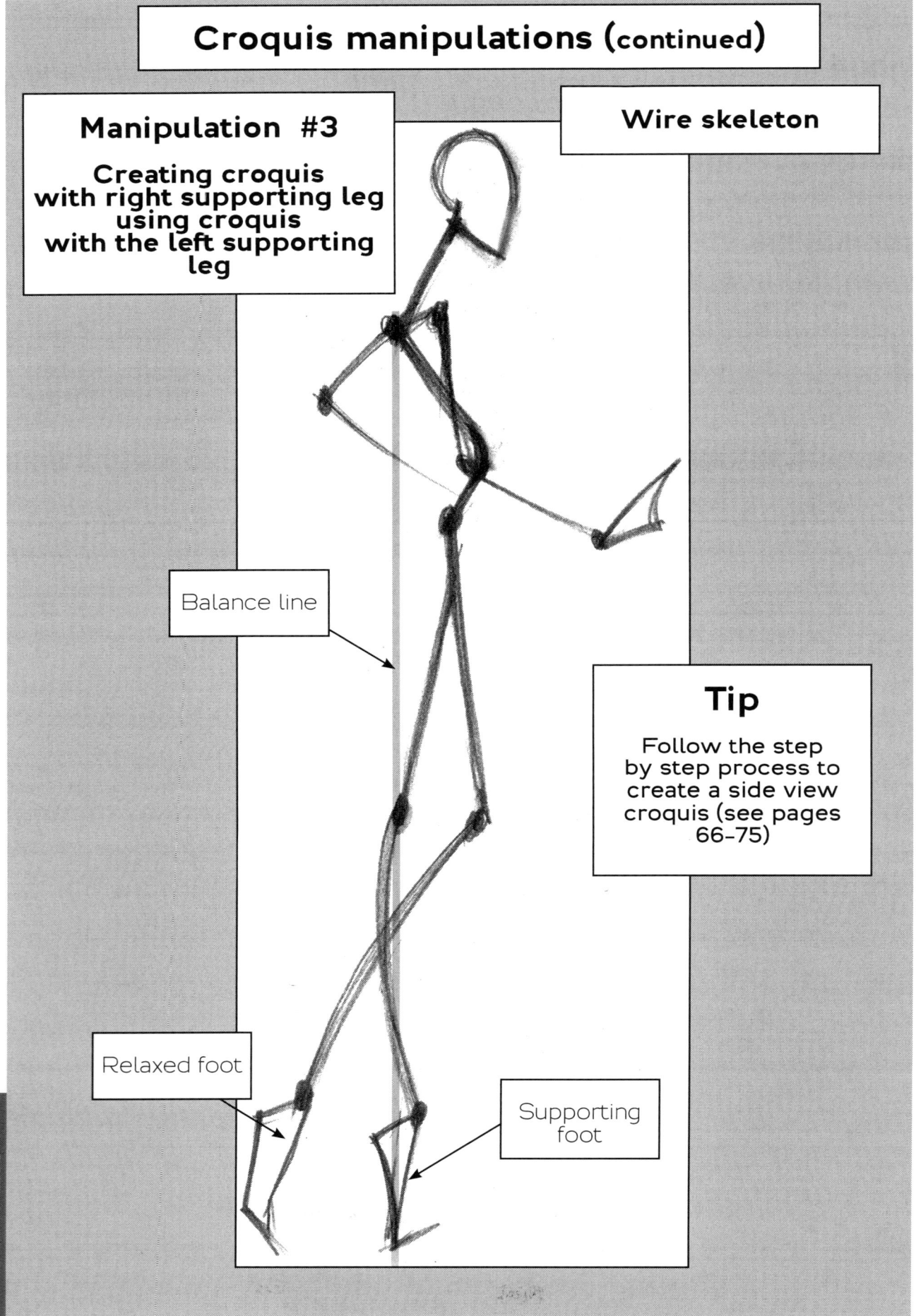

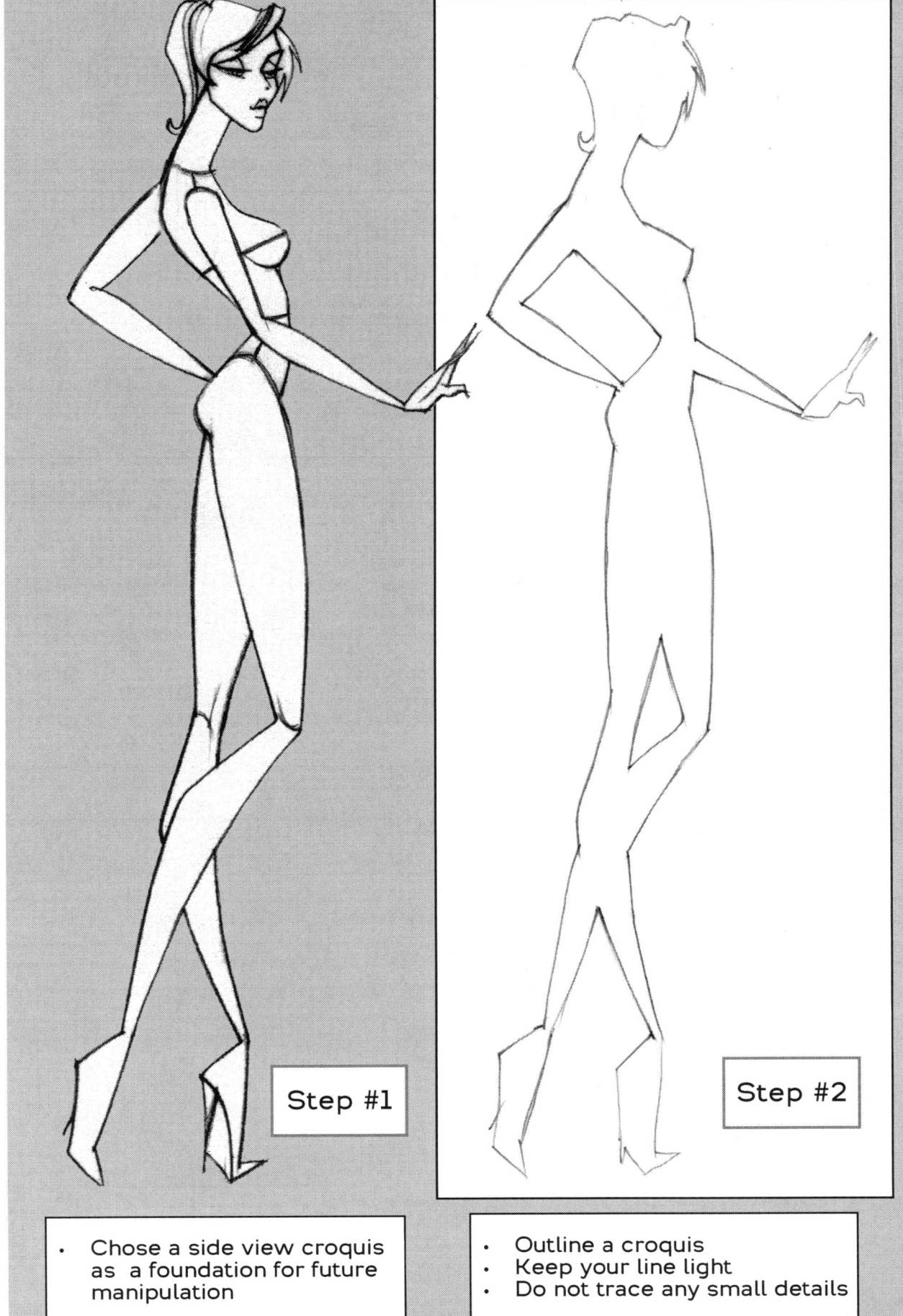

Step #1
- Chose a side view croquis as a foundation for future manipulation

Step #2
- Outline a croquis
- Keep your line light
- Do not trace any small details

How to Draw Fashion Figure Essential figure drawing techniques by Irina V. Ivanova

CHAPTER 7

Croquis manipulations (continued)

Manipulation #3

Creating croquis with right supporting leg using croquis with the left supporting leg (continued)

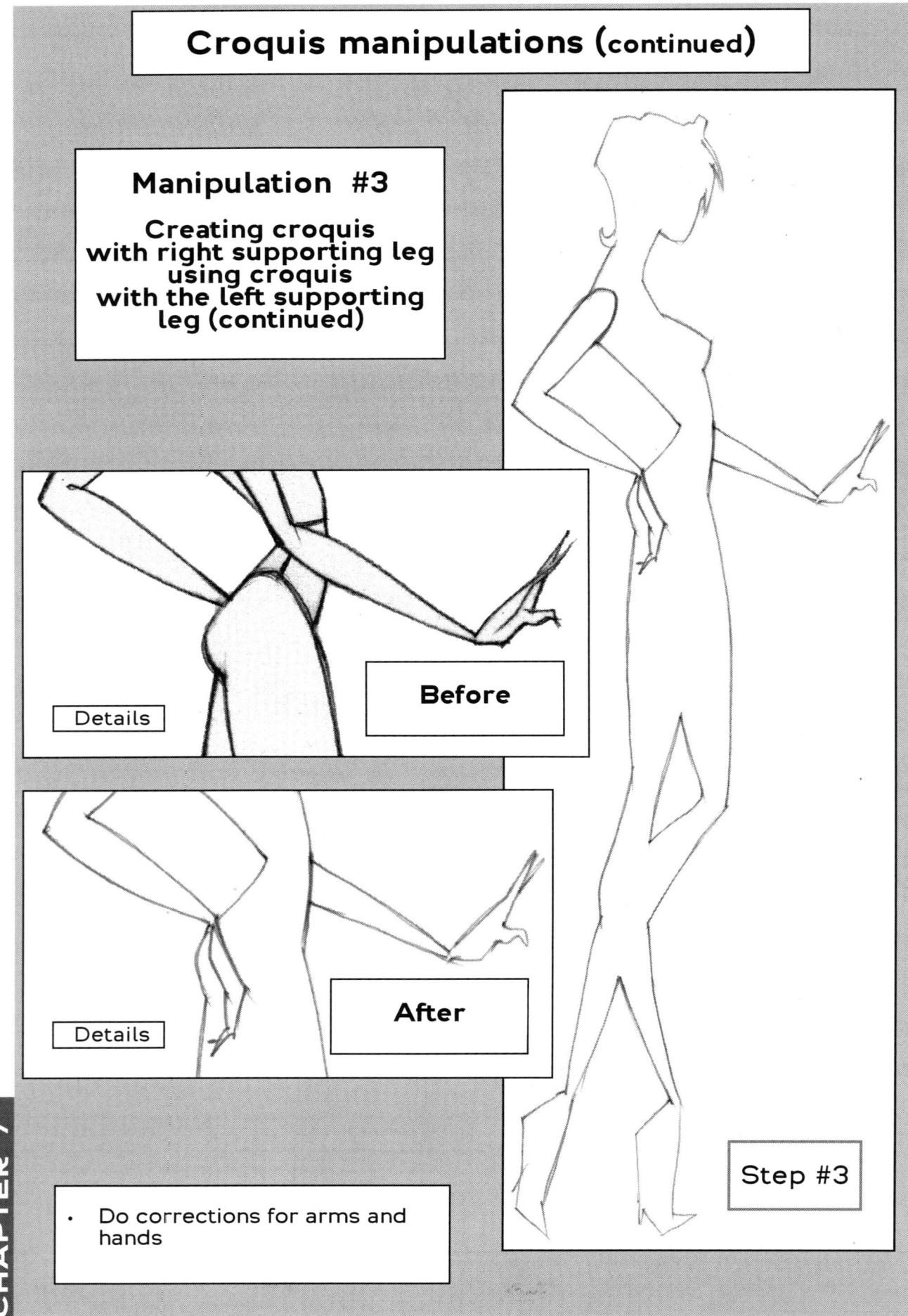

Details — Before

Details — After

Step #3

- Do corrections for arms and hands

Before

Details

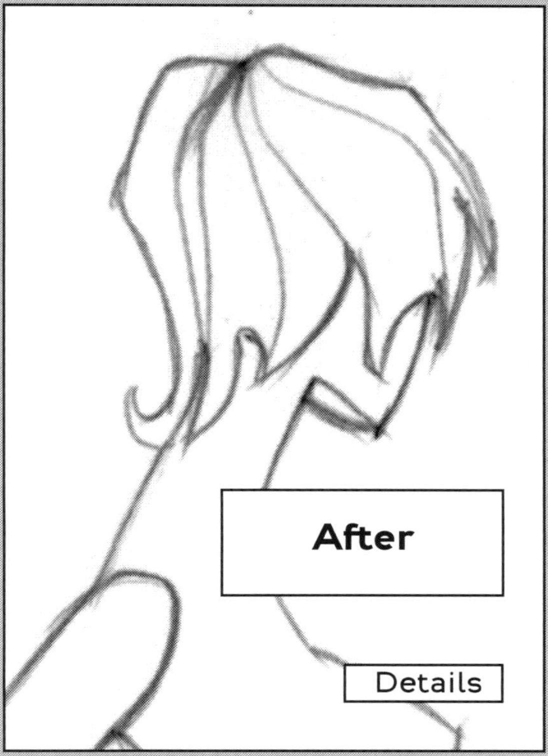

After

Details

Step #4

- Do corrections for head

Croquis manipulations (continued)

Manipulation #3
Creating croquis with right supporting leg using croquis with the left supporting leg (continued)

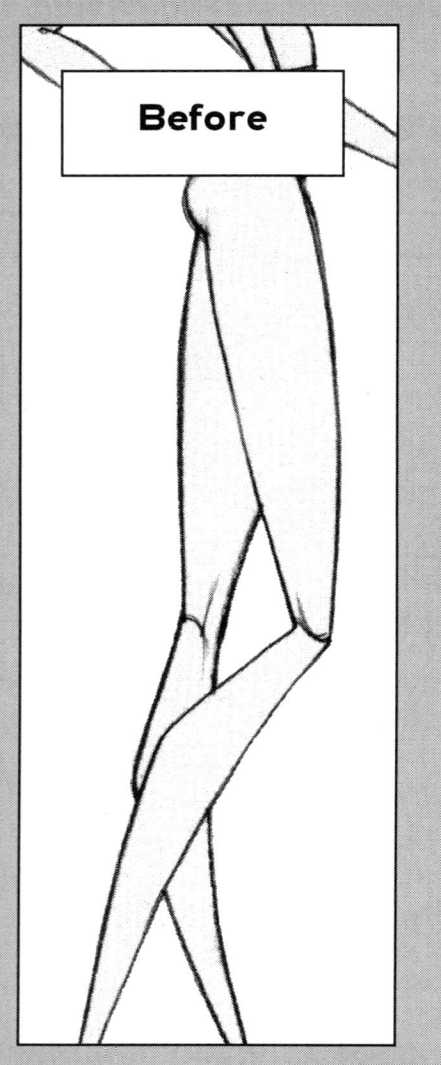

Before

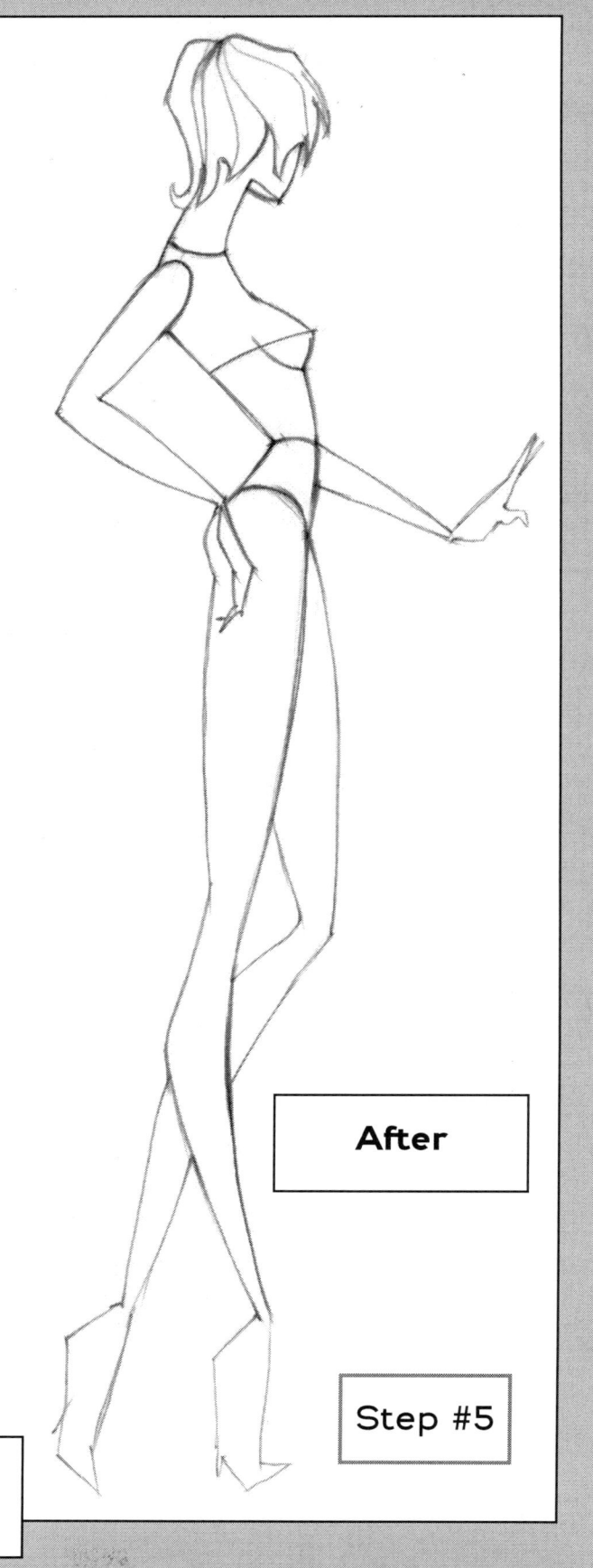

After

Step #5

- Do corrections for legs
- Show neck, bust and waistlines

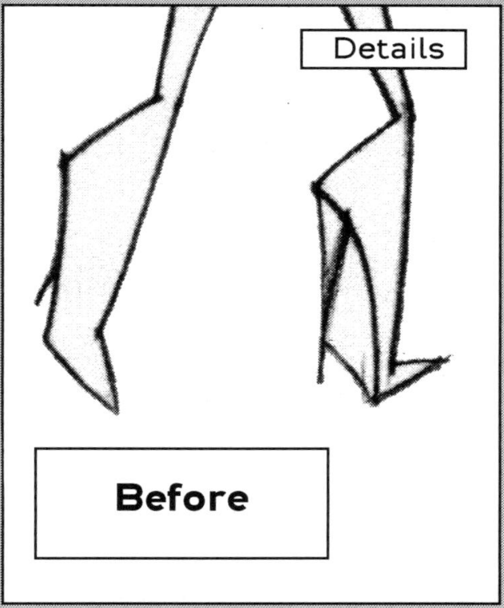

Details

Before

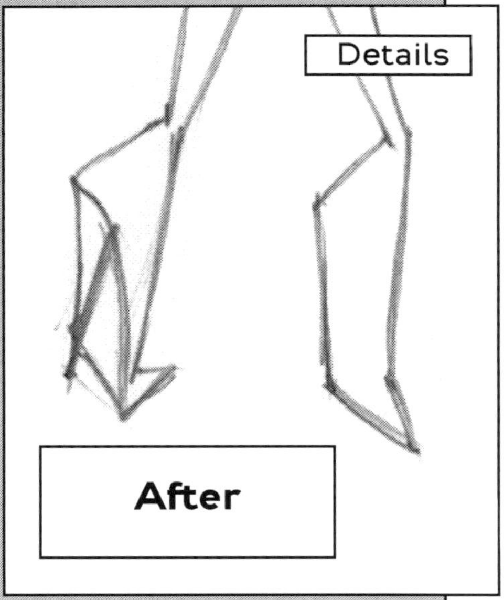

Details

After

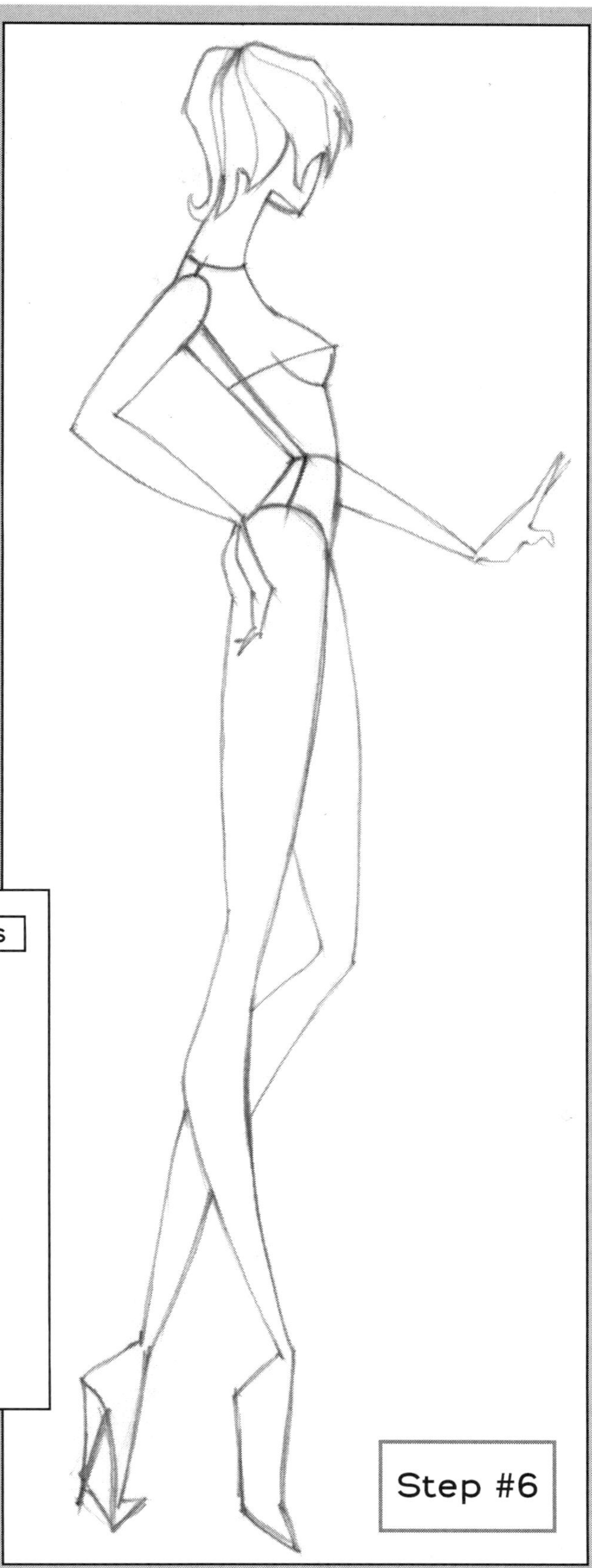

Step #6

- Do corrections for feet

How to Draw Fashion Figure Essential figure drawing techniques **by Irina V. Ivanova**

CHAPTER 7

Croquis manipulations (continued)

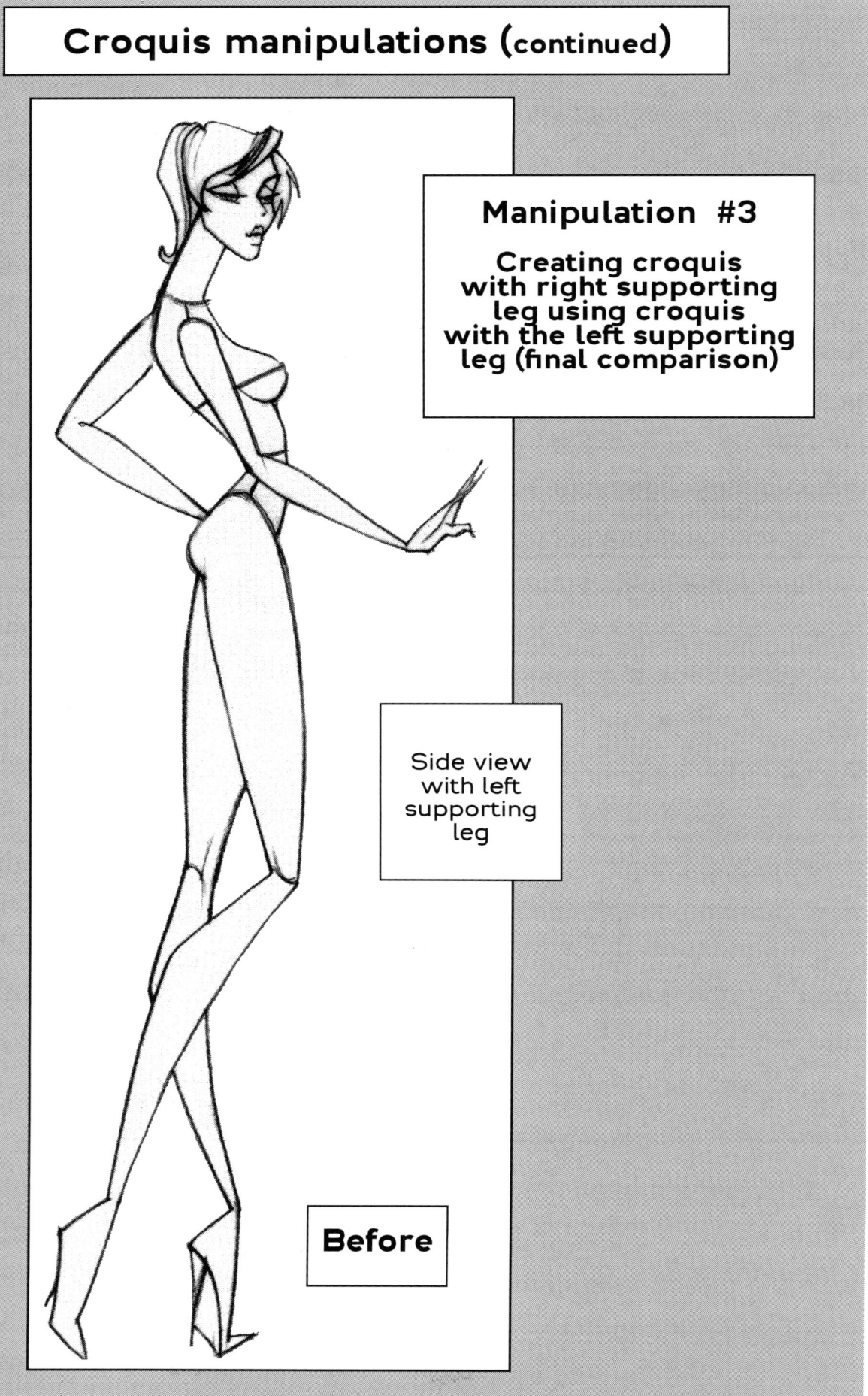

Manipulation #3

Creating croquis with right supporting leg using croquis with the left supporting leg (final comparison)

Side view with left supporting leg

Before

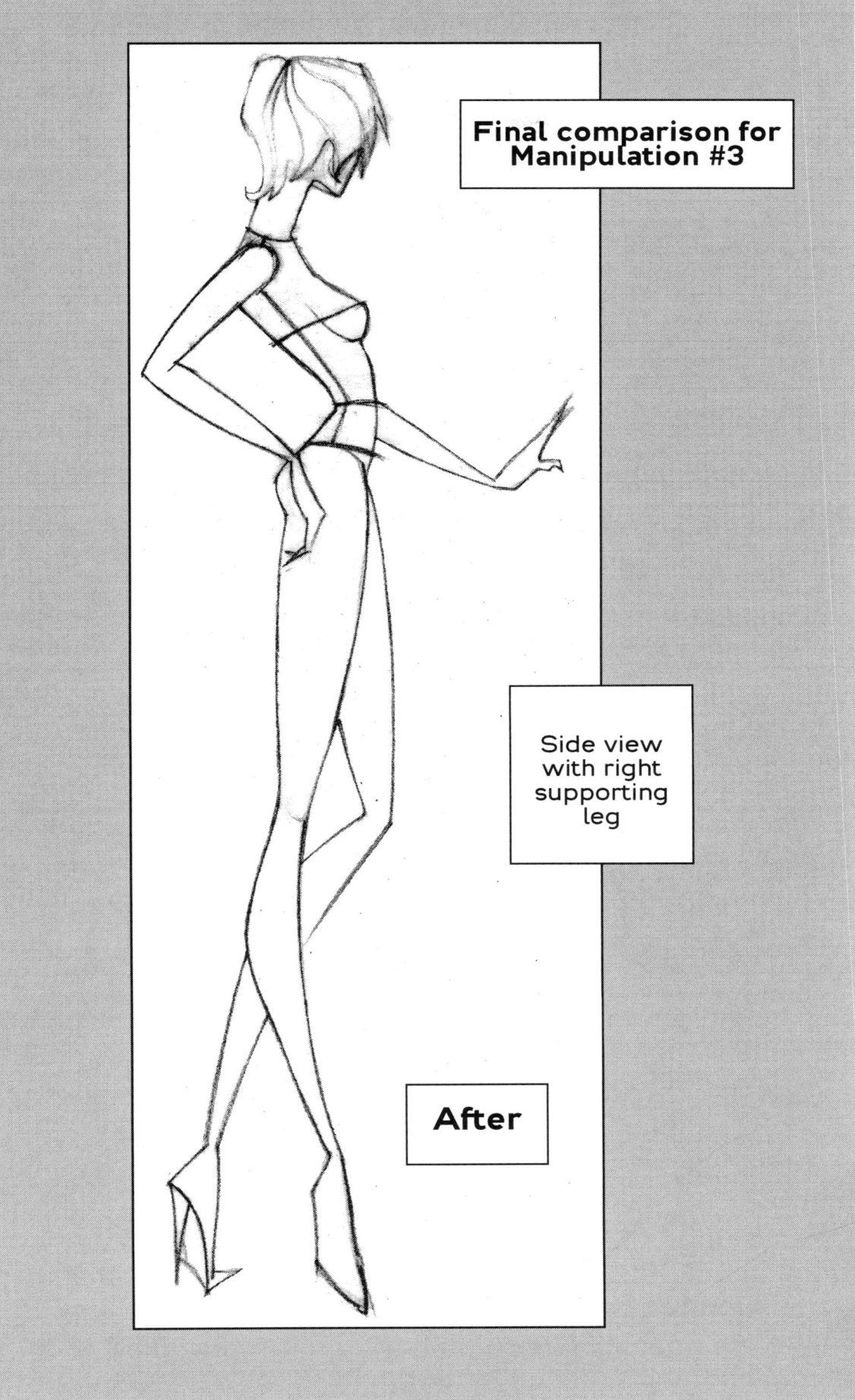

Final comparison for Manipulation #3

Side view with right supporting leg

After

Croquis manipulations (continued)

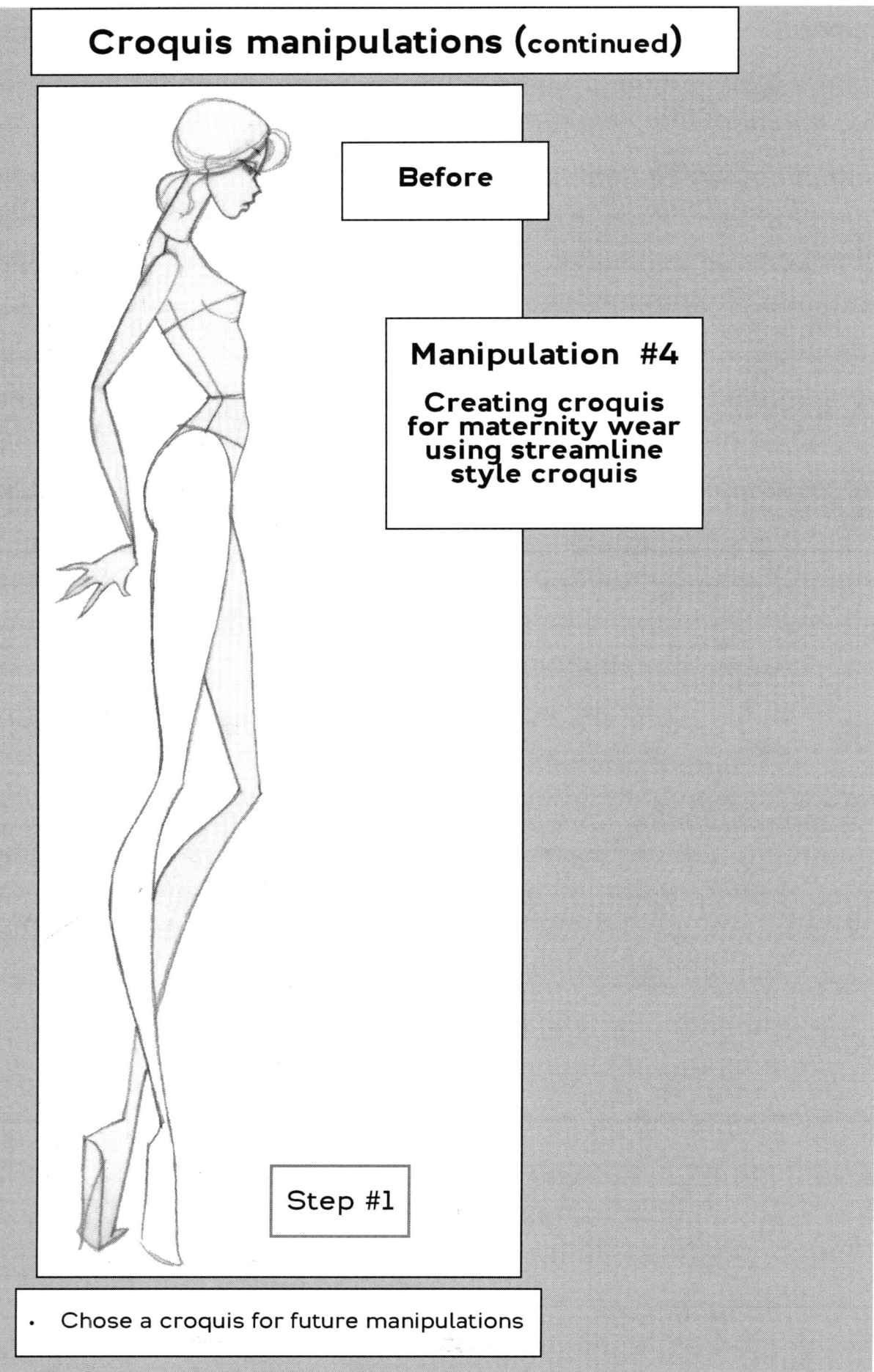

Before

Manipulation #4
Creating croquis for maternity wear using streamline style croquis

Step #1

- Chose a croquis for future manipulations

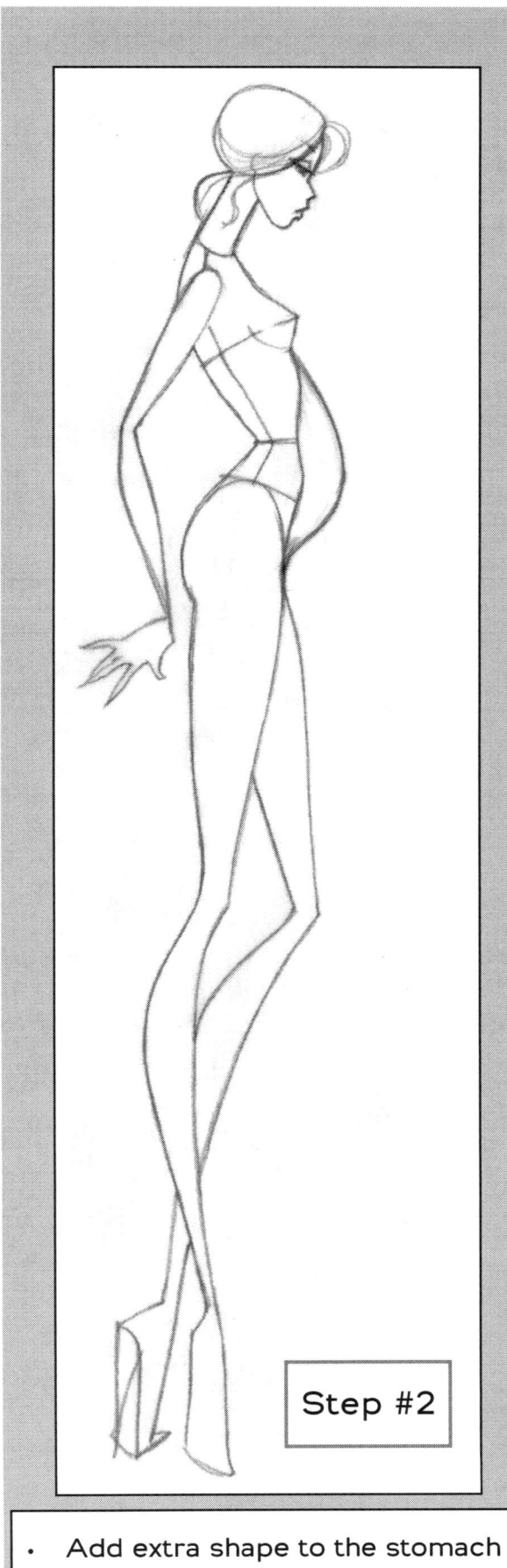

Step #2

- Add extra shape to the stomach area

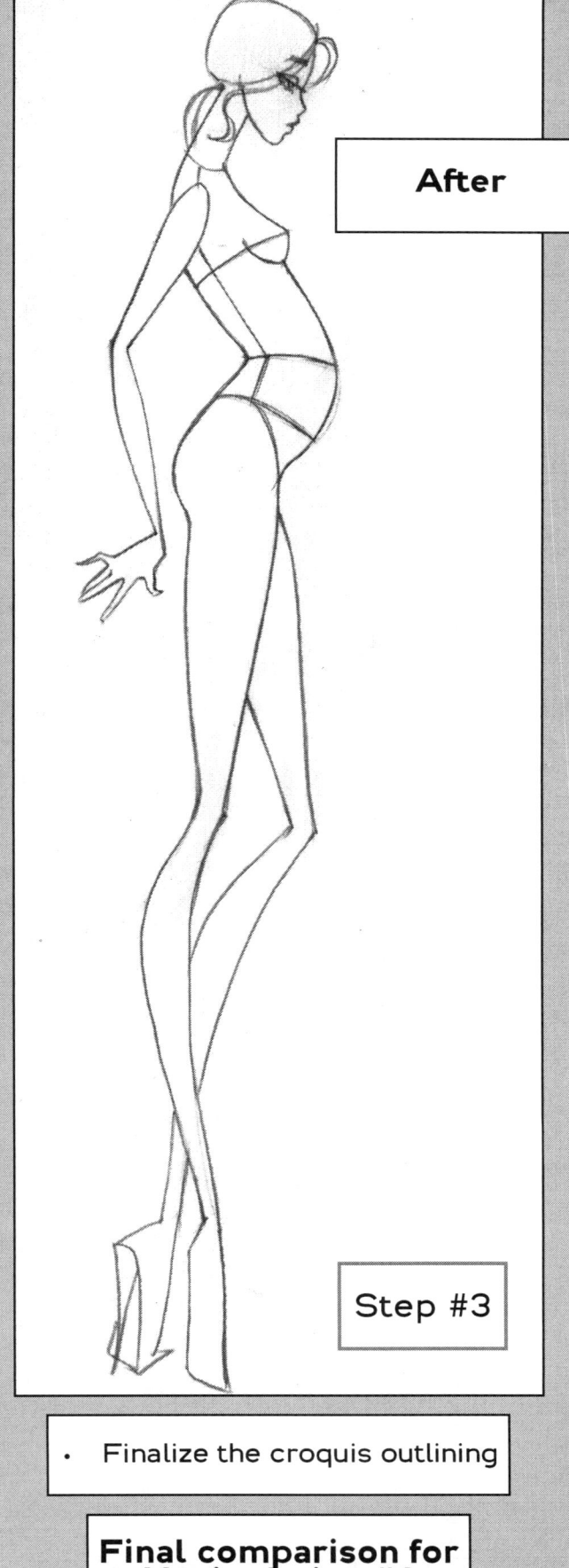

After

Step #3

- Finalize the croquis outlining

Final comparison for Manipulation #4

Croquis manipulations (continued)

Before

Manipulation #5

Creating 9½ and 10½ heads tall croquis using 8½ heads croquis

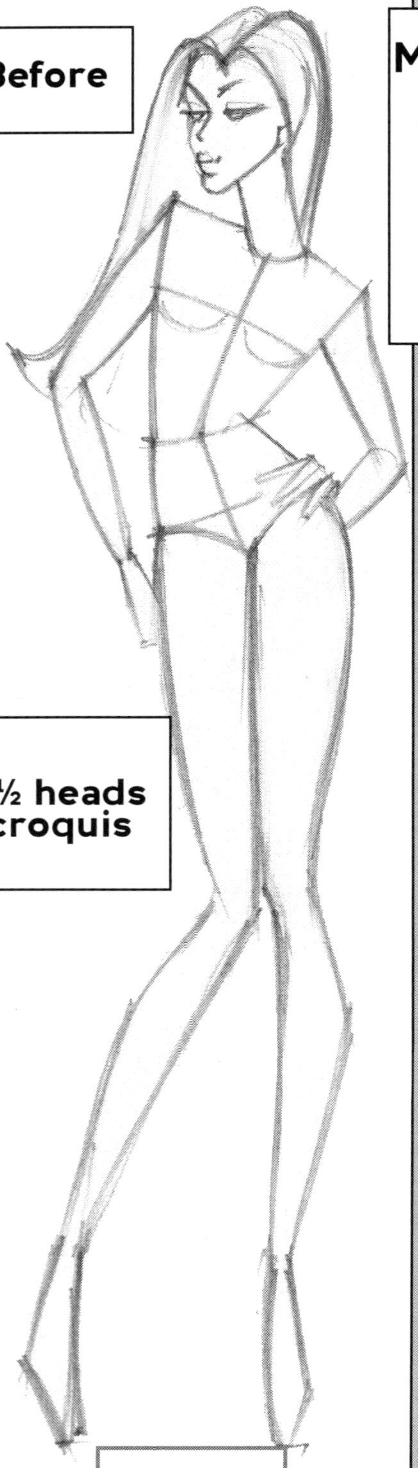

8½ heads croquis

9½ heads croquis

Step #1

Step #2

- Chose a croquis for future manipulations

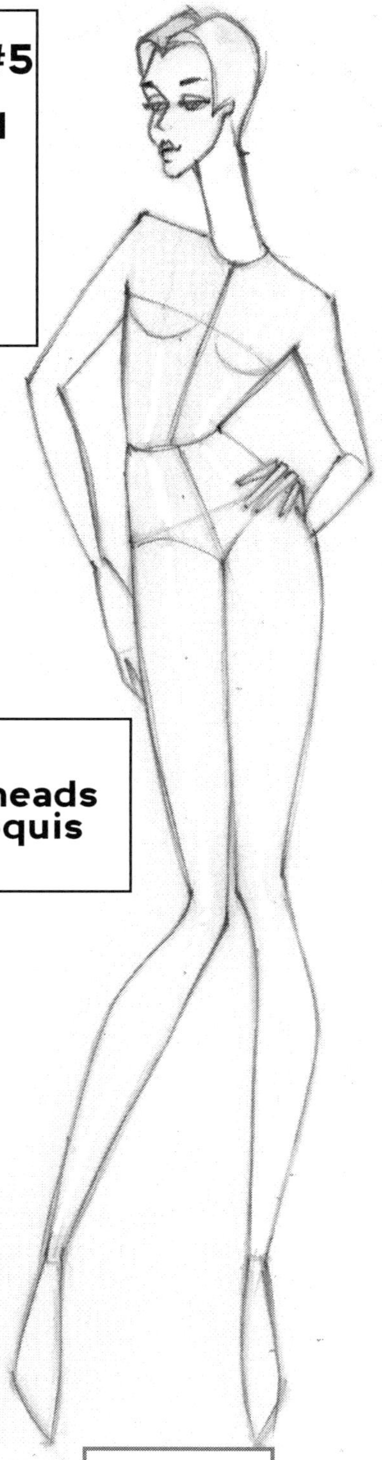

- Redraw the head and make it smaller
- Redraw the neck and make it longer
- Go to step #3 if you need longer legs for the croquis

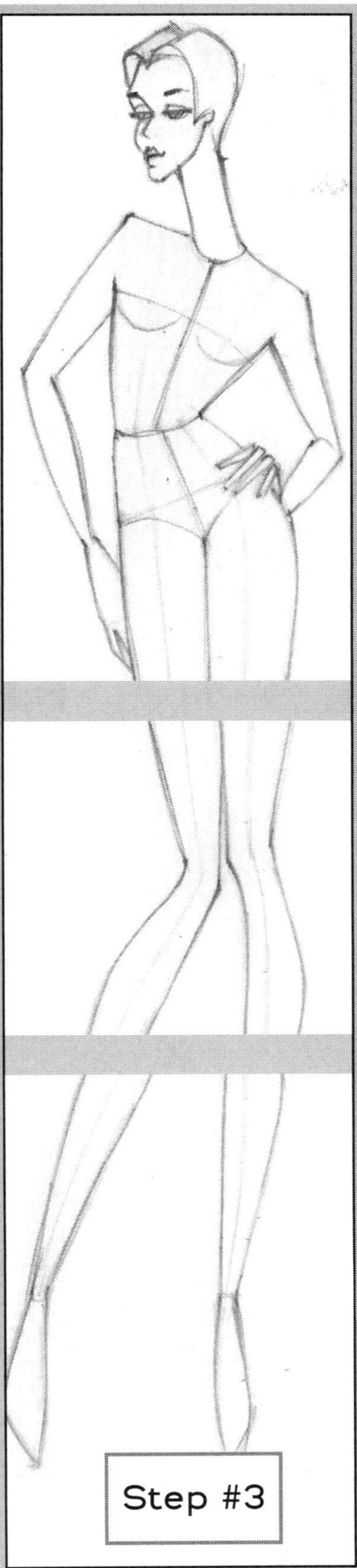

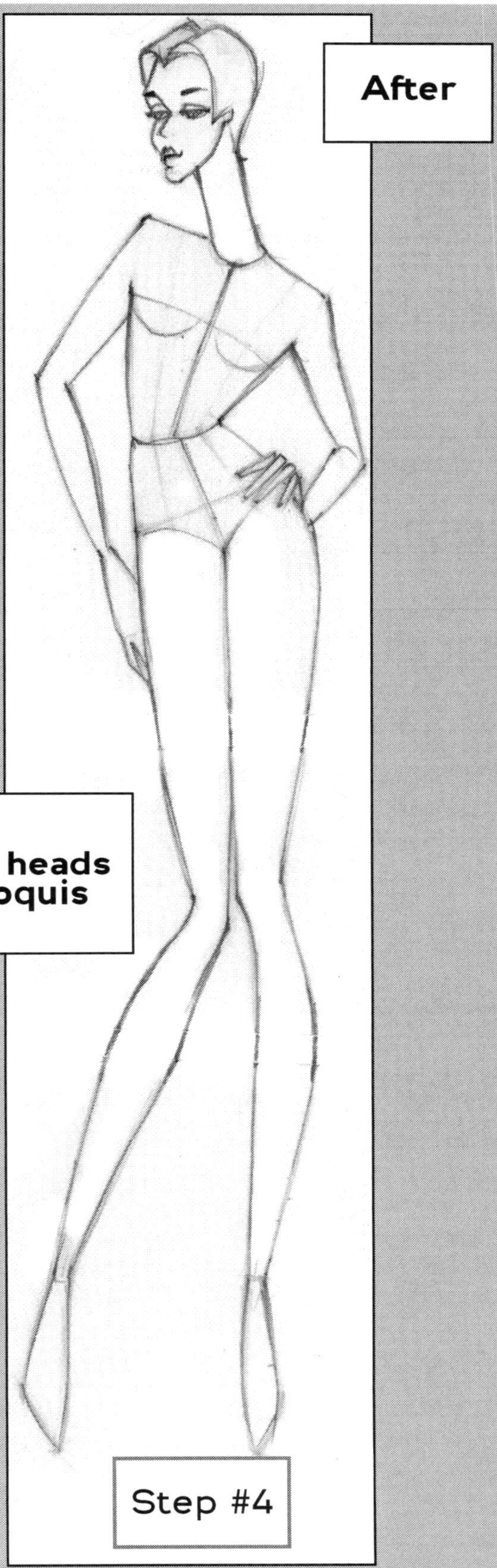

After

10½ heads croquis

Step #3

Step #4

- Cut the croquis in the middle of the upper and lower legs
- Spread your cutouts evenly

- Redraw the croquis and smoothly connect all parts of legs

121

© 2019 Irina V. Ivanova

Croquis manipulations (continued)

Manipulation #6

Using the cutting method for creating a croquis with a new movement for arms and legs

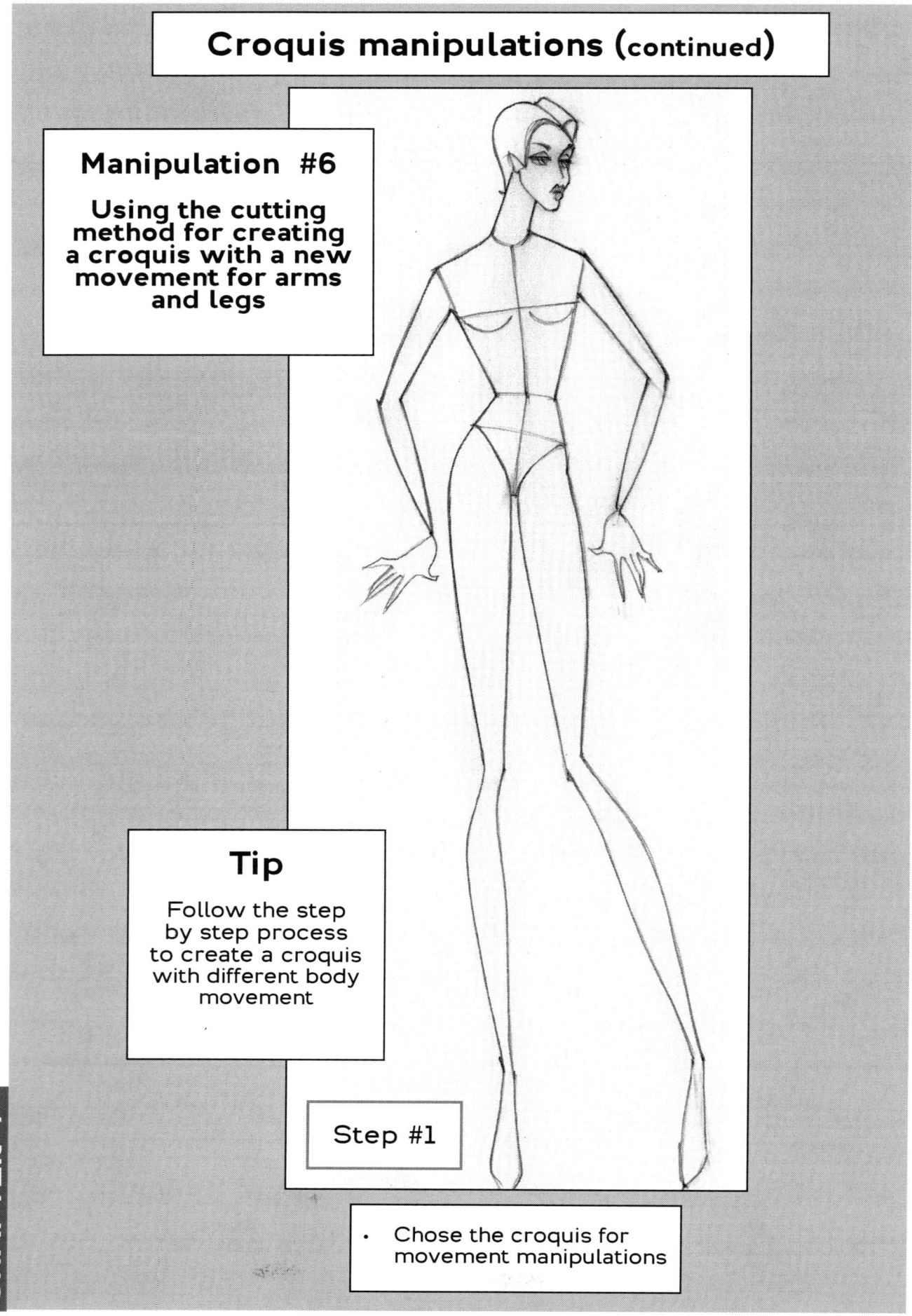

Tip

Follow the step by step process to create a croquis with different body movement

Step #1

- Chose the croquis for movement manipulations

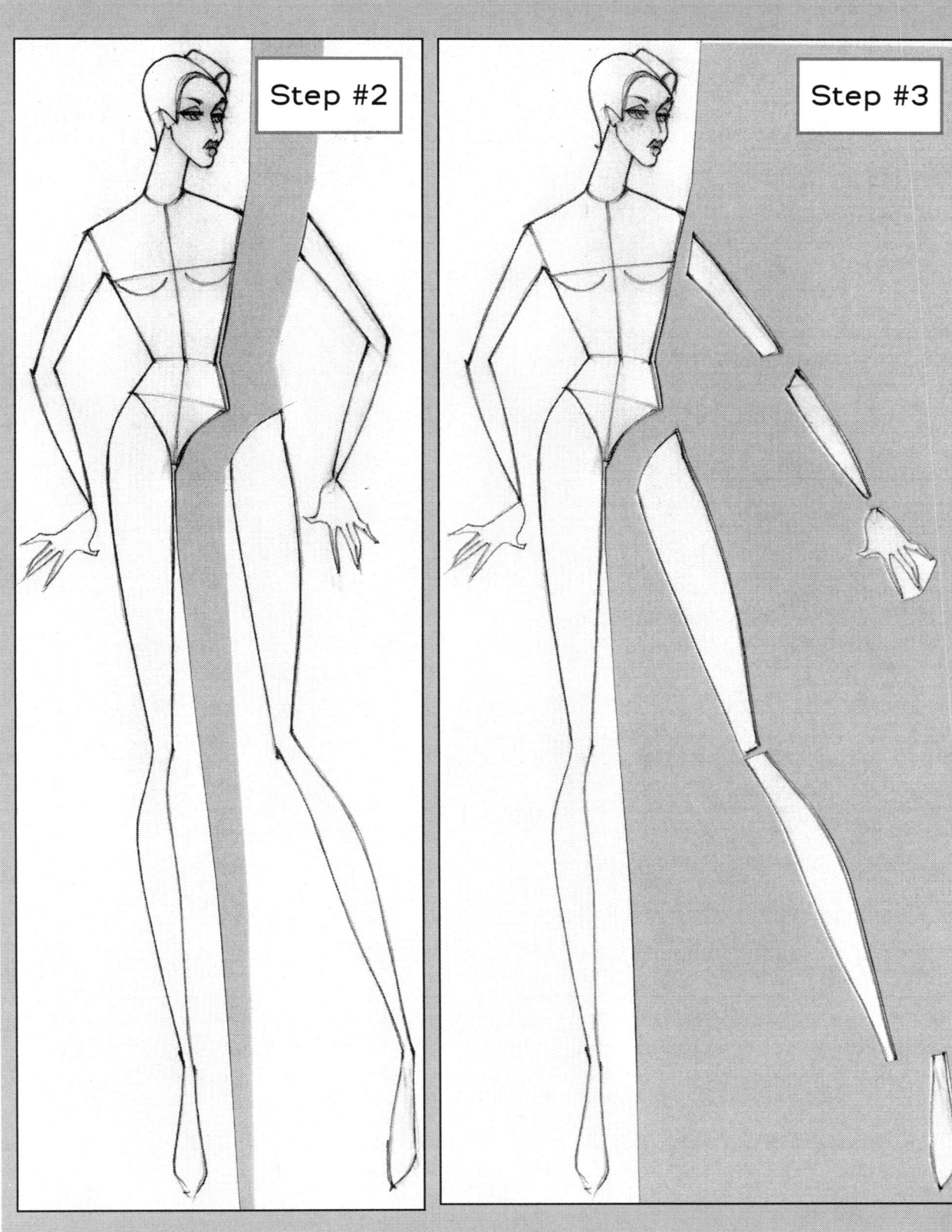

- Cut out arm and leg from a croquis which you want to use for manipulations

- Cut out separately each small portion of arm and leg from a croquis for future manipulations

Croquis manipulations (continued)

Manipulation #6

Using the cutting method for creating a croquis with a new movement for arms and legs (continued)

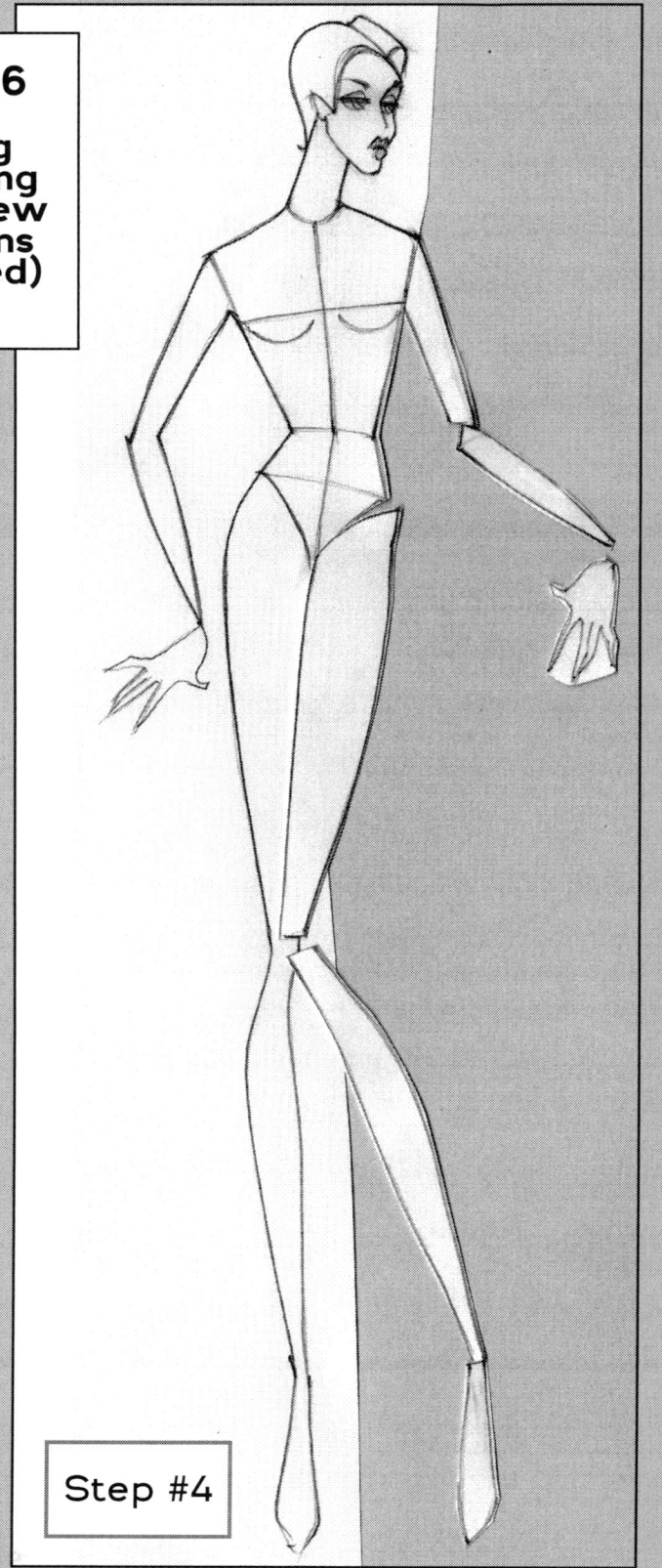

Step #4

- Move all cutouts till you find the desired movement for your croquis

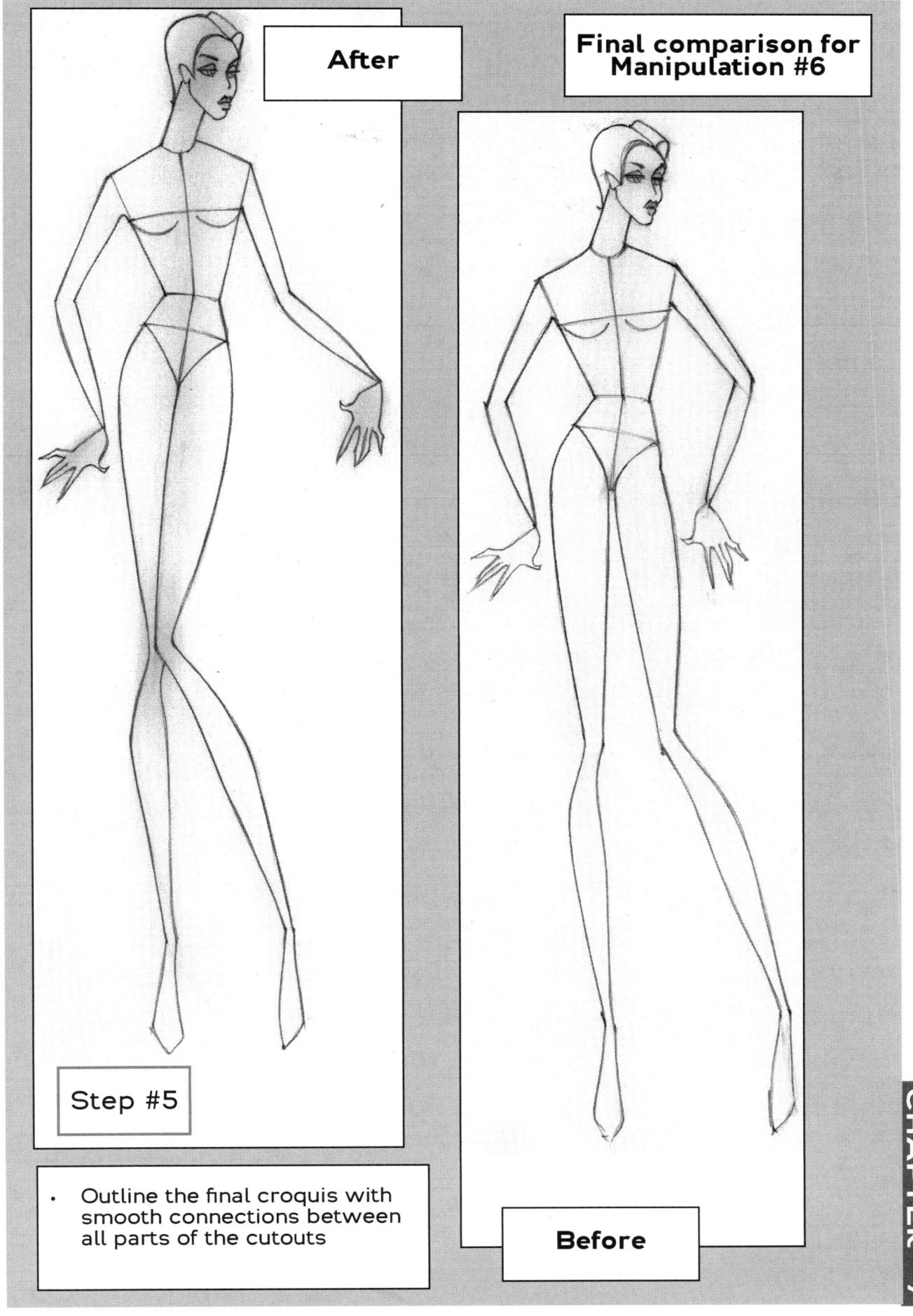

After

Final comparison for Manipulation #6

Step #5

- Outline the final croquis with smooth connections between all parts of the cutouts

Before

Contents:

Chapter 1. Pages 9-25
Basics of body proportions

Chapter 2. Pages 27-35
Fashion figure schematics (wire skeleton study)

Chapter 3. Pages 37-45
Sketching strategy

Chapter 4. Pages 47-61
Freehand sketching for 10 heads tall fashion figure (front view)

Chapter 5. Pages 63-75
Freehand sketching for 10 heads tall fashion figure (side view)

Chapter 6. Pages 77-91
Cutting method for fashion figure croquis

Chapter 7. Pages 93-125
Figure croquis manipulations

Chapter 8. Pages 127-147
Faces and hands drawing

Index
Pages 148-149

About the author
Pages 150-151

Chapter 8

Faces and hands drawing

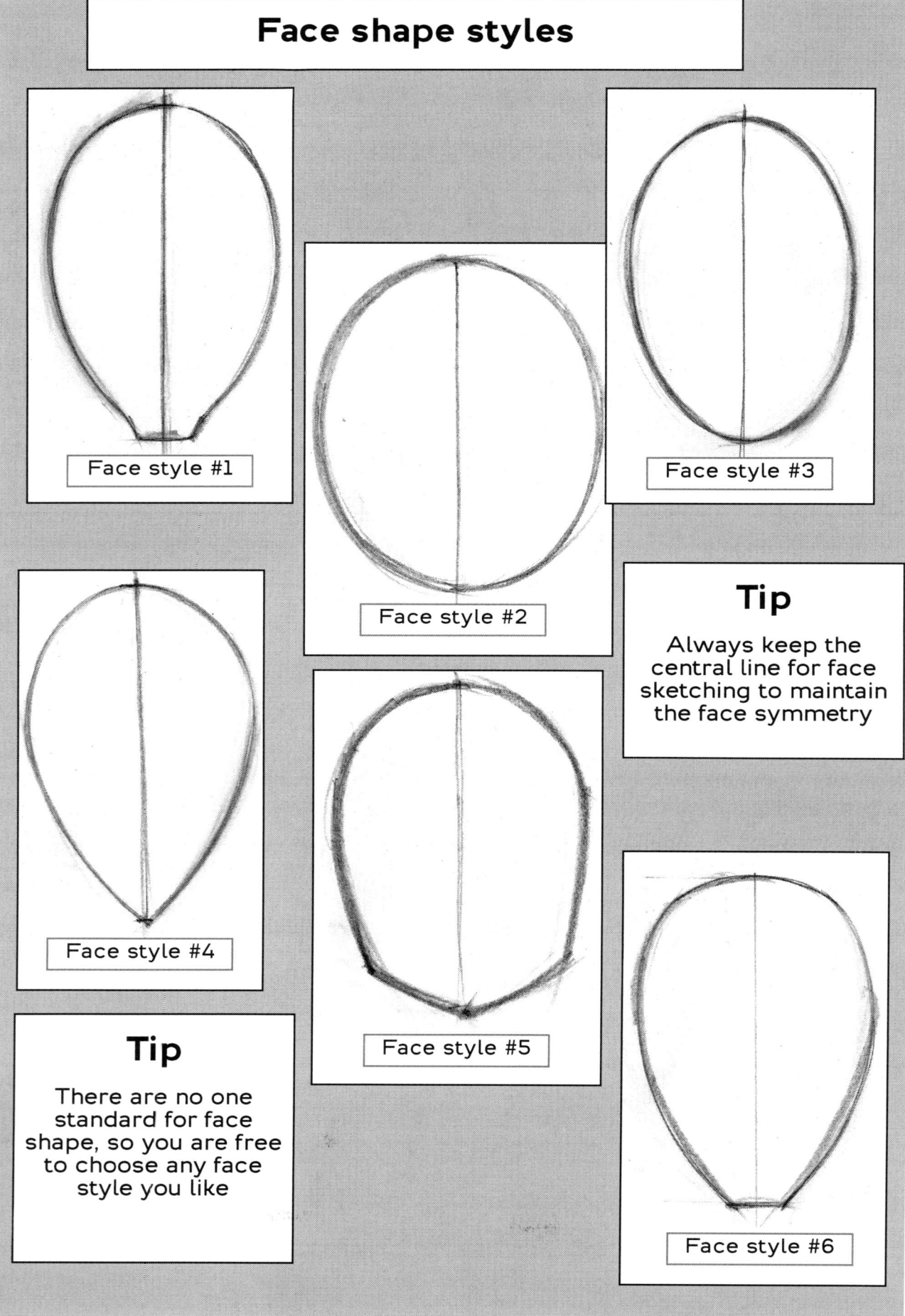

Front view face drawing

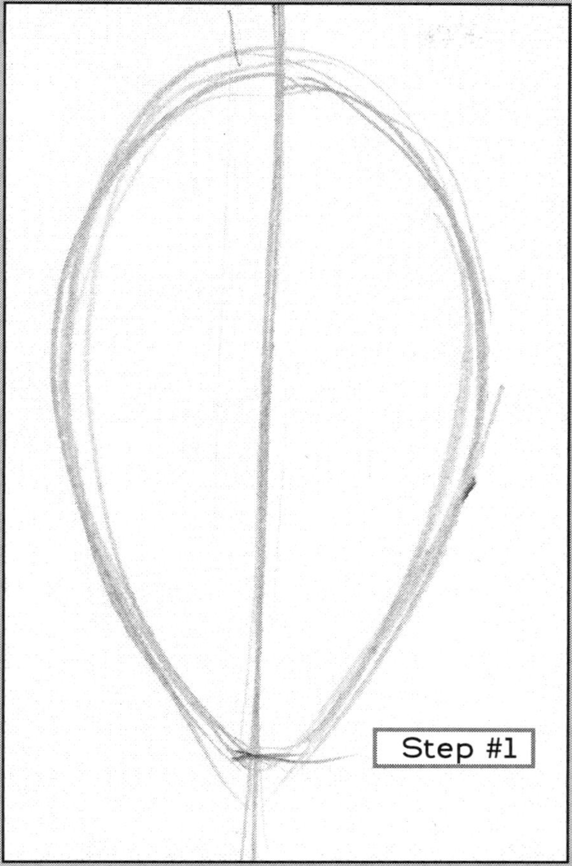

- Outline basic shape for the face
- Do not show any details yet

Tip

Stylize and simplify face drawing as much as you can when create a fashion illustration

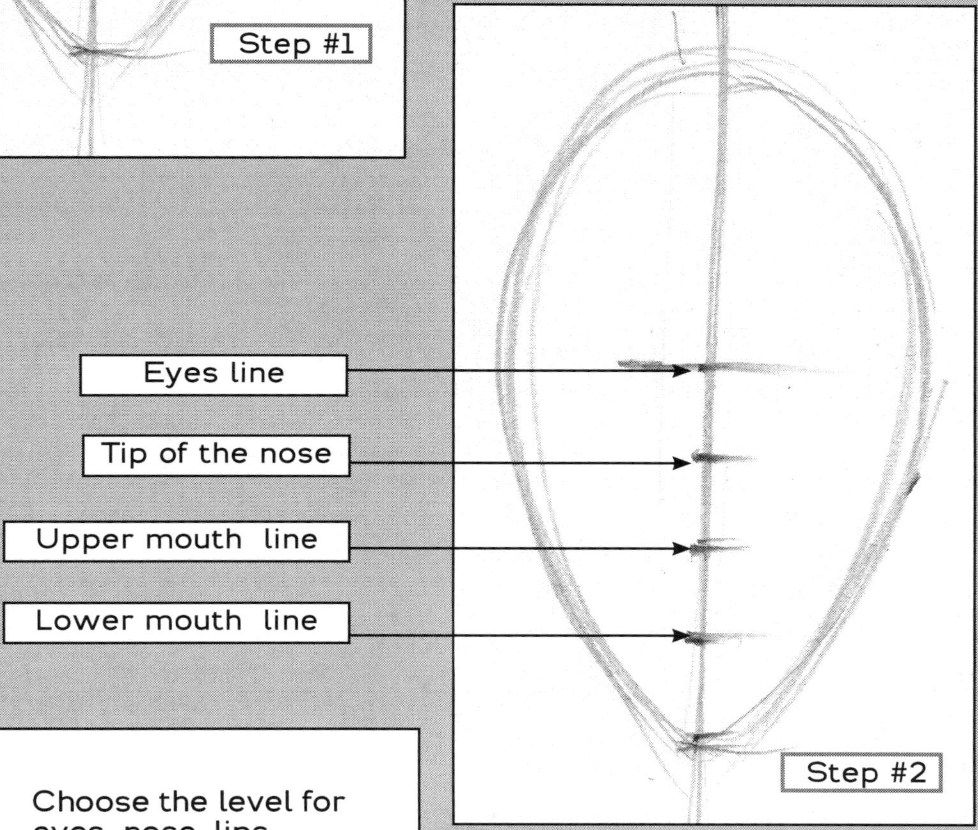

Step #1

- Eyes line
- Tip of the nose
- Upper mouth line
- Lower mouth line

Step #2

- Choose the level for eyes, nose, lips
- Do not show any details yet

Front view face drawing (continued)

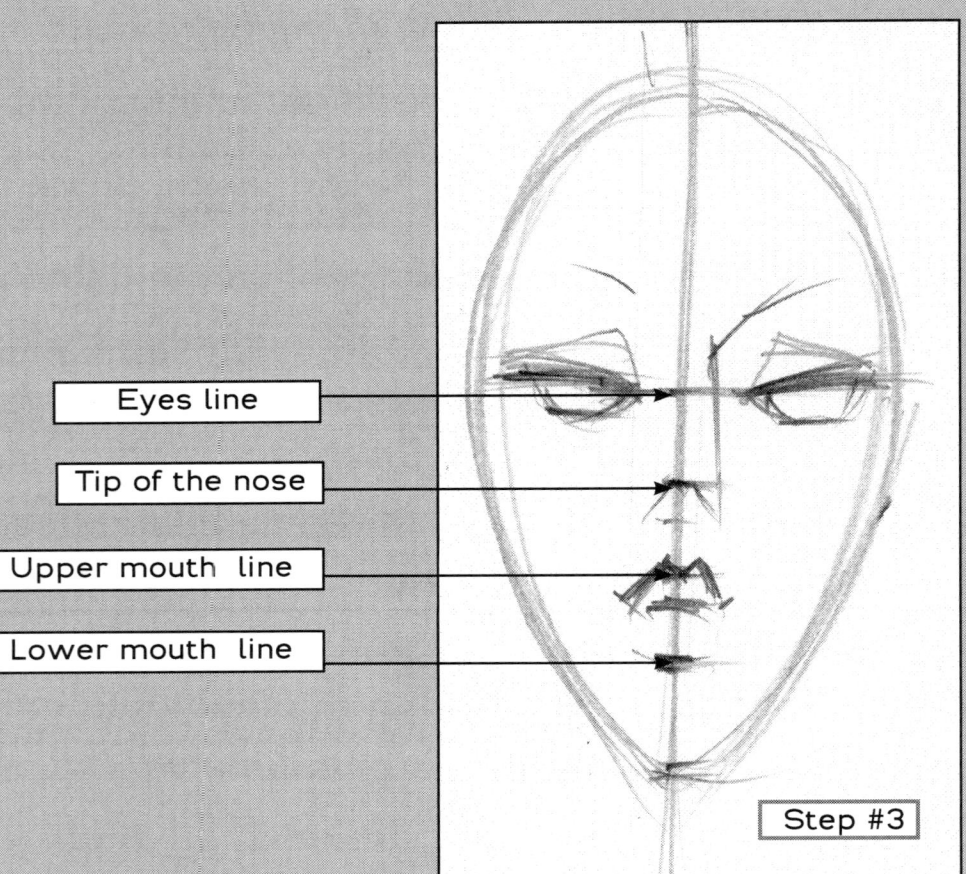

- Eyes line
- Tip of the nose
- Upper mouth line
- Lower mouth line

Step #3

- Sketch basic shapes for eyes, lips, nose, and eyebrows
- Do not rush to finalize face features
- Move to next step only if you satisfy with a basic outlining
- Keep line very light

Tip

There are no right or wrong style for lips, ears, or eyes, so you are free to choose any facial features you like

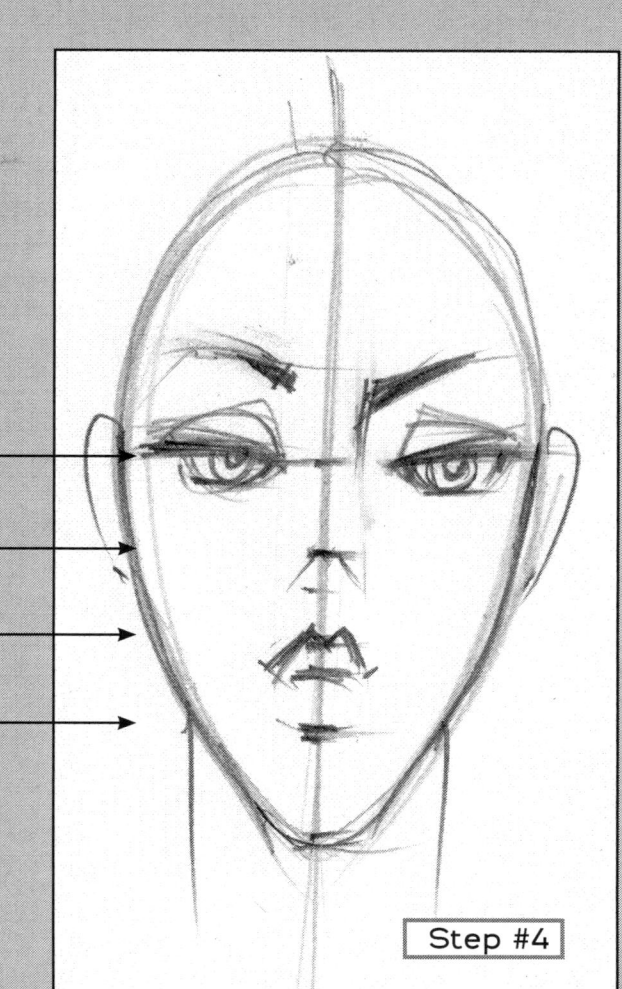

- Eyes line
- Tip of the nose
- Upper mouth line
- Lower mouth line

Step #4

- Add more details
- Show ears somewhere from the top level of eyes till the bottom level of the nose
- Make sure all features are symmetrical

Tip
Try different face styles till you find your way to draw them

Front view face drawing (continued)

Step #5

Tip

Please remember that face drawing is optional. You can create excellent illustration without drawing facial features

- Clean up sketch
- Do not overdo it

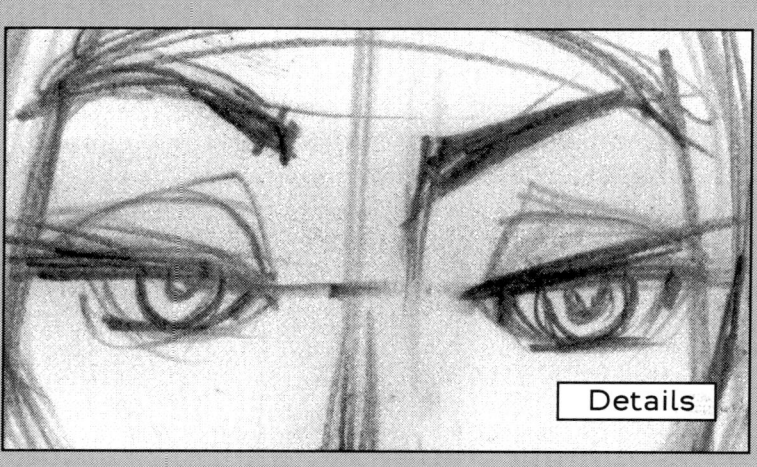

Details

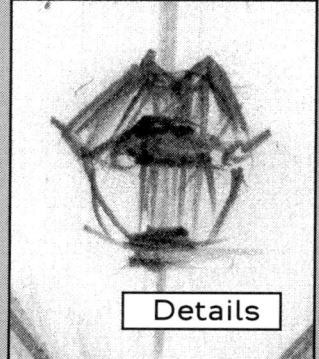

Details

Side view face drawing

Tip
Choose face proportions you like

Step #1

- Outline basic shape for the face
- Do not show any details yet
- Keep it as simple as you can

Step #2

- Eyes line
- Tip of the nose
- Upper mouth line
- Lower mouth line
- Chin line

- Choose the level for eyes, nose, lips
- Do not show any details yet

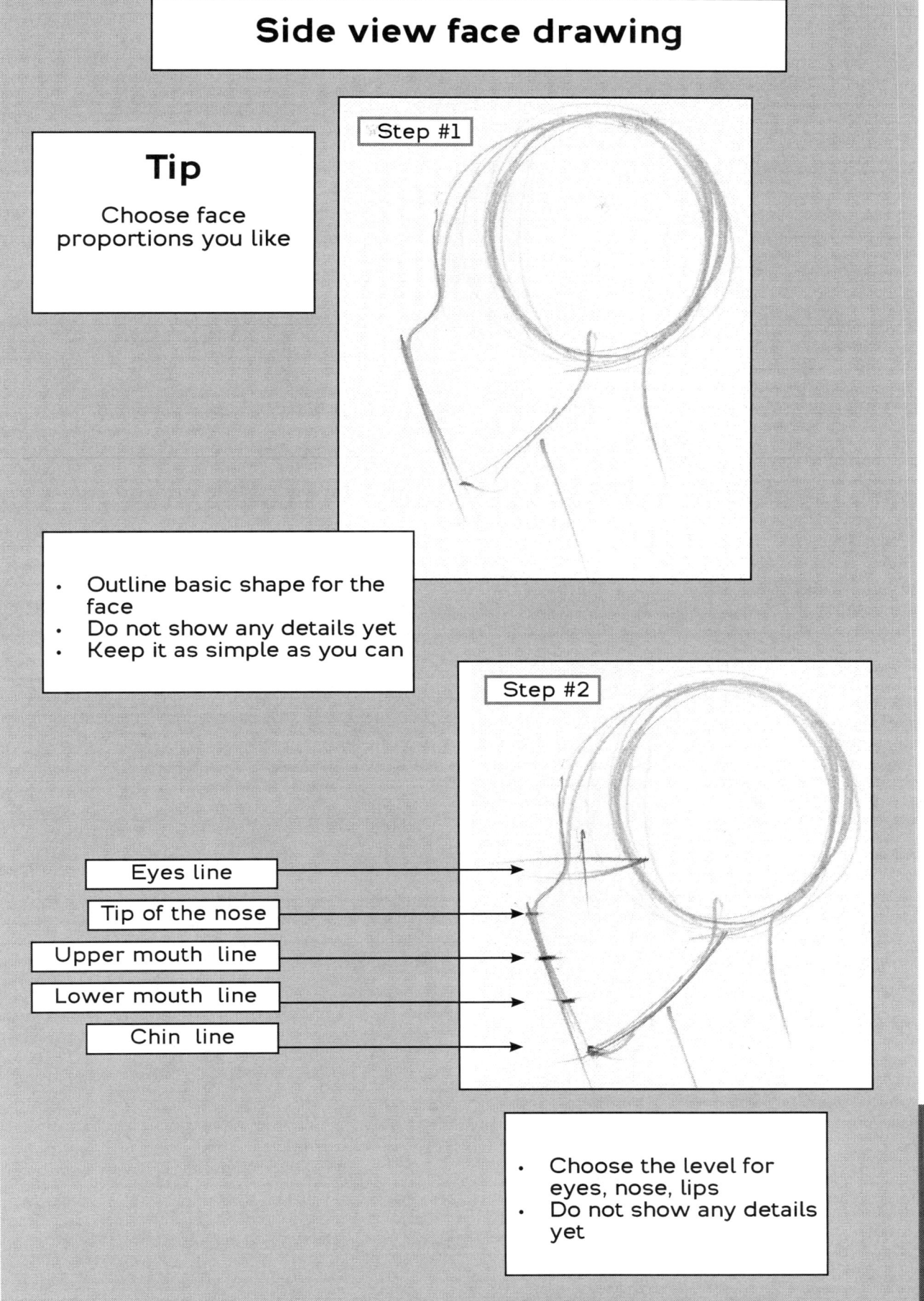

Side view face drawing (continued)

Step #3

- Eyes line
- Tip of the nose
- Upper mouth line
- Lower mouth line
- Chin line

- Sketch basic shapes for eyes, lips, nose
- Do not rush to finalize face features
- Move to the next step only if you satisfy with a basic outlining
- Keep line very light

Step #4

- Add more details
- Show ears somewhere from the top level of eyes till the bottom level of the nose

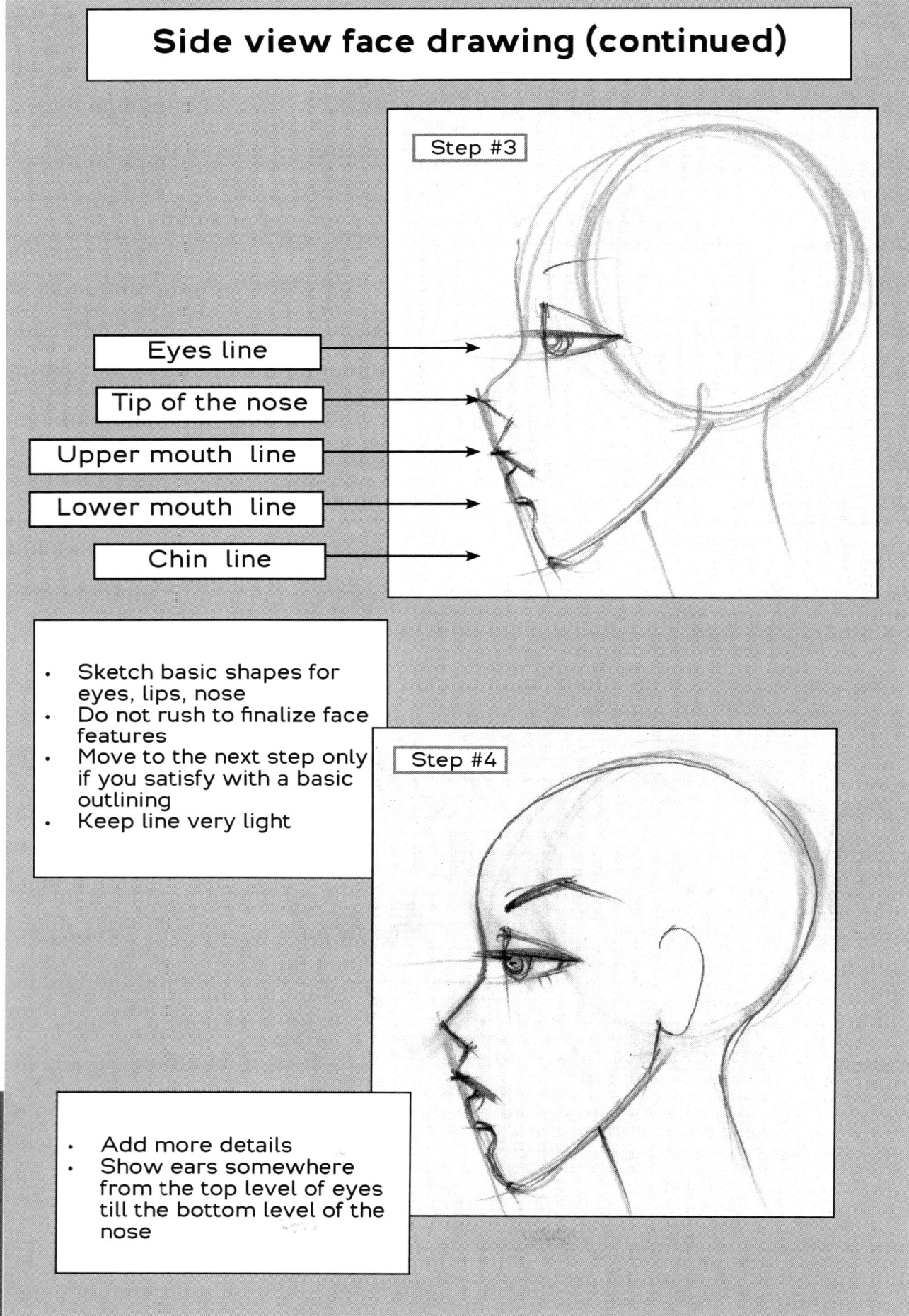

Step #5

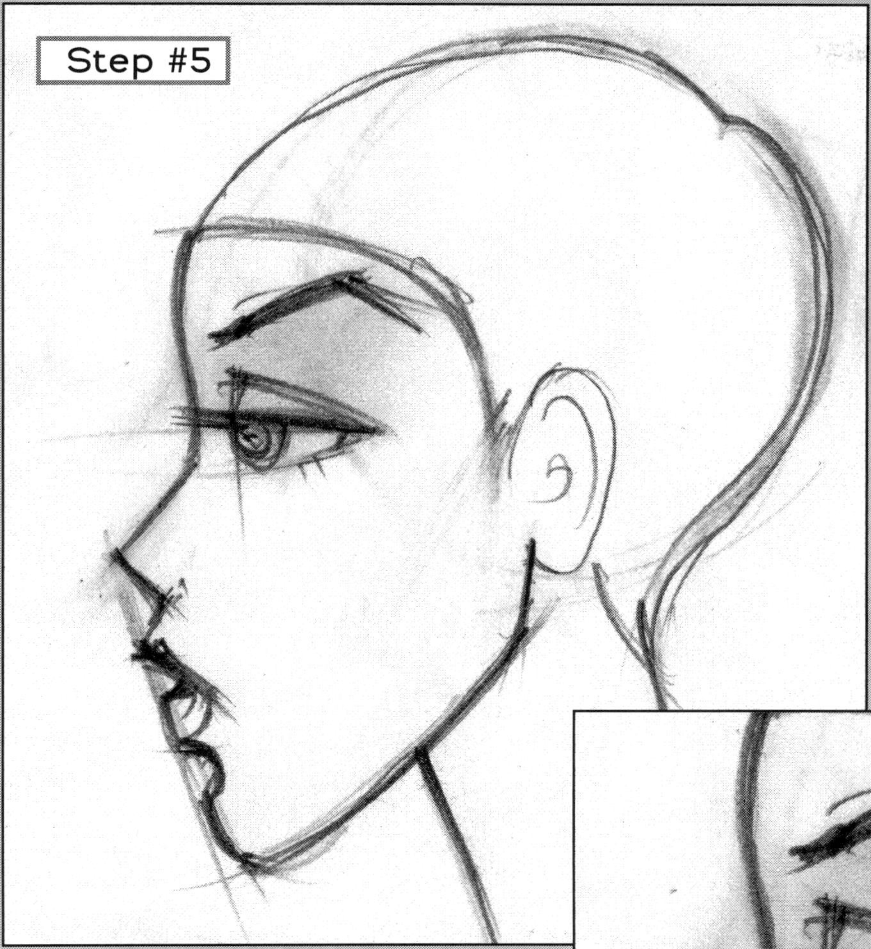

- Finalize face features

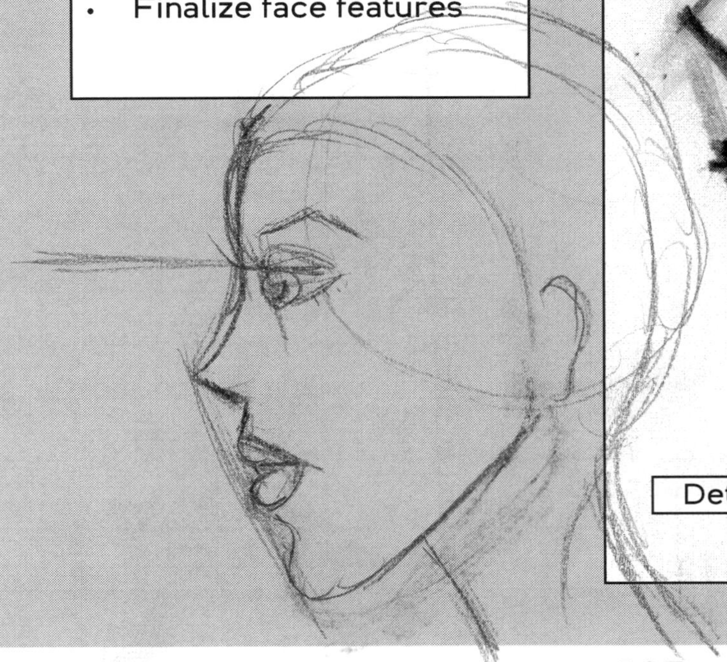

Details

How to Draw Fashion Figure Essential figure drawing techniques **by Irina V. Ivanova**

CHAPTER 8

3/4 view face drawing

- Outline basic shape for the face
- Do not show any details yet
- Always keep the central line for face sketching to maintain the face symmetry

Step #1

- Choose the level for eyes, nose, lips
- Do not show any details yet

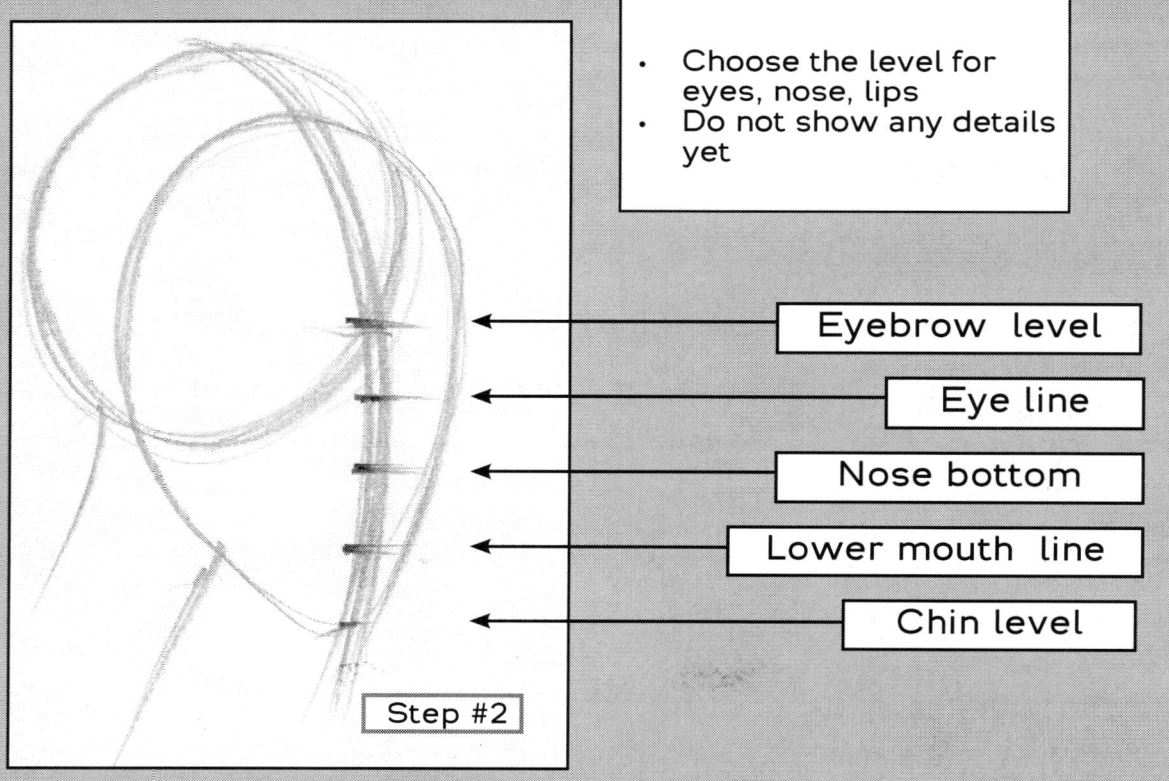

← Eyebrow level
← Eye line
← Nose bottom
← Lower mouth line
← Chin level

Step #2

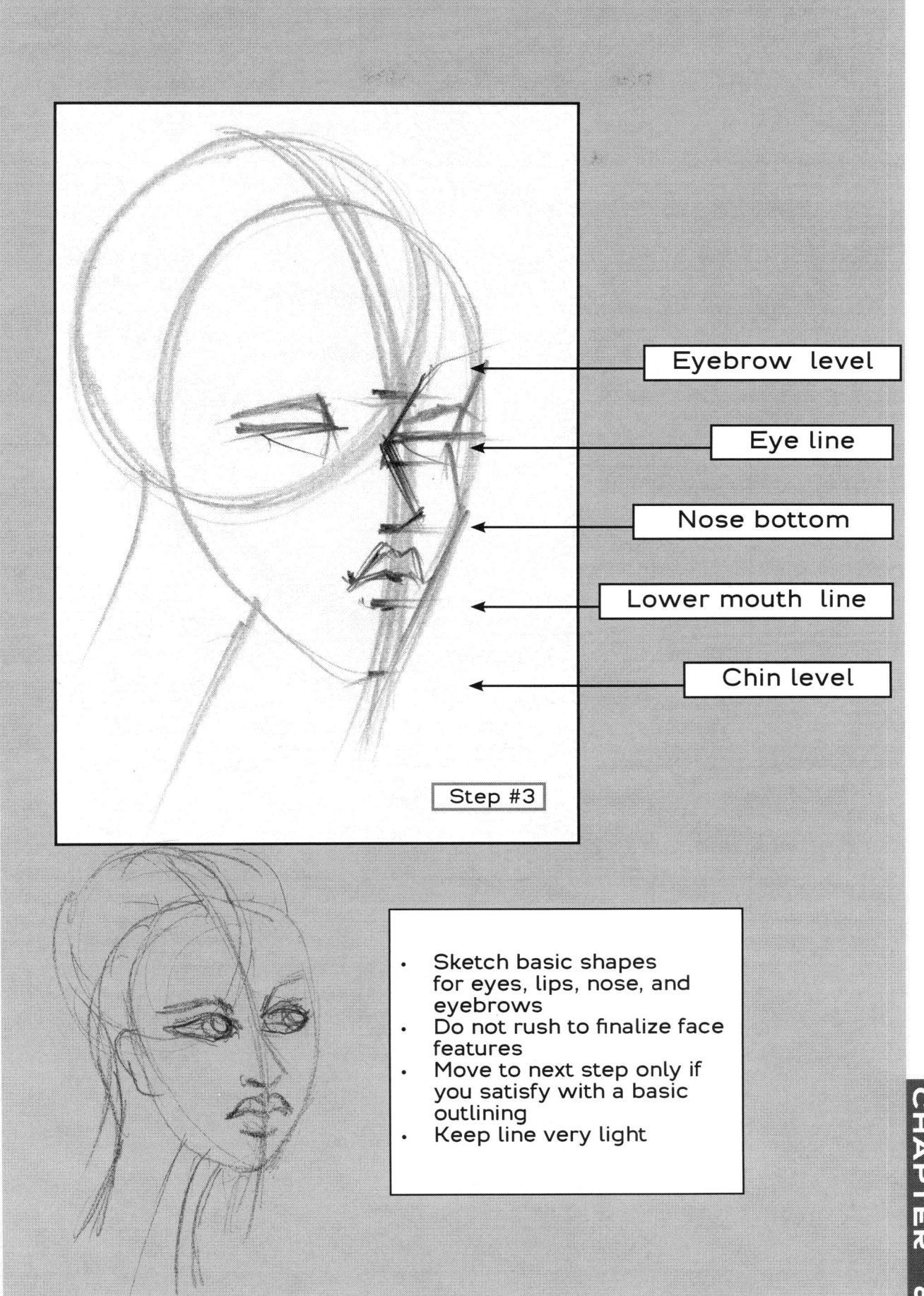

- Eyebrow level
- Eye line
- Nose bottom
- Lower mouth line
- Chin level

Step #3

- Sketch basic shapes for eyes, lips, nose, and eyebrows
- Do not rush to finalize face features
- Move to next step only if you satisfy with a basic outlining
- Keep line very light

How to Draw Fashion Figure Essential figure drawing techniques by Irina V. Ivanova

CHAPTER 8

3/4 view face drawing (continued)

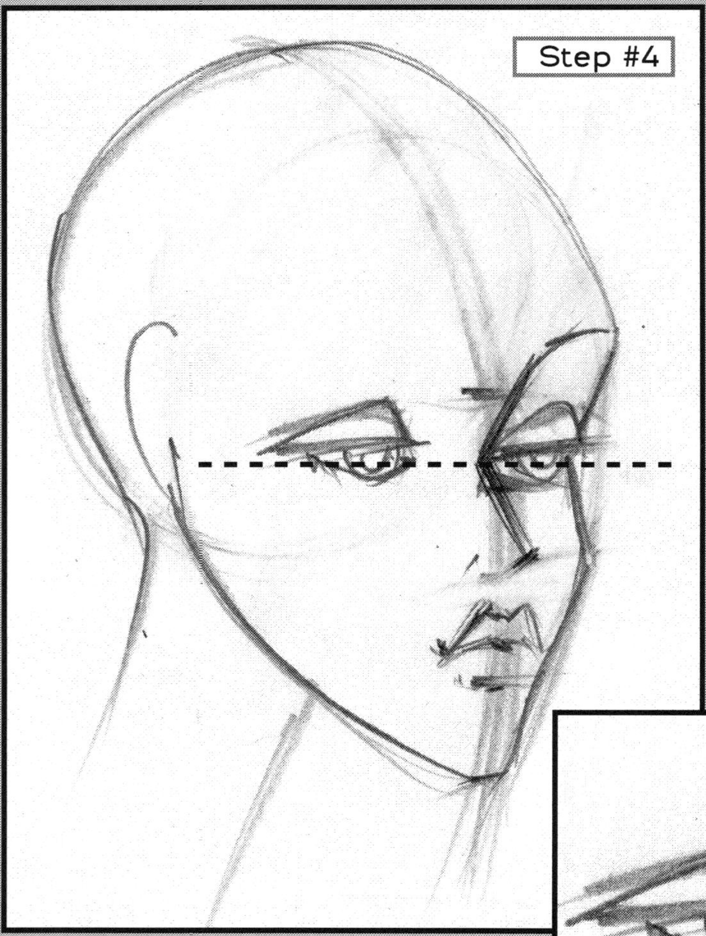

Step #4

- Sketch basic shapes for eyebrows and ears
- Do not rush to finalize face features

← Keep eyes and nose bridge on the same level

- Add more details
- Keep nose and lips on the central line

Details

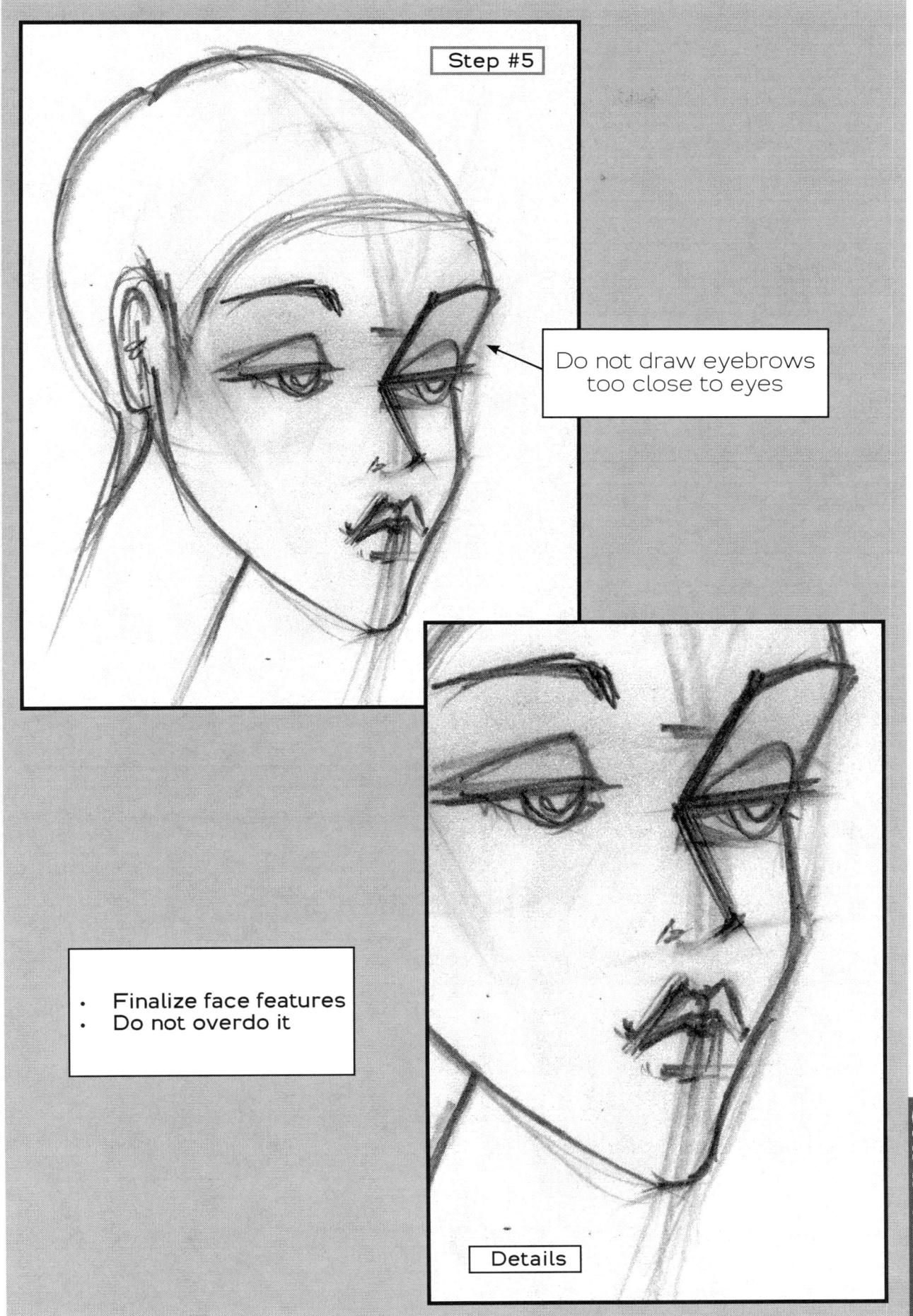

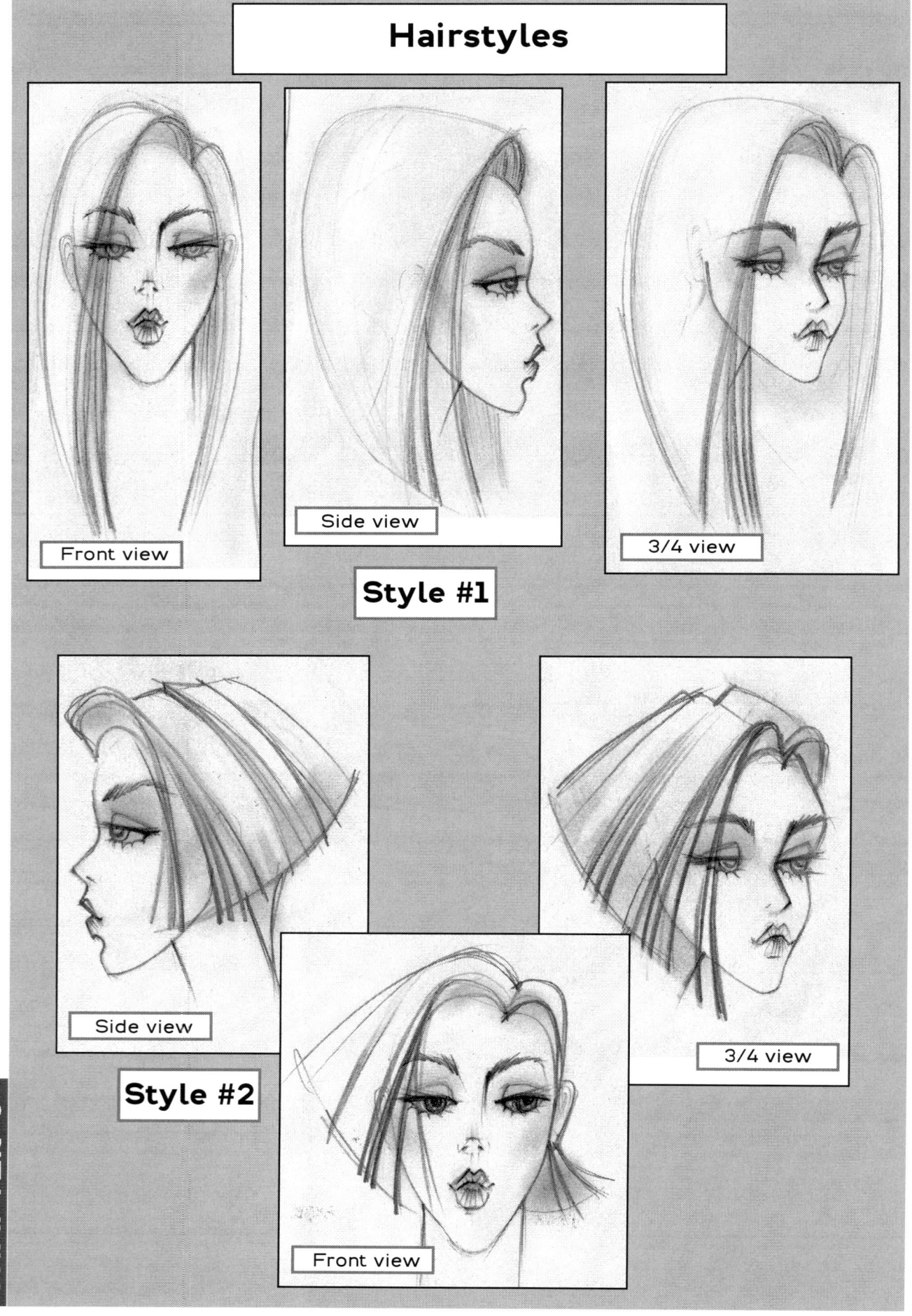

Hairstyles (continued)

Hands sketching

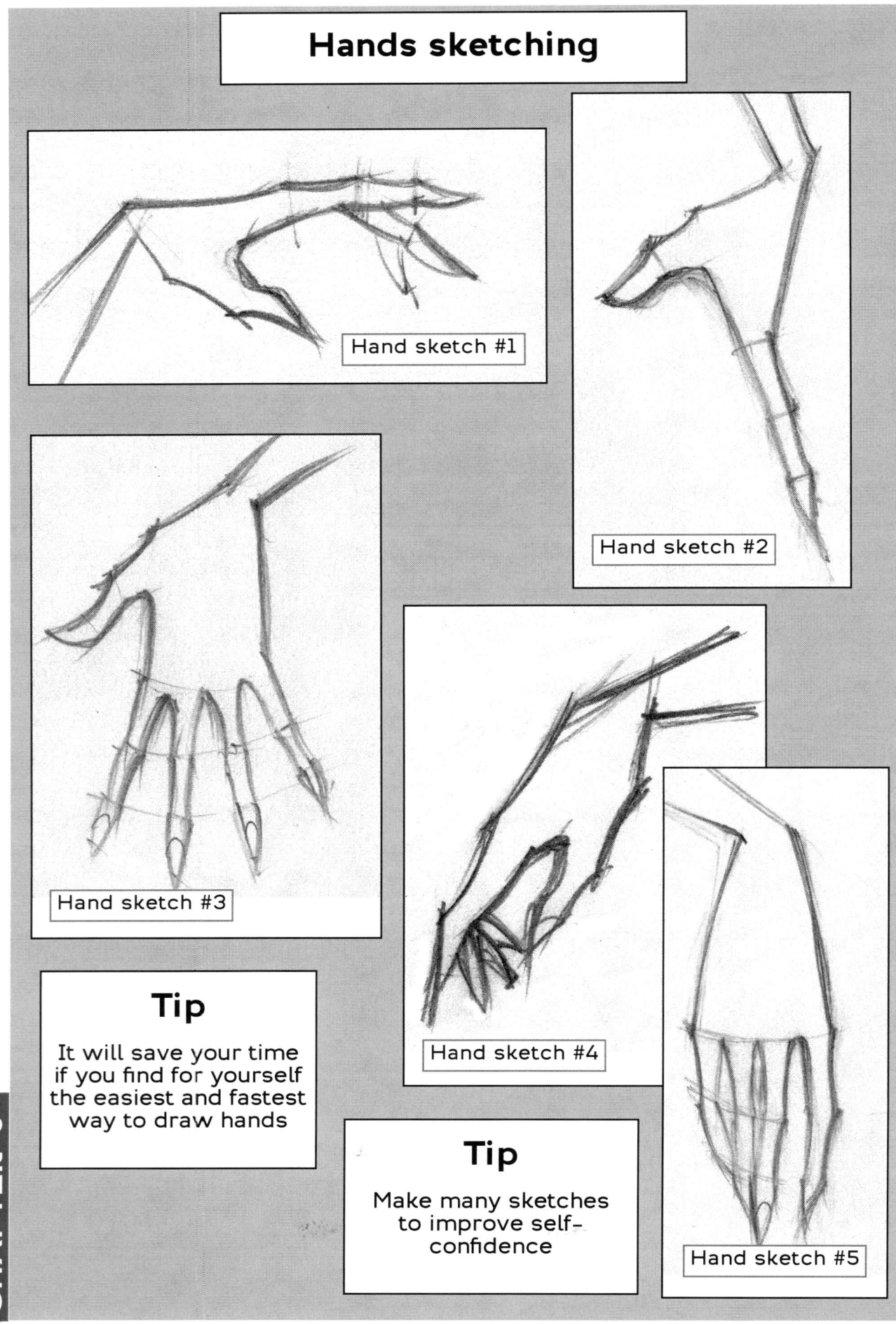

Hand sketch #1

Hand sketch #2

Hand sketch #3

Hand sketch #4

Hand sketch #5

Tip
It will save your time if you find for yourself the easiest and fastest way to draw hands

Tip
Make many sketches to improve self-confidence

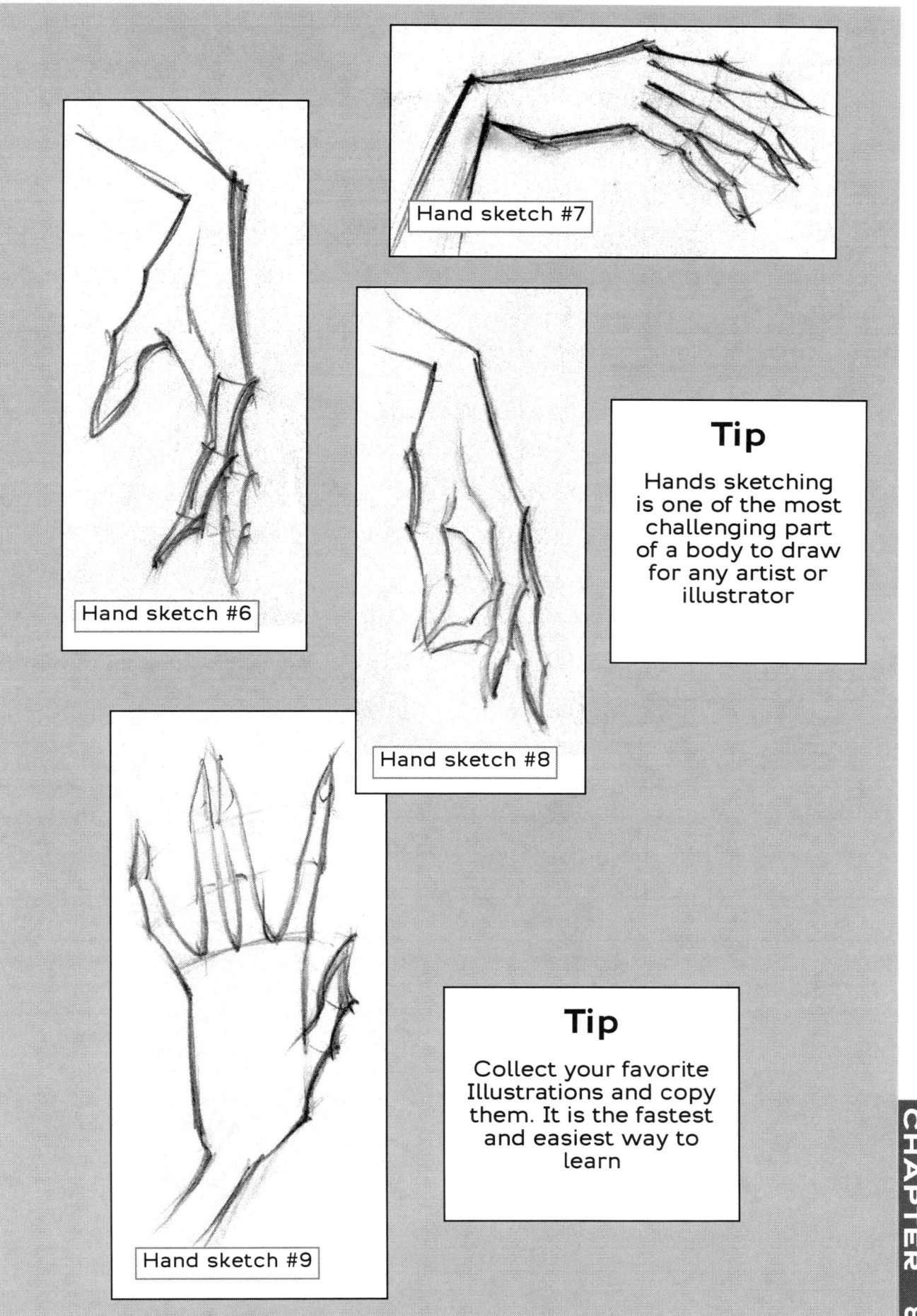

Hand sketch #7

Hand sketch #6

Hand sketch #8

Tip

Hands sketching is one of the most challenging part of a body to draw for any artist or illustrator

Hand sketch #9

Tip

Collect your favorite Illustrations and copy them. It is the fastest and easiest way to learn

Hands sketching (continued)

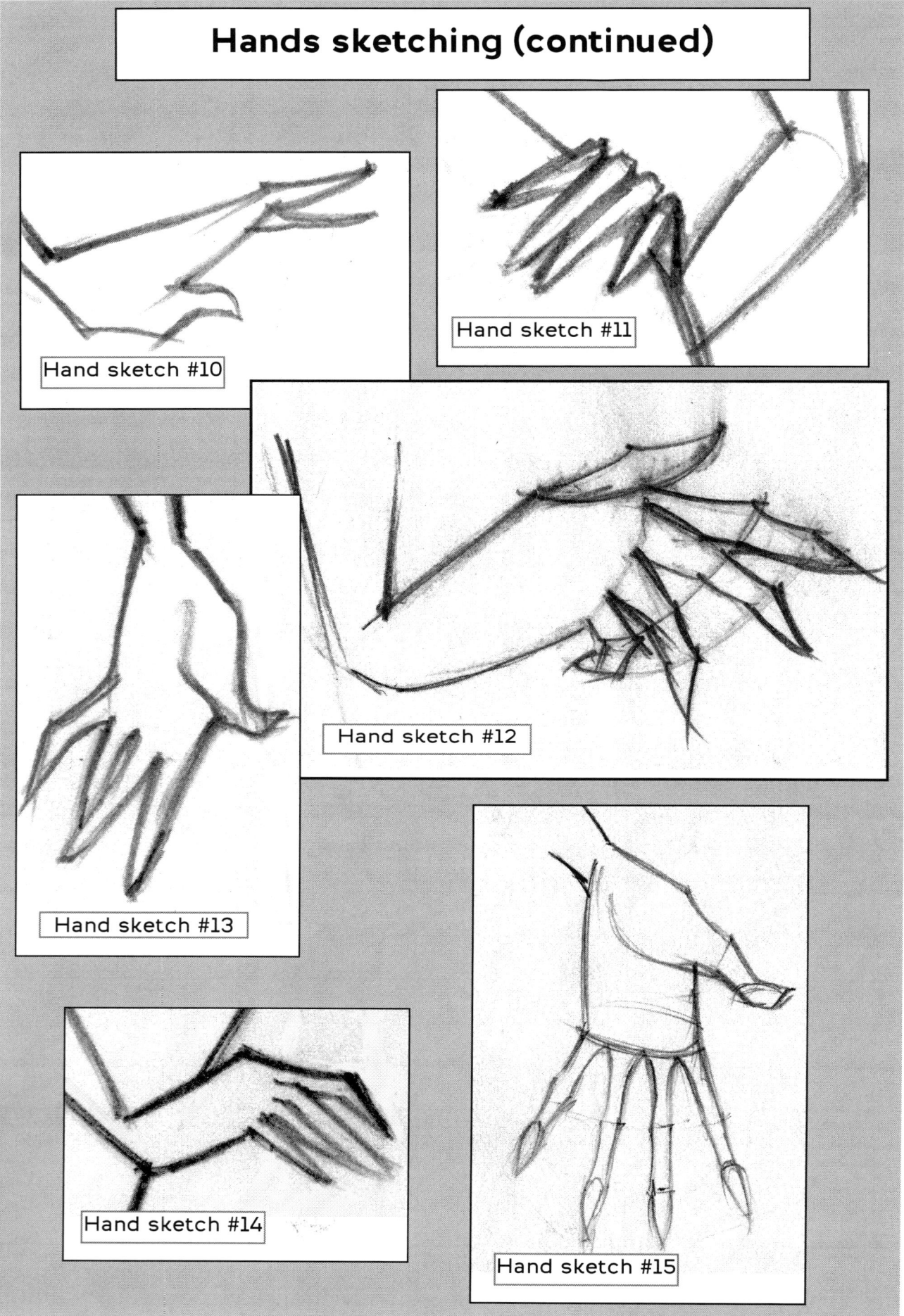

Hand sketch #16

Hand sketch #17

Hand sketch #18

Hand sketch #19

Hand sketch #20

Hand sketch #21

How to Draw Fashion Figure Essential figure drawing techniques by Irina V. Ivanova

CHAPTER 8

© 2019 Irina V. Ivanova

Index

A

apex 12
average figure 16, 17, 18, 19

B

balance line 12, 13, 20, 28, 29, 30, 42, 48, 49, 50, 51, 66, 67, 68, 80, 94, 100, 110
body movement 5, 30
body shape 39, 54, 78
body style 6, 39, 45, 48, 66
body weight 29, 31
body proportion 10, 15
bustline 12, 58, 64, 74, 86, 106

C

chest 29, 49, 53, 58, 67, 69, 79, 80, 81, 86, 96
chin 28, 69, 80, 133, 134, 136, 137
croquis 1, 5, 6, 7, 8, 10, 14, 15, 16, 17, 18, 19, 20, 38, 39, 40, 41, 42, 45, 48, 49, 50, 52, 53, 54, 56, 58, 60, 66, 67, 68, 70, 72, 74, 75, 77, 78, 79, 80, 82, 84, 86, 87, 88, 90, 93, 94, 95, 96, 98, 100, 101, 102, 104, 106, 108, 110, 111, 112, 114, 116, 118, 119, 120, 121, 122, 123, 124, 125
curved figure type 16
cutting method 7, 78, 87, 88, 122, 124

E

ears 130, 131, 134, 138
eyebrows 130, 137, 138, 139
eyes 129, 130, 131, 133, 134, 136, 137, 138, 139

F

face 7, 10, 57, 71, 96, 98, 107, 128, 129, 130, 131, 132, 133, 134, 135, 136, 137, 138, 139
fashion figure 1, 4, 6, 7, 8, 10, 15, 47, 63, 77, 94
freehand sketching 1, 6, 8, 47, 48, 50, 52, 54, 56, 58, 60, 63, 66, 68, 70, 72, 74
front view 5, 28

G

gravity line 29

H

hairstyles 7, 140, 142
hand 71, 144, 145, 146, 147
hands sketching 144, 145, 146
head-body proportions 38, 78
hip point 30, 81

J

jacket 42

L

lips 129, 130, 133, 134, 136, 137, 138

M

motion 5, 6, 10, 12, 13, 28, 29, 31, 64

N

neck pit point 28, 48, 49, 66, 67, 80
nose 129, 130, 131, 133, 134, 136, 137, 138

P

pants 43
pelvis 29, 49, 53, 56, 58, 67, 69, 70, 79, 81, 84, 85, 86
pit point 28, 29, 31, 49, 66, 67, 80
plus size 7, 94, 95
posture 5, 20, 21
princess line 58, 86, 106
proportion 10, 15, 79, 118, 120, 122

R

relaxed foot 31, 51, 55, 82
relaxed leg 30, 51, 82, 83

S

side view 5, 28
silhouette 41
size 5, 7, 10, 14, 15, 16, 17, 18, 19, 22, 38, 39, 49, 67, 68, 69, 80, 94, 95
skeleton 10–155
sketch 66, 67, 78, 132, 144, 145, 146, 147
static 5, 6, 28, 29, 30, 31, 45
streamlined figure 16
supporting foot 30, 31, 50, 51, 68, 81, 82
supporting leg 30, 50, 51, 94, 100

T

template 6, 65, 150

U

underdrawing 48, 49, 66, 67

W

waistline 12, 13, 64, 66, 67, 74, 83, 106
weight distribution 16
wire skeleton 5, 8, 10, 27, 29, 32, 33, 48

ABOUT THE AUTHOR

Author of the book Irina V. Ivanova is a fashion designer and visual artist: the creator of the Fashion Croquis book series.

Irina's expertise in fashion design and visual art is fused in her experience of teaching college-level classes, such as Fashion Illustration, Technical Drawing For Fashion, Fashion Figure Drawing, Costume And Fashion Design.

Irina's classic figure drawing training combined with professional fashion design education and experience makes her an effective teacher for fashion figure drawing. 20 + years of teaching college-level courses made this book possible.

Irina creates her books and visual art in her home-based studio in Hallandale Beach, Florida, USA.

On this page you can see some examples of Irina's fashion illustrations from her *Ruff Couture* collection of drawings.

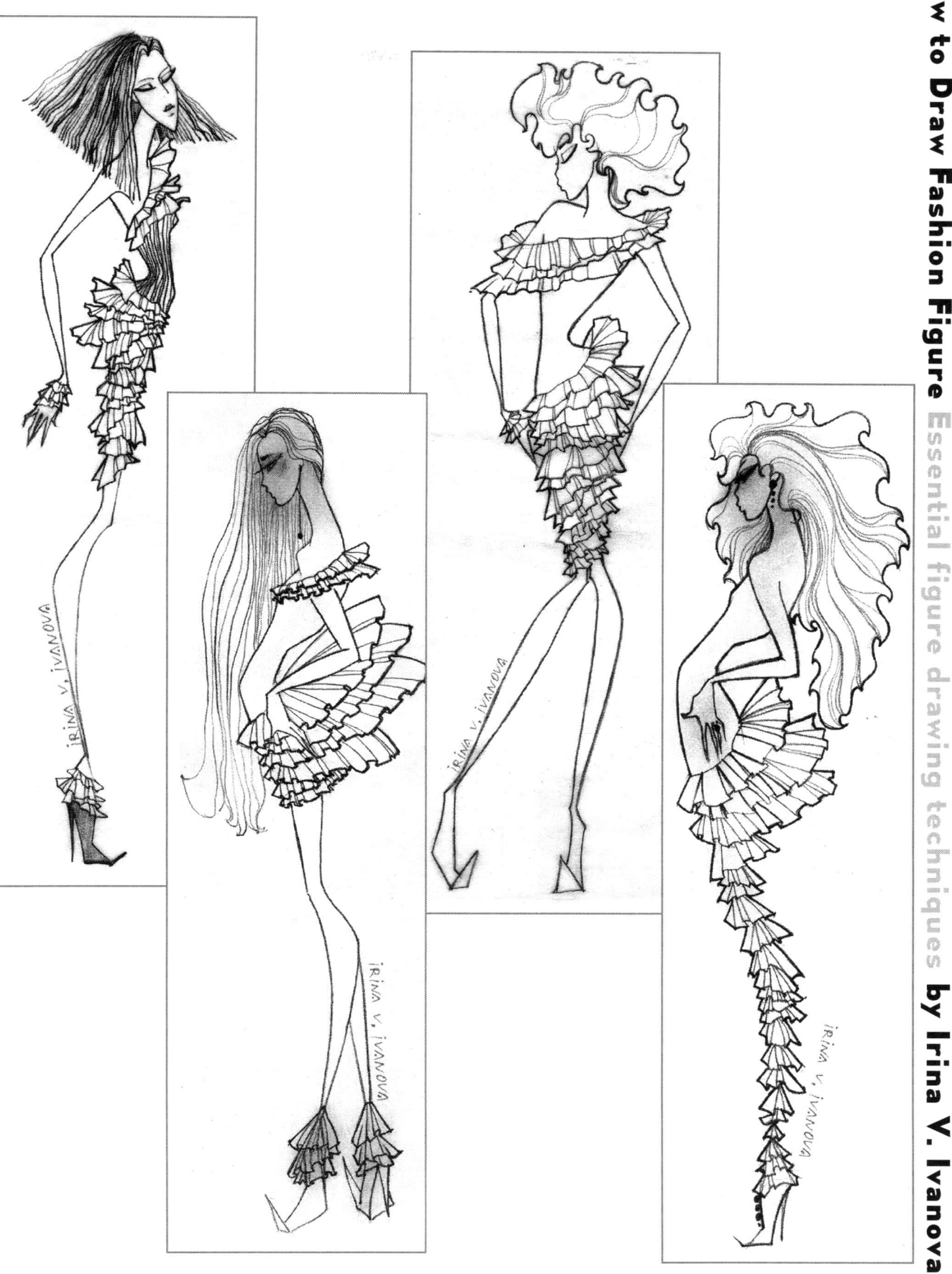

How to Draw Fashion Figure Essential figure drawing techniques by Irina V. Ivanova

Fashion Croquis books series

www.FashionCrqouis.com

Children's wear fashion illustration resource book

Subtitle: *Children's figure drawing templates with fashion design sketches*

ISBN-13:978-0692554074
ISBN-10:0692554076

Page count:132 pages
Trim Size: 8.5" x 11" (21.59cm x 27.94cm)
Color: Black and White
Paper/material: White paper
Publisher: Art Design Project, Inc.
Publication date: 2015-11-12
Language: English

How to draw fashion flats

Subtitle: *A practical guide to fashion technical drawing (pencil and marker techniques)*

ISBN-13: 978-0984356027
ISBN-10: 0984356029

Page count:214 pages
Trim Size:11" x 8.5" (21.59cm x 27.94cm)
Color: Black and White
Paper/material: White paper
Publisher: Art Design Project, Inc.
Publication date: 2016-09-30
Language: English

Fashion Croquis books series

www.FashionCrqouis.com

Haute Couture Fashion Illustration Resource Book

Subtitle: : *How to draw evening dresses and wedding gowns*

ISBN-10: 0984356037
ISBN-13: 978-0984356034

Page count: 261 pages
Trim Size: 8.5" x 11" (21.59cm x 27.94cm)
Color: Black and White
Paper/material: White paper
Publisher: Art Design Project, Inc.
Publication date: 2018-09-16
Language: English

Men's wear fashion illustration resource book

Subtitle: Figure drawing templates with fashion design sketches (pencil drawing techniques)

ISBN-13:978-0692608647
ISBN-10:0692608648

Page count: 184 pages
Trim Size: 8.5" x 11" (21.59cm x 27.94cm)
Color: Black and White
Paper/material: White paper
Publisher: Art Design Project, Inc.
Publication date: 2017-05-29
Language: English

Fashion Croquis Sketch Books

www.FashionCrqouis.com

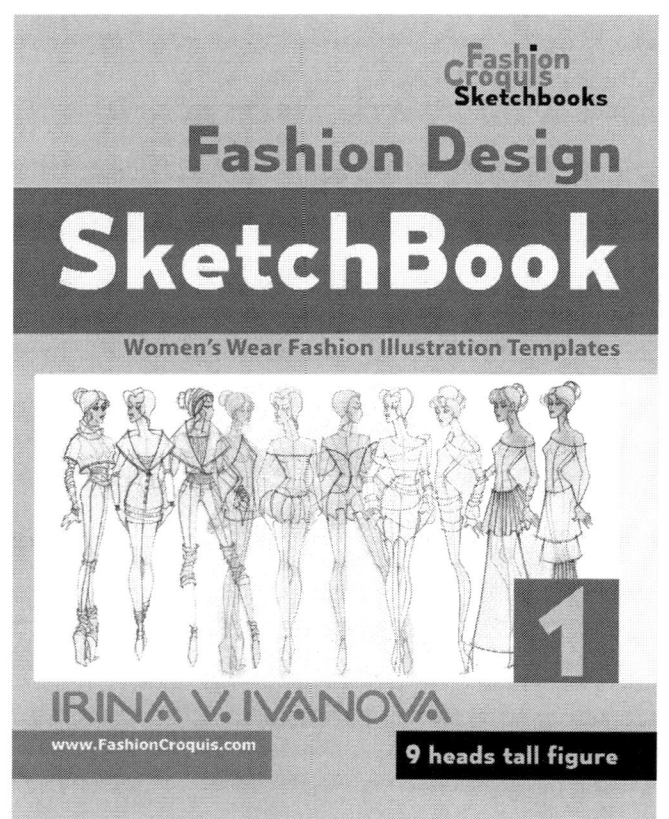

ISBN-13: 978-1731229861

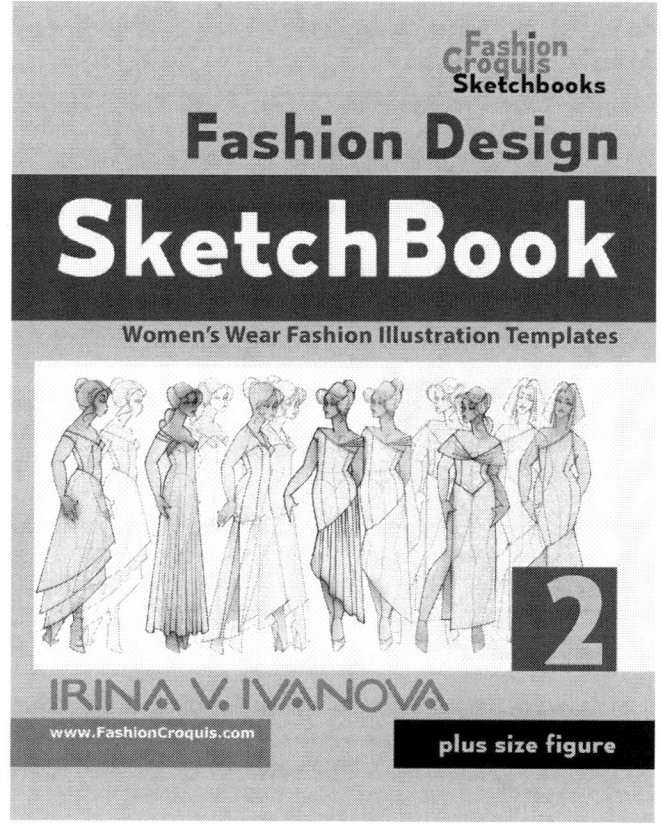

ISBN-13: 978-1792695285

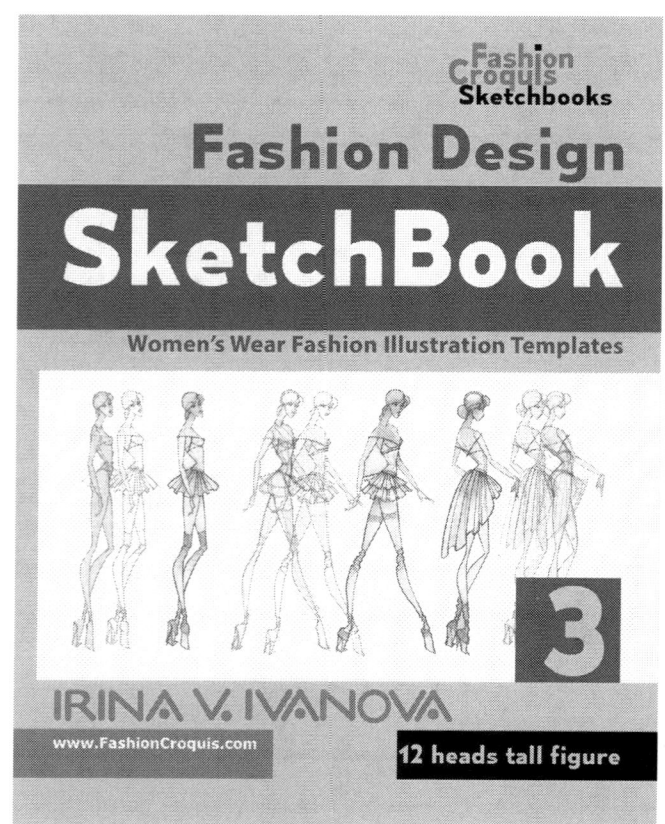

ISBN-13: 978-1794110144

ISBN-13: 978-1795763295

Fashion Croquis

FashionCroquis
shopping cart

Fashion Illustration Resources For Fashion Professionals

Fashion Figure Drawing Templates at www.FashionCroquis.com

Additional learning resources for the book available at
www.fashioncroquis.com/resources/figuredrawing

Made in the USA
Middletown, DE
28 July 2022

70118170R00086